Fortune's Faces

The *Roman de la Rose* and
the Poetics of Contingency

Daniel Heller-Roazen

The Johns Hopkins University Press
Baltimore and London

© 2003 The Johns Hopkins University Press
All rights reserved. Published 2003
Printed in the United States of America on acid-free paper
9 8 7 6 5 4 3 2 1

The Johns Hopkins University Press
2715 North Charles Street
Baltimore, Maryland 21218-4363
www.press.jhu.edu

Library of Congress Cataloging-in-Publication Data
Heller-Roazen, Daniel.
　Fortune's faces : the Roman de la Rose and the poetics of contingency / Daniel Heller-Roazen.
　　p.　　cm.—(Parallax)
Includes bibliographical references and index.
ISBN 0-8018-7191-3 (alk. paper)
1. Guillaume de Lorris, fl. 1230. Roman de la Rose.　2. Jean de Meun, d. 1305.
I. Title.　II. Parallax (Baltimore, Md.)
PQ1528 .H45 2001
841'.1—dc21　　　2002015861

A catalog record for this book is available from the British Library.

For my Mother and Father

L'inconstance du bransle divers de la fortune fait qu'elle nous doive presenter toute espece de visages.
—Montaigne, *Essais,* 1:33

Contents

	Acknowledgments	*xi*
	Note on Citations	*xiii*
	Introduction: The Sense of a Book	1
1	*Inventio Linguae:* The Language of Contingency	11
2	The Nameless Lover, or The Contingent Subject	29
3	Fortune, or The Contingent Figure	63
4	Through the Looking-Glass: The Knowledge of Contingency	100
	Conclusion: Diverse Verses	132
	Notes	*139*
	Works Cited	*181*
	Index	*201*

Acknowledgments

This work has benefited from the thoughts and comments of many readers, and it is a pleasure to be able to thank them here. My greatest debt is to the two scholars who codirected the doctoral dissertation that lies at the origin of this book, Jacqueline Cerquiglini-Toulet and Stephen G. Nichols; without them this study would hardly have been possible. I would also like to extend my warmest thanks to Werner Hamacher and Gabrielle Spiegel, who read and commented on the book at many stages of its preparation, improving it considerably, and to Neil Hertz, whose reflections on an earlier version of the book were a great help. The book has also profited significantly from the expert advice of Simon Gaunt, Sylvia Huot, and my colleague John Fleming. I am keenly aware of the enormous help given to me by Deborah Heller, Justine Landau, and Kevin Ohi, who all shared their thoughts about the manuscript with me more than once. To Patrick Greaney this book, like its author, owes a great deal.

I would like also to express my deep gratitude to the institutions with which I had the good fortune of being associated in the years in which I composed this book: the Humanities Center of the Johns Hopkins University, the École Normale Supérieure of the rue d'Ulm, and, finally, the Department of Comparative Literature of Princeton University, whose faculty has offered me an intellectual and academic environment that is in many respects, for reading and writing alike, nothing short of ideal.

A first draft of this project was completed with the assistance of a generous grant from the Social Sciences and Humanities Research Council of Canada.

Note on Citations

The text and verse numbers of the *Roman de la Rose* cited throughout refer to Félix Lecoy's three-volume edition: Guillaume de Lorris and Jean de Meun, *Le Roman de la Rose* (Paris: Champion, 1965–70 [Classiques Français du Moyen Age vols. 92, 95, and 98]). The English translation that follows is that of Charles Dahlberg's rendition of the poem *The Romance of the Rose,* trans. Charles Dahlberg, 3d ed. (1971; rpt., Princeton, N.J.: Princeton University Press, 1995). At many points I have, however, silently modified Dahlberg's translation, which is based on Langlois' earlier edition of the Old French text. Page numbers in parentheses refer to the corresponding passages in Dahlberg's version.

Unless otherwise indicated, all other translations are my own.

Fortune's Faces

1 *Introduction*
The Sense of a Book

Among its collection of French manuscripts, the National Library of Paris possesses an early-fourteenth-century codex containing the text of a poem divided in two parts. At the point in the manuscript in which the two sections of the text are joined, the scribe who copied the work inserted, in bright red letters, the following remark: "And since the matter pleased so many people, master Jean Chopinel of Meun decided to complete the book and to continue its matter" (*Et pour que la matiere embelissoit a plusors, il plot a maistre Jean Chopinel de Meun a parfaire le livre et a ensivre la matiere*).[1]

The anonymous fourteenth-century scribe thus resolved, in a single sentence, the enigma at the center of the "book" (*livre*) of medieval French literature which was most often copied, read, and debated in the Middle Ages and which, soon after its completion, entered into European literary history as a whole through its translations into Italian, English, and Dutch:[2] the *Romance of the Rose*, begun most likely around 1240 by Guillaume de Lorris and finished approximately forty years later by Jean de Meun. *Continuation* (*ensivre*) and *completion* (*parfaire*) are the terms by which the scribe, copying the romance, defined the activity of the second author of the work and, by extension, the structure of the entire romance as a finished whole. They are the forms, therefore, by which the copyist identified the bipartite structure of the work written by two authors in two cultural, intellectual, and institutional conditions; and they are equally those by which he characterized the double work as still *one* work, a single romance. It is precisely on this issue that the judgment of the medieval copyist diverges most radically from that of modern

1

readers of the poem. The classical nineteenth- and twentieth-century critical assessment of the *Roman de la Rose* can even be characterized as a coherent and repeated negation of precisely the two forms, "continuation" and "completion," by which the scribe conceived of the relation of Jean de Meun's text to the romance of Guillaume de Lorris. In 1856 Paulin Paris already contested the continuity that would appear to bind the "first" *Roman de la Rose* to the "second," writing that Jean treats Guillaume's poem as a mere "occasion" for his own.[3] Gaston Paris repeated the claim in 1888, when he wrote that, for Jean, Guillaume's tale of the "conquest of the rose . . . is nothing more than an excuse [*prétexte*]."[4] In the first critical edition of the *Roman de la Rose* Ernest Langlois articulated the same judgment more fully, stating that "Jean de Meun's frame of mind is in absolute opposition to that of Guillaume de Lorris."[5] The authoritative thesis was then echoed by the great figures of early-twentieth-century Romance philology. In Alfred Jeanroy's 1921 *Histoire des lettres* we read that the poem that Jean de Meun "sets out to bring to its conclusion is clearly of almost no interest to him at all."[6] In his 1924 essay "La littérature allégorique et *le Roman de la Rose*" Edmond Faral argued that the poems of Guillaume de Lorris and Jean de Meun constitute not a unitary work but, rather, merely the agglomeration of "two heterogeneous poems" (*deux poèmes hétéroclites*).[7] By the time C. S. Lewis published *The Allegory of Love,* the first great English consideration of the *Roman de la Rose,* in 1938, the thesis had become canonical: "it is as well to make clear at the outset," Lewis wrote, among his introductory remarks to the second half of the poem, "that Jean's work is only in a very superficial sense the continuation of Guillaume's. . . . He chose to continue a work in which the unity of subject was conspicuous: but he himself had no interest in that subject."[8]

Denying the continuity between the work of Guillaume de Lorris and Jean de Meun, the first critical readers of the *Roman de la Rose* also rejected the claim that the second part of the poem could be said, in the words of the medieval scribe, to "perfect" and "complete" the first. There can be completion only where there has been the articulation and development of an ordered whole, and the nineteenth- and early-twentieth-century philologists were unanimous in arguing that it is precisely such an ordered whole that is absent from Jean de Meun's text. Here, too, Paulin Paris's pronouncement on the *Roman de la Rose* anticipated what soon became the classical position on Jean de Meun: "we cannot ask him for an ordered plan," he wrote, since "the art of composition is not his; he reflects, like Montaigne, upon everything, with the same independence of thought, sometimes the same force of expression, and always the same disorder."⁹ "An infinitely expandable frame" is Gaston Paris's expression for Jean's poem, "into which he forces everything he knows and everything he thinks, higgledy-piggledy, without deliberation or measure."¹⁰ In his 1891 study, *Origines et sources du Roman de la Rose,* Langlois wrote that "it suffices to read a few pages of Jean de Meun's work to be convinced that he started without any plan and without knowing where he was going."¹¹ Jeanroy confirmed the judgment, stating that Jean de Meun "does not have any sense (or even care) for order" and that his poem, as a result, "moves forward only by lurches, interrupting itself at every moment by long speeches."¹² "Under his direction," we read, "the romance is transformed into an encyclopedia in which treatises and anecdotes, which themselves often break off and turn into ardent professions of faith, are piled up without any order or measure. Nothing could be more tattered, more rent [*décousu*]."¹³ "Treatises appear," Faral wrote, "by means of the mere association of ideas, often out of context and at odds with the interests of the tale."¹⁴ Jean de Meun's poem, Louis Thuasne stated in 1929, shows an "almost complete lack of any plan."¹⁵ Lewis, who admits to approaching the second half the *Roman de la Rose* "with despair," was no less severe in his condemnation of Jean's constant recourse to digressions and to *excursus,* which is to say, to that narrative figure that has been defined precisely as "the form that is not one."¹⁶ "We never know, at one page, what we shall be reading about on the next," for Jean de Meun, he wrote, is quite simply "incapable . . . of producing a poem, a ποιημα, a *thing made.*" "He is a bungler";¹⁷ he "produces chaos."¹⁸

The judgment of the modern critics of the poem, at its origins, was thus as clear as it was severe: the work known to the literary tradition as the *Roman de la Rose,* they argued, is not *a* work at all. At best it can be considered the result of an aesthetically senseless, yet historically sanctioned, composition of two utterly disparate texts. The consequences of this judgment for the conception of the structure of the work could only be paradoxical. The very poem that, in the words of the medieval scribe, continued and completed the romance of Guillaume de Lorris appeared, in the works of the first modern critics of the *Roman de la Rose,* to accomplish precisely the contrary: the second part of the poem was understood as breaking the continuity of the first and, by virtue of its very form, as ruining the possibility of any coherence and closure for the romance in its entirety. Rendering the work less ordered than it ever was, Jean de Meun's continuation of Guillaume's poem would thus have consolidated the very fragmentation it sought to remedy. The addition, according to such a reading, subtracts from that to which it is added; the conclusion ensures the definitive incompleteness of the poem it seems to complete. It is thus not the interrupted poem of Guillaume de Lorris but, rather, the finished text of Jean de Meun's poem which, paradoxically, now appears as what cannot in any sense be complete. This much is already clear in the works that Langlois dedicated to the romance, in which the first, literally incomplete text appears, *ordine inverso*, as an essentially complete work, whereas the second, literally complete text figures as a poem necessarily destined to structural fragmentation. While acknowledging, in his critical edition of the *Roman de la Rose*, that "Guillaume did not finish his poem," Langlois thus argued that Guillaume de Lorris was nevertheless "close to the conclusion";[19] in his *Origins and Sources of the Roman de la Rose* Jean de Meun appears, inversely, as "one of those chatterers full of gossip and tales who starts a story [*un récit*] without being able to end it."[20] The chiasmus at work in this account of the bipartition of the romance is unmistakable: the incomplete text is said to be virtually complete, and the complete poem is judged to be essentially incomplete.

A number of twentieth-century critics have questioned this traditional assessment of the unity—or, rather, lack of unity—of the *Roman de la Rose*. Alan M. F. Gunn, in his groundbreaking 1952 study, *The Mirror of Love: A Reinterpretation of "The Roman de la Rose,"* sought to demonstrate that Jean's text, despite appearances, constitutes a genuine development of Guillaume's romance. The grounds of the continuity between the work of the two poets, for Gunn, were thematic: "it is clear," he wrote, "that Jean de Meun understood that Guillaume's theme was love,"[21] for the conclusion of the poem is itself an extended "treatise on the subject of love."[22] The publication of John V. Fleming's *The Roman de la Rose: A Study in Allegory and Iconography* in 1969 marked the next stage in the criticism of the poem. Approaching the work by means of patristic and medieval doctrines of allegory, Fleming called into question the "diagnosis of schizophrenia" that prevailed among the modern critics of the poem, offering in its place an account of the romance as a single, ironic chronicle of the "typical path of sin described by innumerable medieval psychologists."[23] More recently, Roger Dragonetti attempted to vindicate the unity of the romance on altogether different grounds. Guillaume and Jean, he argued, are "but two faces of the same, single narrative structure,"[24] two names for the "one single author,"[25] who, in a sustained play of "specular deformation,"[26] produced the "famous doubling of authors"[27] accepted as a fact by the philological and critical tradition.[28] Dragonetti's thesis, which was initially formal and literary in character, thus ended in a decisive rejection of the single historical presupposition that motivated the entire tradition of modern criticism

Introduction

of the poem: its bipartite structure. As such, Dragonetti's claim is difficult to maintain, for the manuscript tradition furnishes undeniable evidence, as several scholars have demonstrated, for the textual autonomy of the two parts of the poem.[29] But his argument for the single authorship of the poem nevertheless allowed him to bring to light the decisive problem that each of the great critics of the romance before him had confronted: that of the sense of the *Roman de la Rose* as a single, yet bipartite, poem.

There have, to be sure, been important interpretations of the *Roman de la Rose* since Dragonetti's, but it is significant that they have tended, in one way or another, to turn away from the question of the sense of the romance as a whole. The six major books on *Roman de la Rose* published in English in the last two decades are, in this regard, exemplary. For a number of different reasons each one's author chose to set aside the classical critical dilemma of the double authorship of the romance and to offer, instead, an account of specific elements in the literary structure, textual tradition, and intellectual significance of scenes in the work, usually concentrating either on Guillaume de Lorris or on Jean de Meun. In *Reason and the Lover* (1982) John Fleming thus gave a sustained and compelling reading of the famous scene in the second part of the romance in which Lady Reason explains the nature of words and things to the narrator;[30] in *Self-fulfilling Prophecies: Readership and Authority in the First Roman de la Rose* (1986) David F. Hult concentrated, with remarkable critical results, on the "first *Rose*," demonstrating its literary autonomy with respect to the continuation of Jean de Meun;[31] in *False Roses: Structures of Duality and Deceit in Jean de Meun's Roman de la Rose* Susan Stakel focused on the functions of duplicity in the second part of the poem;[32] in *The Romance of the Rose and Its Medieval Readers: Interpretation, Reception, Manuscript Transmission* (1993) Sylvia Huot presented an invaluable account of the textual history of the romance and its medieval reception;[33] in *Internal Difference and Meanings in the Roman de la Rose* (1995) Douglas Kelly considered the relations of Jean de Meun's text to medieval rhetorical literature;[34] and in *Magister Amoris: The Roman de la Rose and Vernacular Hermeneutics* (2001) A. J. Minnis gave a new account of Jean de Meun's Ovidian inheritance.[35] Heather Arden (1987) and Sarah Kay (1995) have each provided critical introductions, in the form of monographs, to many of the notable critical problems provoked by the romance.[36] All of these scholars, moreover, have contributed important articles on the romance, as have Kevin Brownlee, Lee Patterson, and Nancy Freeman Regalado, each of whom has made it necessary to reconsider the interpretation of individual scenes and structures in the two parts of the poem.

The manuscript tradition of the *Roman de la Rose* suggests that the medieval readers of the work perceived the texts of Guillaume de Lorris and Jean de Meun as in every sense a single work. Only two early manuscripts present Guillaume's romance without its continuation by Jean de Meun.[37] At least two explanations, as Pierre-Yves Badel has noted, are conceivable here: "it is possible that the set [of the two poems] eliminated the part; it could also have been the case that Guillaume de Lorris's poem never circulated very widely."[38] It remains the case, for whatever reason, that, as Zumthor wrote in his *Essai de poétique médiévale,* "for the people of the end of the thirteenth century, the two *Romans de la Rose* constitute a single text, despite their evident heterogeneity and the internal contrasts that mark the entire set."[39] The distance that separates medieval literary production from the modern notion of authorship, in its juridical, political, and epistemological force, is particularly clear here: for the Middle Ages, unlike modernity, authors and works are in no sense simply coextensive.[40] The differences that mark the conditions of the historical genesis of the *Roman de la Rose* did not, for medieval readers, efface the literary unity of the poem; despite its double authorship, the *Roman de la Rose,* in the tradition of medieval manuscripts and letters, constitutes one poem.

The subject of *Fortune's Faces* is this single, bipartite work, which was known to the readers of the thirteenth, fourteenth, and fifteenth centuries as the joint product of Guillaume de Lorris and Jean de Meun. The historical authorship of the first "part" of the *Roman de la Rose* is not of great importance in this regard; it matters little whether Jean de Meun's "continuation" followed a text that originally had a different conclusion, that demanded a different conclusion, or that was, in itself, already complete. Once Jean de Meun incorporated the first *Roman de la Rose,* whatever its original form and structure, into his own poem, the romance of Guillaume de Lorris acquired an entirely new status, one that can be defined only through a critical reading of its position with respect to the poetic text that follows and completes it. David Hult has shown that the text attributed to Guillaume de Lorris may well be read as a coherent, unified, and therefore finished work, "insofar as it can be seen to form an artistic whole consistent with stylistic and narrative standards of judgment as well as with medieval poetic traditions."[41] The same clearly cannot be said of the continuation and completion of Jean de Meun. By definition the "second *Rose*" necessarily includes the first, which it integrates into itself as its own opening.[42]

At this point, however, the sense of "the" *Roman de la Rose* as a whole grows only more perplexing, and it is not difficult to understand the bewilderment

Introduction

of critics before the two-part poem. How, after all, is one to understand the order of the work that is produced by Jean de Meun's continuation and completion of Guillaume de Lorris's *Roman de la Rose?* What is the sense of a poem which presents itself not as a single work or even a single fragment but, as we have seen, as a kind of double fragment, produced in the aggregation of a first incomplete poem and a second poem that, in apparently continuing and completing the first, seems in turn to be marked by an essential lack of order and completion?

In its first and second part alike, the *Roman de la Rose* resists the internal harmony, consistency, and completion that, to the eyes of the founders of modern philology, define the form of the aesthetic work. In the text of Guillaume de Lorris this resistance is inscribed in the fragmentary form of the poem, by virtue of which the poetic text constitutes itself as something other than what it could, and perhaps should, have been; in the text of Jean de Meun the poem's capacity to be other than it is is indicated in the very "chaos," "digressions," and perpetual "meanderings" by which the poem, at every turn, calls attention to the fact that it could have had a form different from the one it has.[43] This may well be the sense in which Jean de Meun's work truly continues and perfects the *matiere* of Guillaume's poem, which, for whatever reason, appears to be interrupted before its end. An unfinished work can be no better continued than by a work that, in its very structure, presents itself as irreducibly unfinished; a work rendered fragmentary by chance can only be completed and perfected by a work that, by design, constitutes itself as not necessary and, by virtue of its poetic form, as capable of being otherwise than it is. The two-part *Roman de la Rose,* in this sense, is neither a merely incomplete work nor a simply complete one. Like the *Conte du graal* and so many other medieval works, which have justly been said to "conclude precisely where they are lacking,"[44] the *Roman de la Rose* is, in its very structure, *completely incomplete.* The work shows itself and its own production to be not necessary but, instead, possible and merely fortuitous—in a word, contingent.

The concept of "contingency," in its classical and medieval philosophical sense as "what is capable of being and not being," thus proves crucial here. It is, in a certain sense, implicit throughout the history of the critical evaluations of the *Roman de la Rose.* If the faults for which nineteenth- and early-twentieth-century philology reproached the *Roman de la Rose* were that its form appears in some way arbitrary, that its development seems unpredictable, and that it gives the impression of not being necessary, then it can be said that the one trait for which the collective work of Guillaume and Jean has traditionally been faulted is simply its contingency. When the critics lamented that they were obliged to engage in mere "speculation" concerning how Guillaume "would have ended" the first part of the *Rose*,[45] when Langlois suggested that in his continuation Jean "did not know where he was going," when Jeanroy remarked that his text "moves forward only by lurches, interrupting itself at every moment," and when Lewis complained that when confronted with Jean's poem "we never know, at one page, what we shall be reading about on the next," they all condemned the romance for the same trait: the contingency of its form and structure.

Fortune's Faces takes this canonical judgment of the *Roman de la Rose* as its point of departure, formulating a principle that at once draws on the nineteenth- and twentieth-century criticism of the poem and breaks with it: one of the defining characteristics of the two-part romance, this book argues, is that, at each of the fundamental levels of its construction, it presents itself as capable of being otherwise than it is. Building on the classic nineteenth- and twentieth-century interpretations of the romance, this book therefore seeks to bring to light a critical perception of the work which has been implicit in the history of its modern reception but which has never been considered as such: the perception, namely, that a certain contingency marks the unfolding of the romance from its opening to its close. Once rendered an object in its own right, the contingency of the romance, however, acquires a new form; it no longer appears, as it did to the eyes of the first critics of the work, as a single and indeed regrettable characteristic that can be set aside in the final literary evaluation of the poem. When its presence in the romance is considered as such, contingency no longer appears as a phenomenon external to the work which leaves its traces within it as residues of an empirical process of production from which the artwork itself would remain autonomous. Contingency emerges, instead, as a complex force that the romance itself explores at each of the fundamental levels of its construction; it acquires a positive poetic function in the romance, as a *materia* that is in every sense fundamental to the articulation of the joint work of Guillaume de Lorris and Jean de Meun.

The literary art of the *Roman de la Rose* is examined, in this book, in four chapters. Each considers, in a different way, the functions that contingency plays in medieval poetic language, stressing the depth and complexity of the relations between medieval philosophical discourse in its most precise and technical form and medieval literary production. Chapter 1 articulates the general theoretical and philosophical problematic of the study as a whole; it argues that, in the tradition of medieval philosophy and logic, speech that bears

Introduction

on contingency constitutes a limit form of discourse which can be defined as a model for the vernacular literary language of the Middle Ages. The following chapters then examine the literary functions of contingency in the "art of love" of Guillaume de Lorris and Jean de Meun through an analysis of three exemplary poetic, rhetorical, and philosophical aspects of the *Roman de la Rose*. Chapter 2, which opens the discussion of the *Roman de la Rose*, considers the *ego* of the poem with reference to medieval grammatical, logical, and philosophical accounts of the first-person pronoun, arguing that the common "I" of Guillaume and Jean constitutes the cipher of a literary subjectivity that marks the form of the entire romance as an essentially contingent work. Chapter 3 offers an interpretation of the figure of Fortune in the romance with reference to the literary history of the figure in late antiquity and the Middle Ages as well as to the concept of fortune (*fortuna*) as it was defined in opposition to chance (*casus*) in thirteenth-century physics and metaphysics; it treats the Lady Fortune of Jean de Meun, in a simultaneously literary and philosophical context, as the fundamental *persona ficta* of the contingency at work in the construction of the romance. Chapter 4 analyzes the extended discussion of free will and divine prescience in the concluding part of the romance, assessing the extent to which this discussion represents both an appropriation and a displacement of the philosophical and theological problem of future contingents in thirteenth-century theology. Taken together, the steps by which the argument of this study proceeds can therefore be easily summarized: the book defines contingency as a fundamental problem in medieval philosophy of language and poetics and subsequently examines its poetic operation in the *Roman de la Rose* as a formal structure, a rhetorical figure, and, finally, a literary and philosophical topic.

Fortune's Faces lays no claim to comprehensiveness in its readings. It aims neither to give an account of everything in the twenty-one thousand verse poem nor to explain the sequence by which the romance, according to the elaborate literary architecture that has been studied by other scholars, proceeds from scene to scene.[46] Eschewing the methods and the critical aspirations of the "total interpretation," the book instead seeks to consider closely a series of forms, figures, and moments of contingency in the romance which prove exemplary for an understanding of the structure of the work as a whole. Such a procedure allows the book to move from the detailed reading of a set of passages to the identification and elaboration of a coherent "poetics of contingency" which animates both parts of the romance, determining its rhetoric, its form, and its topics. The many interruptions long ago recognized in the *Ro-*

man de la Rose, from the rupture at the end of its first part to the sudden awakening with which the poem concludes, acquire a new sense in this light. They appear not as the signs of an aesthetic imperfection to which the benevolent critic must turn a blind eye but, rather, as critical junctures at which the two-part romance indicates its own capacity to be different from itself. The multiple breaks and discontinuities in the romance emerge as points at which the language of Guillaume of Lorris and Jean de Meun speaks not only contingently but about contingency and, moreover, about itself and its own existence *as* this very contingency. Such is the novel significance that the infamously "tattered" masterpiece of European literature then acquires. In its characteristic interruptions and digressions, the romance appears as a work that incessantly explores its own capacity to be otherwise than it is; in the staging of its very "accidents," the poem reveals itself to be dedicated to nothing other than its own bare capacity to take place (*accidere*): to take place as it is, to take place otherwise than it is, and, *a limine,* not to take place at all—to be cut short and interrupted, like Guillaume's poem, by death.

1 ■ *Inventio Linguae*
The Language of Contingency

I

At the opening of *De Interpretatione* Aristotle defines the nature of speech in terms that are both logical and metaphysical and which, to a large extent, determine the ancient, medieval, and many of the most modern theories of language and its operation. "Spoken sounds" (literally, "the things in the voice" [τὰ ἐν τῇ φωνῇ, *ea quae sunt in voce*]), Aristotle explains, are signs of impressions on the soul (παθήματα, *passiones*), which, in turn, are the images of things (πράγματα, *res*).[1] Speech is thus tied, in two steps, to the world of things: its sounds point, as symbols, to psychic imprints that, for their part, attest to the beings with which the soul is already familiar.[2] The significance of this claim, for the philosophy of language and its history, could not be more decisive. Once *De Interpretatione* determines the canonical form of speech as a "meaningful utterance" (λόγος σημαντικός, *vox significativa*) and, more precisely, as a "proposition" (λόγος ἀποφαντικός, *oratio enuntiativa*) bearing truth or falsity, and once it situates truth and falsity in the composition (σύνφεσις, *compositio*) of autonomous elements,[3] the conclusion is inevitable: the paradigmatic form of true speech must be that of a "statement of one thing concerning another thing" (λέγειν τι κατά τινός, *enuntiatio*, in Boethius' translation of the Greek, *alicuis de aliquo*).[4] Even at its end, language, according to such a conception, thus hardly leaves the things from which it arises. It reaches its final form, the predicative assertion, in reducing itself, through the terms of its logical composition, to the subject on which it bears; it fulfills its function in dissolving itself, according to the canon of analysis (ἀνάλυσις, literally, "loosening up") into the "one thing" of which it states "another thing." At its origin and its end, speech, by definition, remains the speech of what exists; the integrity and identity of language is altogether founded on the consistency and stability of the things that it bears.

Aristotle's treatise, in this way, confronts all speech with a limit beyond which it cannot easily venture: it must remain a question whether language can bear on what does not exist. *De Interpretatione* does not conceal this limit, nor does it retreat before the radical consequences it implies for the form of the statement and its truth. Aristotle, on the contrary, places this limit at the center of his discussion of language and the utterance, giving it a name: contingency. *Contingency* (τὸ ἐνδεχόμενον in Greek, which Boethius renders as *contingens*) is the term by which Aristotle refers to that of which language speaks when, at the limit of its canonical operation, it refers to what is not a thing and what, in a certain sense, is not at all. The steps that lead Aristotle to consider the problem of contingency in his reflections on language and the statement can be easily summarized. Having defined truth, in numerous passages of his logical and metaphysical works, as the correspondence between things and thought, such that the necessities of speech are also those of Being, Aristotle locates truth in the judgment and the proposition that expresses it.[5] A proposition is therefore considered to be true when, in the form of affirmation or negation, it states what exists. Given the stability and irrevocability of the past and present, Aristotle writes, all statements that refer to past and present things are therefore necessarily bearers of truth and falsity: "with respect to what is and what was," we read, "it is necessary that affirmation and negation be true or false" (ἐπὶ μὲν οὖν τῶν ὄντων καὶ γενομένων ἀνάγκη τὴν κατάφασιν ἢ τὴν ἀπόφασιν ἀληθῆ ἢ ψευδῆ εἶναι, *in his quae sunt et facta sunt necesse est adfirmationem vel negationem veram vel falsam esse*).[6]

"In singular and future matters," however, Aristotle adds, "the case is not the same" (ἐπὶ δὲ τῶν καθ' ἕκαστα καὶ μελλόντων οὐχ ὁμοίως, *in singularibus vero et futuris non similiter*).[7] Aristotle's reasoning here is perfectly consistent with the principles that found his treatment of language; his claim follows directly from his initial derivation of the statement and its truth from the determinacy and presence of that of which it speaks. In each case the necessary truth or falsity of the statement has as its condition the presence and actuality of that which it signifies. Aristotle's example is of a sea battle that may, or may not, take place tomorrow.[8] The proposition "Tomorrow there will be a sea battle" (or its negation: "Tomorrow there will not be a sea battle") could be said to be true or false only if the future itself were already determinate and actual; it could be said to have the form of all other statements only if the future itself were, in its actuality and irrevocability, no different from the present and the past. The necessary truth or falsity of statements about a singular term in the future would, in short, imply that speech can signify the future as it can signify the past and the present; it would imply, therefore, that the indeterminate character of the future—what constitutes the future *as* future—does not exist. If one accepts such an implication, Aristotle writes, then one must conclude that "nothing happens by chance or fortuitously, and nothing will be or not be; instead, everything takes place by necessity and not fortuitously" (οὐδὲν ἄρα οὔτε ἔστιν οὔτε γίγνεται οὔτε ἀπὸ τύχης οὔθ' ὁπότερ ἔτυχεν, οὐδὲ ἔσται ἢ οὐκ ἔσται, ἀλλ' ἐξ ἀνάγκης ἅπαντα καὶ οὐχ ὁπότερ' ἔτυχεν, *Nihil igitur neque est neque fit nec a casu nec utrumlibet, nec erit nec non erit, sed ex necessitate omnia et non utrumlibet*).[9]

Such a conclusion, Aristotle writes, is plainly false, for "it is apparent that not everything is or happens by necessity" (φανερὸν ἄρα ὅτι οὐχ ἅπαντα ἐξ ἀνάγκης οὔτ' ἔστιν οὔτε γίγνεται, *manifestum est quoniam non omnia ex necessitate vel sunt vel fiunt*).[10] Aristotle's recognition of the existence of events that are not necessary thus forces him to restrict the principle that modern logicians call the "law of bivalence," according to which all statements, regardless of their subjects and the time to which they refer, are necessarily either true or false.[11] After having defined the statement as an affirmation bearing truth or falsity, Aristotle must posit the existence of propositions that cannot yet be said to say "one thing concerning another thing" and that cannot yet, for that reason, be either true or false. It would be difficult to overestimate the significance of this gesture, by which Aristotle admits the existence of utterances that, while formally indistinguishable from statements, are in no sense bearers of determinate truth and falsity. This is the price of Aristotle's recognition of the existence of what, in the present, cannot properly be said to *be:* chance, possibility, freedom, the future—in Aristotle's word, "contingency." In accordance with the Aristotelian principle that "the truth of the statement consists in being adequate to things (πράγματα, *res*),"[12] if, at the moment at which a statement is uttered, that to which the statement refers does not yet exist, then the statement, as a consequence, must itself not yet be either true or false.

In Aristotle's text the existence of such a thing as contingency therefore necessarily implies the existence of statements of a very particular kind. Indeed, in *De Interpretatione* the problem of contingent events is inseparable from the problem of the linguistic expression of contingent events; the examination of the event that is not yet necessary cannot be told apart from the study of the utterance that is not yet necessarily either true or false. This much is demanded by the correspondence established by Aristotle between speech and things: the reflection on what, in a certain sense, does not exist must entail a reflection on what, according to the criterion of assertion and predication, is not speech. Here, however, Aristotle's solution to the problem only complicates matters further. For what, then, does it mean to say, "Tomorrow there will be a sea battle," if such a statement is neither true nor false but, rather, at once potentially true and potentially false? If to speak, as Aristotle suggests, is always to speak of what is present and of what is, then what can it mean to speak of what, at the moment of speaking, does not exist? What, in short, is the language of contingency?

With the appearance of Christianity and the concept of an omniscient deity, Aristotle's problem of what it means to speak about "future and singular matters" is soon tied to the theological problem of the reconciliation of divine prescience and what appears as fortuitous and indeterminate in human action and thought. The question posed by Aristotle with respect to the speech of contingency becomes inextricably linked, in this way, to the question of the divine knowledge of contingency.[13] But the initial problem raised by Aristotle does not lose its force in the Middle Ages; on the contrary, it remains in some sense the decisive question for every philosophy of language and semantics which, in the tradition inaugurated by the linguistic theory of *De Interpretatione,* seeks to ground the stability of speech in the presence of the things signified by language. The theological significance of the medieval *quaestio de futuris contingentibus* can even be said to have lent Aristotle's discussion an importance it never had before, transforming the Stagirite's one chapter on the speech of "future and singular matters" into the locus classicus for every discussion of the specifically human expression of time. In their commentaries and expositions of *De Interpretatione,* the philosophers and theologians of the Middle Ages did not fail to consider the linguistic form identified by Aristotle in his discussion of statements concerning the future. Nor did they cease to reflect, as we shall see, on the limit point indicated by *De Interpretatione,* at which language, in its canonical sense, breaks down, displaced from the terrain of the *oratio enuntiativa* to that of fundamentally different utterances—utterances whose form and structure remain to be examined and which in many ways recall those instances of speech which, in Aristotle's words, are "neither true nor false" (οὔτε ἀληθὴς οὔτε ψευδής, *neque vera neque falsa*) and which

must be said to belong, therefore, "to the province of rhetoric or poetry" (ῥητορικῆς γὰρ ἢ ποιητικῆς οἰκειοτέρα, *rhetoricae enim vel poeticae convenientior consideratio est*).[14]

II

Before turning to the works of the medieval philosophers and theologians themselves, it is worth briefly recalling the importance and persistence of Aristotle's treatise on interpretation throughout late antiquity and the Middle Ages. The fundamental work on this subject remains J. Isaac's *Le Peri Hermeneias en Occident, de Boèce à Saint Thomas: Histoire littéraire d'un traité d'Aristote*,[15] to which any consideration of the transmission of *De Interpretatione* to the Middle Ages must be indebted. Isaac notes that, although Marius Victorinus already translated *De Interpretatione* into Latin in the middle of the fourth century, Boethius' Latin rendition of the treatise was the only version known to the Latin Middle Ages until William of Moerbeke translated it again, on the basis of Byzantine manuscripts, in the second half of the thirteenth century.[16] The Latin version of the work that Greek commentators entitled Περί ἑρμηνείας thus owes its existence, like the other works of *Aristoteles latinus* (such as the *Kategorica*, the *Analytica*, and the *Topica*), to Boethius' unrealized project to translate all the dialogues of Plato and all the works of Aristotle into Latin, "transposing the wealth of Greek letters into the treasure of the Roman language" (*ea quae ex opulentia litterarum in romanae orationis thesaurum sumpta conveximus*).[17]

De Interpretatione, however, constitutes a text of particular importance in Boethius' philosophical corpus, on account of the two commentaries that he dedicates to it and the fifth book of *De Consolatione Philosophiae*, in which Boethius reproduces a number of formulations that are clearly borrowed, often word for word, from his commentaries on Aristotle's treatise.[18] The *distinguo* that Boethius ascribes to *De Interpretatione* is in some way prophetic for the thinkers of the Middle Ages, for whom Aristotle's treatise proves central to any reflection on language and signification. For the thinkers born after the invasions of Rome, Aristotle's treatise on interpretation is not only the only work, together with the *Isagoge* and the *Kategorica*, still accompanied by commentaries by Boethius; it is also, more significantly, the only logical work of Aristotle other than the *Kategorica* that survives the destruction of so much of Greco-Latin letters and, therefore, the only classical philosophical treatise on the form of the statement to which medieval thinkers, at least before the recovery of the whole *Organon* in 1159, could turn in their own reflections on language.

Other works, to be sure, also transmitted Greek logic and philosophy of language to the authors of the Middle Ages. Most notably, the Latin Περὶ ἑρμηνείας, or *De Syllogismis Categoricis,* composed in the second century by the rhetorician Apuleius of Madaura,[19] must be considered in a discussion of the transmission of Greek linguistic theory in the Middle Ages; it, and not Aristotle's work, constitutes the source from which Martianus Capella, for example, draws much of his own treatment of dialectics in the fourth book of *De Nuptiis Philologiae et Mercurii.*[20] And yet, if Apuleius' treatise, which considers the form of the phrase, the utterance, and the figures of the syllogism, was widely read and studied in the centuries following the destruction of Rome, it in no way displaced Aristotle's own Περὶ ἑρμηνείας, of which it has been said to constitute a kind of "summary."[21] In its success Apuleius' treatise could rival Boethius' own works on logic and the philosophy of language, as Isaac suggests;[22] but it did so precisely as an introduction to the thought expressed in the work of the Stagirite.

Throughout the Middle Ages Aristotle's text continued to be copied and studied, generally together with Boethius' two commentaries *in librum Peri hermeneias.* The manuscript tradition demonstrates that by the ninth century the corpus of the *logica vetus* already assumed the form that it maintained for the rest of the medieval period, consisting of the *Isagoge,* the *Kategorica,* and *De Interpretatione.*[23] Topics and problems drawn from Aristotle's *De Interpretatione,* as a consequence, are already clearly present in the works of the first theologians of the Middle Ages. In his *De Divina Omnipotentia Reparatione Corruptae et Factis Infectis Reddendis* Peter Damian thus considers the categories of possibility and impossibility and their relation to God's will in terms that owe much to Aristotle's discussion of contingency and possibility in the final chapters of *De Interpretatione.*[24] Anselm of Canterbury's own treatments of divine omnipotence in *De Divina Omnipotentia, Cur Deus Homo* and *De Concordia Praescientia et Praedestinationis et Gratiae Dei cum Libero Arbitrio,* which often rely on the classical Aristotelian distinction between absolute and conditioned necessity, could also not have been carried out without a precise knowledge of Aristotle's text.[25]

Abelard's glosses on *De Interpretatione* in his *Dialectica,* his *Editio super Aristoteles,* and his *Logica Ingredientibus* bear witness to the presence of Aristotle's text in the twelfth century. We are in possession of a sufficient number of

The Language of Contingency

study programs and syllabi from the period, moreover, to register the continued importance of Aristotle's treatise in the curricula of the new *scholae* of Chartres and Paris.[26] By the middle of the twelfth century the study of logic, which is undertaken in the field of dialectics, includes Aristotle's *Topica* and *Elenchica* (and, in Paris, also the *Analytica Priora* and *Posteriora*) yet continues to have the *Organon* at its center.[27] In the thirteenth century the transmission to the Latin West of Aristotle's *Physica, Metaphysica,* and the works of *philosophia rationis* which form the *logica nova,* inevitability displaces *De Interpretatione* from its position as the only extant Aristotelian text on the organization of statements; but it in no way functions to diminish the attention given in the faculties of arts to the text of Περὶ ἑρμηνείας. Aristotle's treatise is "constantly taught" at the end of the end of the thirteenth century,[28] as shown by Albert's *Commentarius* of around 1250 and Thomas's *Expositio in Libri Periermeneias* of 1270. No instruction in the *trivium* in the thirteenth century could fail to include a detailed examination of *De Interpretatione;* no study of language and the arts of speech, at this point, could not involve a consideration of Aristotle's doctrine of the proposition and its interpretation.

It is hardly an exaggeration, therefore, to consider Aristotle's *De Interpretatione* as a genuine sourcebook for medieval reflections on language and its operation. Wherever the arts of the *trivium* are considered, taught, and studied and wherever these arts are at play in literary and poetic texts, the concepts and categories of the Aristotelian treatise, implicitly or explicitly, are never far removed. As we shall see, the medieval discussions, from Boethius to St. Thomas, of speech on "future and contingent matters" demonstrate as much; and it is to them that we must now turn.

III

In the history of classical philosophy, the passage from Greek to Latin constitutes so radical a displacement in the vocabulary and idiom of thought that it would be more correct to speak of a transposition and transformation, rather than translation, of Hellenic thought in Rome. The text of Boethius' *De Interpretatione,* like that of his *Kategorica,*[29] is an exemplary testament to this transformation; in its lexis it registers the fundamental alteration that Aristotle's concepts undergo in being reformulated in Latin. The formation and use of the term that interests us here, *contingentia,* is particularly telling in this regard. *Contingens* is, first of all, the word with which Boethius renders Aristotle's ἐνδεχόμενον and δυνατόν.[30] As such, it functions to designate Aristotle's concept of "two-sided" possibility in *De Interpretatione*, which "can be and can also not be" (ἅμα γὰρ δυνατὸν εἶναι καὶ μὴ εἶναι, *simul enim possibile esse et non esse*).[31] *Contingentia* indicates, furthermore, the notion of contingency (ἐνδέχεσθαι) which Aristotle defines in the *Analytica Priora*, when he writes that "to be contingent is said in two ways" (τὸ ἐνδέχεσθαι κατὰ δύο λέγεται): first, as "what falls short of being necessary," and, second, as "what is capable of happening in a certain way and also of not happening in such a way" (ὃ καὶ οὕτως καὶ μὴ οὕτως δυνατόν).[32] *Contingentia* is, in this sense, the logical equivalent of the metaphysical "possibility" or "potentiality" (δυναμία) of which Aristotle writes in Book 9 of the *Metaphysics*, which is defined as potentiality to (do or be) and potentiality not to (do or be), being in this sense both "potentiality" (δυναμία) and, as Aristotle writes, "impotentiality" (ἀδυναμία).[33]

In his 1932 study, *Die Vorgeschichte des philosophischen Terminus "contingens,"* Albrecht Becker-Freysing notes, however, that in Boethius' translation of Περὶ ἑρμηνείας the term *contingens* does not merely function as a Latin equivalent of the terms used by Aristotle to designate possibility and potentiality. It also appears, in accordance with the primary meaning of the verb *contingere* in classical Latin, as a synonym of *accidere* and *evenire*, to designate what happens and takes place.[34] In such cases *contingens* refers not to the Greek ἐνδεχόμενον or δυνατόν but, rather, to an entirely different term that, in Aristotle's text, is neither lexically nor conceptually associated with potentiality: συμβαίνειν, "to happen," which designates the event as such, without particular reference to possibility and impossibility. Becker-Freysing demonstrates that in Boethius' translation the two senses of *contingere* can hardly be distinguished. In a single passage of *De Interpretatione*, *contingens* may refer to either ἐδέχεσθαι or συμβαίνειν; at certain crucial points in Aristotle's treatise, such as in the chapter dedicated to statements "on singular and future matters," it even refers to both at once, appearing in one sentence to express the concept of possibility and in another to indicate the idea of taking place and occurrence.[35]

"Why," Becker-Freysing asks, "was Boethius not more exact in his translation of Περὶ ἑρμηνείας"?[36] His answer is that Boethius' striking use of the term *contingere* in the sense of the Greek ἐδέχεσθαι is not of his own invention; instead, he argues, it follows the translation practice established several hundred years before him by Marius Victorinus in his own Latin rendition of Περὶ ἑρμηνείας, with which Boethius, as we know from Cassiodorus, was familiar.[37] In the absence of Victorinus' *De Interpretatione*, Becker-Freysing demonstrates his hypothesis with reference to the extant fragments of Victorinus' translation of the *Isagoge*. Here the word ἐνδέχεται figures in Porphyry's definition of accident (συμβεβηκός), and Victorinus indeed renders it, as Boethius will, by the Latin *contingit*.[38]

Becker-Freysing's explanation for Boethius' use of the term *contingens* in his translation of Aristotle cannot be called into question on philological and historical grounds; as such, it is certainly sound. But it fails to address the properly philosophical significance of Boethius' lexical usage, which determines the form in which Aristotle's notion of possibility (δυνατόν, ἐνδεχόμενον) is transmitted to medieval thought.[39] By rendering the Greek συμβαίνειν and ἐνδέχεσθαι (or δύνεσθαι) by the same verb, *contingere,* Boethius binds the notion of the event to that of possibility, such that, in his text, what is capable can no longer be separated from what takes place. After Boethius the *contingentia,* in short, will concern *contingere* as such; contingency will constitute a mode of "happening," a way of taking place.

Despite appearances, Boethius' "translation" is in this sense faithful to Aristotle's text. For, when Aristotle considers the nature of contingency and possibility, his aim is not merely to define a logical category that is expressed in statements; he seeks, rather, to conceive at the same time of the nature of a faculty that exists as such. Hence Aristotle's account, in the *Metaphysica,* of the "potentiality to play" that persists in the kithara player even when he does not play and the "potentiality to build" which continues to be present in the architect even when he does not build;[40] hence, too, Aristotle's treatment, in *De Interpretatione,* of contingency precisely in terms of future events—events such as tomorrow's sea battle—which may, or may not, take place. In this sense Boethius' rendition, far from being a matter of mere philological oversight or deference to tradition, constitutes a genuine philosophical decision, which radicalizes, rather than distorts, a fundamental trait of Aristotle's notion of potentiality: namely, that it designates not an abstraction or a merely hypothetical possibility but something that exists and which, as such, takes place. This is the sense in which Boethius can truly be said to be the inventor of contingency, not merely as a *terminus technicus* but as a concept in its own right, one that carries the Aristotelian notion of potentiality (as τὸ ἐνδεχόμενον and τὸ δυνατόν) beyond itself, to the point at which, in Boethius' *contingentia,* it functions to indicate a complete coincidence of possibility and the event, potentiality and existence, being capable and being tout court.

In his two commentaries on *De Interpretatione* Boethius specifies the conditions that an event must fulfill to be properly termed "contingent." Not all future events, he explains, are capable of both being and not being; many, Boethius writes, "have a certain necessity in their very nature" (*quoniam in natura propria quandam habent necessitatem*).[41] There are those things, for example, that are necessary by virtue of their natural characteristics: thus fire is necessarily hot, even as snow is necessarily cold and man is necessarily mortal.[42] And there are those things, furthermore, which are necessary by virtue of natural laws: for example, the movement of earthly and astronomical bodies and the effects they imply.[43] Such things, which may certainly belong to the future, do not satisfy the definition that Boethius, citing "the Aristotelian doctrine" (*sententia Aristotelica*), offers of contingency: "that which happens by chance, or comes from free choice and one's own will, or which, by virtue of the readiness of nature, can be said to be in either of its parts, that is, as happening and not happening" (*quodcumque aut casus fert aut ex libero cuiuslibet arbitrio et propria voluntate venit aut facilitate naturae in utramque partem redire possibile est, ut fiat scilicet et non fiat*).[44] To predicate contingency, according to this definition, is simply to predicate possibility; the two terms, *contingentia* and *possibilitas*, Boethius writes, are coextensive (*convertuntur*) and "signify the same thing (*idem*)."[45] Contingent things are those "that *are* not, but that, rather, are capable of happening in the future" (*sunt contingentes, quae cum non sint, eas tamen in futurum evenire possibile est*).[46]

As such, contingent events, for Boethius as for Aristotle, imply the existence of utterances of a singular nature. Indeed, the link between contingent events and the speech that refers to them becomes so strong in Boethius that one term, *future contingents* (*contingentes futura*), functions to refer both to statements and to things, *propositiones* and *res*.[47] Boethius devotes great attention to the problem of the status of such future contingents as bearers of truth, falsity, or something other than either truth or falsity. Given two contradictory *propositiones* referring to a future contingent, Boethius writes, it cannot be the case that one is definitely false and one definitely true, for the "truth of the statement," according to the Aristotelian principle to which he often refers, "follows from the necessity of the thing" (*veritas propositionem sequitur necessitas rei*),[48] and the future contingent, by definition, is not necessary. But it cannot be the case, moreover, that, of two such statements concerning a future contingent, both are true or both false. Such claims, which admit the existence of contradictory statements that are both true or both false, cannot be reconciled with the fundamental logical law of the excluded middle. Finally, it cannot be said, Boethius writes, that, of two contradictory statements about the future, both are neither true nor false (*nec veras . . . nec falsas*), as the Stoics argue in their interpretation of Aristotle;[49] for the future contingent, although not yet determinately true or false, will, after the realization of the contingent event, necessarily refer to an event either truthfully or falsely.

Boethius concludes that future contingents are all, as such, bearers of "indeterminate" or "indefinite" (*indefinita*) truth and falsity. His thesis is in perfect accord with the fundamental Aristotelian principle to which Boethius, as we have seen, always holds: language speaks of things, from which it draws its existence. Since contingent events, according to Boethius, are those events that "tend equally toward being or toward not being" (*vel ad esse vel ad non esse aequaliter sese habent*) and which, in this sense, "have being or not being indefinitely" (*indefinitum habent esse et non esse*), the speech that bears on them must, as a result, itself "have indefinite truth or indefinite falsity" (*indefinitam veritatem vel falsitatem*).[50] That which is "unstable" (*instabile*),[51] "changeable" (*mutabiliter*),[52] and "variable" (*variabile*)[53] thus has its exact counterpart in a language that is itself indeterminate, which "affirms no more than (*non magis*) it denies,"[54] and which "bends equally toward truth and falsehood" (*aequaliter ad veritatem mendaciumque vergentibus*).[55] Here speech and the "things themselves" (*res ipsae*)[56] are bound together by the "indistinction" or "indiscretion" (*indiscretio*)[57] they share: by the literal impossibility of a *discrimen,* a distinction, separation and de-cision, between the possibility of being and not being, taking place and not taking place, and, therefore, between the possibility of affirmation and denial, truth and falsity. Even as the contingent event, according to Boethius' definition of *contingentia,* takes place as possible, the language that expresses it, too, is therefore irreducibly contingent: it takes place not in the form of an actual statement but as the mere possibility of predication, assertion, and truth—as the mere possibility, therefore, of *oratio* as such. Language, in future contingents, thus makes itself adequate to what it says: signifying what is merely capable of being and what cannot yet be said to be, language renders itself potential, reduced to a point at which, in total "indefinition," it is not yet itself.

IV

The early medieval philosophers do not develop the radical logical and linguistic consequences implied by Boethius' analysis of future contingents. When Anselm of Canterbury, for example, considers what it means to predicate the future of a thing (*futurum dicitur de re*), his concern is to establish that divine omniscience, although necessary, in no way compromises the freedom of the will (*libertas voluntatis*).[58] He does not call into question the specific truth value of statements concerning future contingents, for he supposes that, insofar as they are known by God, future contingents are in some sense necessary; and for Anselm the necessity of the event, whether absolute or conditional, demands that the proposition that refers to it be either true or false, both after and before its realization.[59]

Peter Abelard is the first medieval thinker to offer a sustained treatment of the linguistic form of future contingents in *De Interpretatione,* which repeats Boethius' analysis of the problem even as it carries it beyond the terms of Boethius' two commentaries. In the brief treatment he accords to *propositiones de praeterito et de futuro* in *De Dialectica,* Abelard thus offers a concise summary of the conclusions to which Boethius is led in his own *Commentarii.*[60] The event that Boethius terms *indefinitum* here appears as *indeterminatum,* and the specific truth of the statement bearing on the future contingent is renamed accordingly; but, despite its introduction of the concept of indetermination, Abelard's text follows Boethius' account of the metaphysical and logical status of the future contingent. "Just as the event of a future contingent is indeterminate," Abelard writes, "so the statements that speak of such events are said to be indeterminately true or false" (*Sicut autem eventus contingentis futuri indeterminatus est, ita et propositiones quae illos eventus enntiant indeterminate vel falsae dicuntur*).[61]

In his *Editio super Aristotelem de Interpretatione* and his *Logica Ingredientibus* Abelard offers far more sustained treatments of the indeterminacy constitutive of the future contingent, which lead him to formulate altogether novel conclusions.[62] Here Abelard considers contingency as "fortuitousness" (*utrumlibet*),[63] which he defines in the *Logica Ingredientibus* as "that which is no more inclined to take place than not to take place, tending equally to whichever" (*non magis se habet ad fieri vel ad non fieri, sed aequaliter ad utrumque*).[64] As such, however, the notion of contingency implies a paradox. According to the letter of Abelard's definition, that which is contingent is capable of taking place precisely to the extent that it is capable of not taking place; it is "no more" capable of happening than of not happening. This is the very aporia that I. M. Bochenski, in his *Formale Logik,* formulates as the characteristic paradox of contingency: if x is said to be contingent, then it follows that x is possible if and only if x is impossible and that, conversely, x is impossible if and only if x is possible.[65] This paradoxical existence, for Abelard, is implied in the concept of possibility as such. "For possible things," Abelard writes, "are those things that exist when they do not exist and do not exist

The Language of Contingency

when they exist, and that are thus naturally capable of turning over into either of the two by virtue of the ease of their nature" (*Possibilia enim sunt esse, cum non sint, et non esse, cum sint, et ita in utrumque partem facilitate naturae verti possunt*).[66] To exist in the mode of not existing and not to exist in the mode of existing—this, according to Abelard, therefore constitutes the very nature of contingency.

But how, then, is it possible to speak of what is contingent? Abelard addresses the question most forcefully in his commentary on Aristotle's example of the sea battle that may, or may not, take place tomorrow. At the end of the ninth chapter of Περὶ ἑρμηνείας, Aristotle had resolved the dilemma of statements on singular and future matters in the following terms:

> Dico autem, necesse est quidem futurum esse bellum navale cras vel non esse futurum, sed non futurum esse cras bellum navale necesse est vel non futurum esse, futurum autem esse vel non esse necesse est.[67]

> I say that it is necessary for there to be a sea battle tomorrow or for there not to be a sea battle tomorrow. But I do not say that it is necessary for there to be a sea battle tomorrow, or that it is necessary for there not to be a sea battle tomorrow; rather, what is necessary is that it will be or will not be.

Commenting on this passage, Abelard draws a fundamental distinction between the modes of necessity expressed by propositions: *necessitatas dividentem,* which holds for a single statement (in Aristotle's example, "there will be a sea battle tomorrow" or "there will not be a sea battle tomorrow"); and *necessitas sub disiunctione,* which holds for a disjunctive utterance as a whole (the entire phrase, "there will be a sea battle tomorrow, or there will not be a sea battle tomorrow").

Necessitas dividentem is the necessity expressed by a statement concerning a necessary event; it corresponds, Abelard writes, to *esse determinatum*.[68] *Necessitas sub disiunctione,* by contrast, is the necessity of "all things concerned with future contingents";[69] it corresponds, in metaphysical terms, to *esse impermutabiliter*.[70] This typology of necessity, for Abelard, founds the specific truth expressed in the statement on the future contingent. Abelard writes:

> Futurum esse vel non esse hoc totum scilicet est necesse, categorica est vera, in qua "necesse" praedicatur et haec oratio "esse futurum vel non esse futurum" subicitur.[71]

> What will be or will not be, as a whole, is necessary. The statement concerning what will be is true when "necessary" is predicated in this manner, from which "it will be or will not be" follows.

In accordance with the Boethian dictum that "the truth of the proposition follows from the necessity of the thing,"[72] Abelard thus derives the truth of the contingent statement from the specific necessity it articulates. The necessity of happening or not happening, taking place or not taking place, being or not being, therefore implies a singular form of logical truth: *veritas sub disiunctione,* one could say, coining a term that is not to be found in Abelard's texts, the necessary truth expressed in the tautology "there will be *x,* or there will not be *x.*"

In considering future contingents, Abelard is thus led to rethink not only the modal category of necessity but, equally, the structure of the proposition and the modes of its truth. *Necessitas sub disiunctione* is nothing if not a modality conceived in the closest relation to language, a modality that, by definition, requires the formulation of a specific utterance—namely, the disjunctive proposition—such as Aristotle's "there will be a sea-battle, or there will not be a sea-battle." In such a proposition, however, language is displaced from the register of its classical form. Nothing can said to be stated as such, for what is affirmed ("there will be a sea battle") is immediately followed by the possibility of its negation ("or there will not be a sea battle"). Here the logical element of predicative assertion, the *categorema,* must be set aside; at issue, instead, is a mere *syncategorema,* on which the possibility of the disjunctive proposition as a whole can be said to rest. *Or, vel,* is the single term that, without reference and signification, renders possible the alternative statement as a whole. It is the linguistic operator of contingency, without which no *necessitas sub disiunctione* could be formulated as such. Were there no *or,* nothing, after all, could be said to take place *or* not take place; all speech would, instead, be the speech of necessity. *Or,* which has justly been said to constitute "a linguistic element that is neither a noun nor a demonstrative and which expresses neither an affirmation nor a negation,"[73] is therefore what language says when, at the limit of speech, it no longer speaks of what must be. It is what language says when, instead, it announces what may, *or* may not, take place and when it thereby announces itself, in its essential irreducibility to affirmation and negation alike, as contingent.

V

In the thirteenth century Abelard's treatment of future contingents is so well known that it is hardly an exaggeration to consider it, together with Boethius' *Commentarii,* as the principal *auctoritas* with which any account of

The Language of Contingency

the logical and linguistic status of future contingents must reckon. This much is registered, for example, in Albert the Great's commentary on *De Interpretatione,* which was probably composed in 1262 and which Thomas Aquinas, in his own *Expositio in Libri Periermeneias* of a few years later, follows in its explication of the logical status of future contingents.[74] Clearly referring to Abelard's treatment of future contingents, Albert writes that the truth of the future contingent can only be expressed *sub disjunctione indeterminate;*[75] only such a form, he argues, corresponds to "what takes place in matters of contingency" (*contingit in contingenti materia*)—namely, the specific "potentiality" (*potentia*) constitutive of what is fortuitous (*utrumlibet*).[76]

At the same time, Albert's text, however, registers a fundamental displacement with respect to the tradition of reflection on the logical and linguistic status of contingency inaugurated by Boethius' *Commentarii in Librum Aristotelis Peri Hermeneias.* There are "some," Albert writes, at the end of his exposition of the problem of future contingents, who will ask further questions at this point.

> Quærunt etiam hic quidam de necessitate ordinis causarum, de fato, de fortuna, de consilio, de casu, de certitudine divinæ providentiæ in singularibus voluntariis contigentibus. Sed de his hic quærere stultum est: quia quæstiones istæ ex istus scientiæ principiis (cum logica procedat ex communibus quæ in pluribus vel in omnibus inveniuntur) non possunt determinari: ista autem determinari volunt ex propriis.[77]

> There are some who will also ask here about the necessity at work in the order of causes, fate, fortune, deliberation, and chance; and there are some who will ask here about the certitude of divine providence with respect to contingent singular matters of the will. But it is senseless to ask about these things in this field, for these questions can only be resolved on the basis of the principles of science that we study, given that logic is based on the common principles that are to be found in a multitude or in all things. These questions must be resolved on the basis of their own principles.

The series of concepts that medieval philosophy, at least since Boethius, articulates on the basis of the logico-linguistic problem of contingency are thus to be explained, according to Albert, with reference to the specific "principles of science" which, as such, lie outside the field of logic. The study of chance and fortune, Albert suggests, is now to be accomplished in the discipline of physics; that of deliberation, in ethics; that of divine prescience, in theology. The specific problem of the language of contingency, as a consequence, is dissolved. Here *contingentia* no longer functions, as it did from Aristotle and

Boethius to Abelard, to name the limit of language as such. Contingency, instead, is reduced to a matter of specific natural, metaphysical, and theological phenomena—fate, chance, fortune, divine will—to be studied in independence of language and its forms.

At the same time that Albert writes his *Commentarius,* however, a different investigation into the problem of contingency is already under way. Yet the authors of this exploration are not philosophers; they are, rather, poets. The point should not be entirely surprising. For the definition that, in one way or another, functions to characterize the language of contingency, from Boethius to Abelard, Albert and Thomas, is also, in truth, a precise definition of poetic language as such: *that speech that, while formally indistinguishable from speech in its canonical form, does not predicate, assert, or bear truth and falsity, and therefore is not, in any established sense, speech.* For what is poetry if not a linguistic usage that carries speech in its classical forms to a limit point at which it can no longer be said to retain any of its characteristic traits? What is literary language if not a discourse that, while formally identical to meaningful speech, accomplishes something other than the work of signification and reference? The set of idioms classed under the concept of "literature" consists of nothing if not of forms of speech which, in the terms of Boethius' definition of the language of contingency, "affirm no more than they deny,"[78] forms—or, rather, non-forms—of speech irreducible to the classical canons of communicative discourse. In poetry the structures of meaningful discourse are repeated, cited, recited, and thereby fundamentally altered; the figures of speech are displaced onto a terrain in which they no longer function in the service of the consolidation of meaning. In poetic discourse, language, in its classical sense, exceeds itself. No longer speaking of what exists, speech now concerns itself solely with what might, or might not, take place, dedicated entirely to what can and cannot be. In this sense poetry may be defined precisely as the language of contingency: that form in which language, speaking of what is merely possible, shows itself as something other than what it has been thought to be at least since its canonical, Aristotelian determination in terms of reference and signification, predication and assertion.

The birth of vernacular verse in the Middle Ages constitutes the emergence of precisely such a novel speech, for which classical terms and concepts for language (φωνή, λόγος, *vox, oratio*) may very well be inadequate. This is perhaps the ultimate sense in which medieval poetry constitutes an "invention" of languages. For, in composing in the vernacular, medieval poets do not merely write texts in languages (such as Old Occitan or Old French) which are homologous to the ones that precede them in time (for example, Latin). In the history of literature and thought, the first vernacular poetry of the Middle Ages marks a far more radical event: a genuine *inventio linguae* in which the forms of meaningful discourse, transposed and translated to unknown idioms, no longer function in the service of *vox significativa* in its traditional sense. In their use and transformation of the figures and structures of classical speech, the vernacular poetic texts of the Middle Ages mark the emergence of entirely novel languages, poetic idioms irreducibly to predicative and assertive *oratio*.

The first literary texts in the vernacular constitute poetic experiments with precisely such languages. They are significant because, instead of operating in the service of reference and signification, they present themselves as mere "fables": *fabulae, fables,* and *gabes,* works that by definition cannot be dissolved into that of which they appear to speak. Their verse, according to the famous phrase of the first troubadour, is "a verse of absolutely nothing" (*un vers de dreit nien*), which gives rise to a composition whose origin, form, and sense remain obscure to the poet himself: a speech of what in no sense exists and, therefore, for the reasons we have seen, something other than speech as such.[79] The singular *locutio* that Dante, in his works on poetry and poetics, defines as the "illustrious vernacular" (*vulgare illustre*) can be read the concept of precisely such a language. For Dante does not only distinguish the language of the classical *auctores* from the idioms of the vernacular poets, in that the first represents an ancient tongue and the second, by contrast, are fashioned in the mother tongue, which is "absolutely close to everyone" (*massimamente prossimo a ciascuno*) and "first in the mind" (*uno e solo è prima nella mente*), in the terms of the *Convivio*.[80] The author of *De Vulgari Eloquentia*, more significantly, treats the difference between the vernacular and Latin as a distinction between two fundamentally different forms of expression. As a "first speech" (*prima locutio*), the language of vernacular poetry is, in itself, irreducible to all "grammatical language" (*lingua gramatica*) in both senses of the medieval Latin term *gramatica:* "grammar" and "Latin."[81] Without *gramatica* medieval poetry, for Dante, is by definition foreign to all "science" and, for this reason, the form of its articulation, the predicative assertion; it cannot become the means of theoretical reflection, for it does not function in the service of the consolidation of learning. The first speech of which the vernacular writers make use, therefore, at once conditions and exceeds the "second speech" (*locutio secundaria*) of knowledge. By virtue of its constitutive "agrammaticality," the language of the vernacular *poëtas* is quite literally unruly and irregular; with respect to all previous forms of speech, it constitutes another language and, perhaps, something other than any language at all.

The *Roman de la Rose* of Guillaume de Lorris and Jean de Meun is perhaps the most perfect *exemplum* of the medieval project to compose verse in the novel language of this first speech. For the *Roman de la Rose* presents itself from the outset as capable of being otherwise than it is and, *a limine*, of not being at all; and its language, as a result, appears as a language that speaks, above all, of contingency. Carrying the medieval philosophical problem of the language of contingency to an extreme point, the language of the romance presents itself and its own taking place as the very contingency of which it speaks. As a work that, in its rhetorical and poetic organization, incessantly brings to light its own capacity to be interrupted and to take place otherwise than it does, the *Roman de la Rose* thus radicalizes the medieval reflections on the linguistic form of contingency in displacing them into the domain of poetic composition. We shall see that, in this case, three of the structures that criticism recognizes as fundamental in the medieval literary work—the subject of discourse, the organization of figural language, and topics—concern nothing other than the taking place of the text itself, in its irreducible possibility to be and not to be. In the *Roman de la Rose* these structures are thus not so much charged with new meanings as emptied of meanings and of meaning in general, discharged from the task of stating "one thing concerning another thing." Each structure is carried to its own limit point at which, portraying neither an individual subject nor a general doctrine, neither a set of figures nor a collection of ideas, it exposes what is, strictly speaking, no thing: the bare possibility of language to occur in the form of a poetic work. Such is the sense, as we shall see, of the poetics of contingency at work in the poem of Guillaume de Lorris and Jean de Meun: in its fundamental form as the discourse of an irreducibly contingent poetic subject, who is himself in being capable, at the same time, of being someone other than himself and no longer being at all; in its deployment of the figure of Fortune, which, as the allegorical personification of contingency, constitutes a figure for that of which one cannot properly speak; and, finally, in its treatment and transformation of the philosophical and theological problem of the reconciliation of human possibility and divine knowledge, in a language that, in its poetic form, marks the event of its own taking place as purely possible.

2 *The Nameless Lover,*
or

The Contingent Subject

I

It would be difficult to find a figure that has attracted more attention among historians and critics of medieval literature than the one in the poem that, with an apparently simple gesture, says "I." Since Leo Spitzer's early essay "Note on the Poetic and Empirical 'I' in Medieval Authors,"[1] numerous works have been dedicated to the speaker of medieval poetry: works on the literary "I" in the context of the medieval doctrines of allegory, such as Charles S. Singleton's studies of the exemplary "I" of the *Commedia*;[2] works on the condition of the poet as a lover, such as Roger Dragonetti's essays on the "total submission, dispossession, and complete powerlessness" characteristic of the *trouvère*;[3] and works on the structural position and function of the poetic self in the literary codes of medieval literature, such as Paul Zumthor's writings on the "perception of the individual in a poetic language that determines its topical structure,"[4] to name only several of the most eminent contributions to the field. The interest in the poetic "I" of medieval literature has grown further in recent criticism. To a large degree, this growth is due to Michel Zink's important work, *La subjectivité littéraire*, which defines medieval literary history in its entirety as the gradual emergence and development of poetic subjectivity. "The appearance of French literature," Zink writes, "coincides with the moment in which literature recognizes that it has no truth other than that of the subjectivity incarnated in it."[5]

The recent scholarly works on literary subjectivity have thus made it possible to pose a critical question that is of the greatest importance for the study of literature: who, in the text, is speaking? The question, despite its apparent simplicity, cannot easily be answered. The critical works on the problem of the medieval poetic "I" concur precisely in their uncertainty about the referential status of the first-person pronoun; and in many instances they deny, implicitly or explicitly, the possibility of attributing the "I" of a medieval author to a historical individual. Spitzer, for example, argued that the *ego* of medieval authors referred to two figures, the "universal" self and the "empirical" self, thereby suggesting, at least in principle, that the "I" was not the sign of an actual individual but the mark of a fundamental fracture.[6] In his essays on "Le je du poète," Zumthor also argued, albeit on different grounds, against any identification of the poetic "I" with a physical and historical being. The *ego* of the poet, he wrote, is not formed "in accordance with what is outside the text [*le hors-texte*]" but, rather, "forms itself" on the basis of the "types" of medieval poetic writing.[7] In *Le mirage des sources* Dragonetti reached a similar conclusion, arguing that "the 'I' is not an empirical subject, but a fictive identity."[8] And the formation of a subject that Zink considered in *La subjectivité littéraire* was a specifically literary phenomenon, tied not to historical individuals but to the development of forms of poetic discourse in the Middle Ages. Many of the strongest figures in the tradition of medieval criticism have maintained, for a number of different reasons, that the literary "I" is not the sign of an actual being but, rather, a specifically poetic figure.

If the *ego*, however, is not a lexeme whose referential function can be presupposed, if the "I" is not the name of an actual individual but essentially the product of a rhetorical operation, then the *significatum* of the first-person pronoun in medieval poetry cannot be presupposed by criticism; it cannot be considered as an actual being whose nature and structure are already established. In a significant portion of the recent criticism of medieval literature, however, the ultimate referent of the poetic "I" tends to be treated precisely as such a being, which is increasingly referred to by a single name: the subject. The term *subjectivity* itself has gained such currency in contemporary critical discourse that its pertinence to medieval literature is rarely considered; and when it is examined as such, it presents considerable resistance to analysis. It is significant, in this regard, that as keen a critic as Sarah Kay, the author of a book titled precisely *Subjectivity in Troubadour Poetry*, remains unable to define the meaning of *subjectivity* without recourse to the term *subject* itself: "By 'subjectivity,'" she writes, "I mean above all the elaboration of a first-person (subject) position in the rhetoric of courtly poetry."⁹ What, or who, however, is this "subject," which, presupposed within parentheses, functions to define the sense of poetic "subjectivity" in general? And in what sense can the "I" of medieval literature be said to constitute the "elaboration" of such a thing as a subjectivity?

It is worth noting that the use of the term *subject* with reference to the first-person pronouns of medieval texts involves a certain anachronism; it is, in a purely lexicographic sense, foreign to the Middle Ages. The only subject with which the medievals were familiar is that expressed by the Latin *subjectum,* a term that, in medieval philosophical parlance, functions as the Latin translation of the Greek ὑποκείμενον and the Arabic *mawḍuʻ*: to render literally, "that which lies beneath," "that which is posited," or "that which is presupposed."¹⁰ But this subject in no way bears the traces of a human individual; it does not function in medieval thought either to define or to characterize the form of a human being. For the philosophers of the Middle Ages who follow in the wake of Aristotle's science of the *ens inquantum ens,* the term *subjectum* designates, rather, the fundamental structure of all substance insofar as it "lies beneath" all accidental determinations. The identification of the "I" with "subjectivity," by contrast, is a specifically modern phenomenon, whose origin lies in the work of the very thinker commonly taken to seal the irrevocable end of medieval thought, namely, Descartes. Only after the Cartesian project to conceive of *certitudo cognitionis humanae* as the sole and absolute *fondamentum inconcussum veritatis* is the "I" considered as a subject, such that consciousness and existence, egoity and substantiality, become strictly correlative.¹¹

Even the most cursory glance at the definitions of the "I" to be found among the medieval philosophers suffices to show the distance that separates the thought of the Middle Ages from the modern project to conceive of the "I" as the expression of an actual and determinate subject. Peter Abelard's commentaries on Porphyry and Aristotle are especially significant in this context. They demonstrate the great subtlety with which twelfth-century grammatical and logical reflection could treat the complex referential structure of the first-person pronoun, the very structure that, in the twentieth century, Émile Benveniste placed at center of his linguistics of enunciation and Roman Jakobson sought to classify with reference to C. S. Peirce's distinction between symbol and index.¹² In his *Glossae super Porphyrium* Abelard defines the "I," in accordance with its linguistic status as a "shifter,"¹³ or means of deixis, precisely as belonging to a class of terms that "determine no nature or properties" (*nullam naturam vel proprietatem determinent*).¹⁴ "For instance, when I say 'I' or 'this,'" Abelard writes, "singular beings are signified, and yet the individual beings are not spoken of with any greater characteristics":

> Veluti cum dico: "ego, hic," singularis sunt significationis, nullius tamen superioris proprie individua dicuntur, quia ex sola discretione inventa sunt et meras significant substantias, quarum nullam naturam vel properitatem determinant, quia "hic" per se dictum neque dicit "haec substantia" neque "hic homo" neque "hoc ratione" vel "hoc album," sed simpliciter secundum discretionem personalem inventum est.[15]

> For instance, when I say "I" or "this," singular beings are signified, and yet the individual beings are not spoken of with any greater characteristics. For they are used only by specification or demonstration, and they signify mere substances of which they determine no nature or properties. For in itself, "this" does not say "this substance," "this man," "this reason," or "this white thing"; rather, it operates more simply, in accordance with the personal specification used.

In Abelard's text the personal pronoun appears, together with the demonstrative pronoun, as a part of speech whose meaning, in itself, is necessarily indeterminate. It may function as a means of reference in discourse, Abelard argues, only if it receives further specification by a noun or substantive (in such a way that *hoc,* to take Abelard's example, is defined as *hoc ratione* or *hoc album*). In itself the only signification the pronoun can accomplish is an "indifferent" one (*indifferenter*), as we read in the *Glosae super De Interpretatione;* for, as such, it indicates neither an actual thing nor the attributes of a thing.[16] In accordance with a tradition of linguistic reflection which has its origins in Apollonius Dyskolos' definition of pronouns as the signs of unqualified Being,[17] Abelard thus argues that the first-person pronoun "signifies bare substance"; as such, he writes, it "barely signifies" (*significat meras substantias, idest mere*).[18] It "determines no form" (*nullam formam determinat*), for it cannot express a qualified substance.[19]

Long before twelfth-century dialectics, however, the grammatical tradition of late antiquity had already distinguished the "I" as a term that, by virtue of its very nature as a pronoun, could not be said to signify any definite substance or subject. The *Artes Donati,* which remain canonical works for the instruction of grammar throughout the Middle Ages, are exemplary in this regard. "What is a pronoun?" we read in the *Ars minor.* "It is that part of speech," Donatus answers, "which, placed before the noun, signifies almost the same thing and, at the same time, expresses a *persona*" (*Pronomen quid es? Pars orationis quae pro nomine posita tantundem paene significat personamque interdum recipit*).[20]

Here Donatus does not merely define the *pronomen,* as one might expect, as a substitute for the noun.[21] In accordance with a tradition of grammatical reflection which stretches from Dyonisius Thrax and Apollonius to Priscian, Donatus also assigns the pronoun a specific and positive function among the parts of speech: *personam recipere,* to "express," or, more literally, to "receive" or "assume" a *persona.*[22] *Persona,* the equivalent of the Greek grammatical term προσώπον, is to be understood here in the classical sense the word still had in Donatus' fourth-century Latin, as "mask, especially that used by players," and, by metonymy, the "character" or "part" shown by it.[23] In being marked by *personae,* pronouns, for the grammarians, express such "false faces"; they articulate not distinct subjectivities presupposed by language but, rather, purely discursive functions (such as "the one who speaks," "the one spoken to," and "the one spoken of") which are determined by the grammatical structure of language alone.[24] According to such a conception, to say "I" is in no way to express oneself as an existing and substantial individual; it is neither to "incarnate oneself in literature," to invoke Zink's phrase, nor to "elaborate a first-person (subject) position," to return to Kay's formulation of her subject. It is, instead, *personam recipere,* to "assume," "receive," and "welcome" a mask, an empty shell through which the sound of the voice then passes (*per-sonat,* according to a possible classical etymology of the term which can still be found in Boethius).[25]

The distance that separates the modern critical ideas of the literary "I" from the medieval logical and grammatical considerations of the first-person pronoun, therefore, could not be more pronounced. *I,* the very word that is invoked by Zink, after Hegel, as the expression of a substantial individual to which one may give the name "subjectivity," is defined by a tradition of medieval thought as a term that defines no substance, refers to no actual properties, and expresses a mere function of discourse. The "I," which for many recent critics of "literary subjectivity" is what names an actual being, is precisely what, for many medieval authors, appears to express a fundamental anonymity: something without any determined nature or properties, a work of artifice and *fictio* in every sense.

The definition of the "I" as the sign of an existing subject, which appears almost self-evident today, is therefore foreign to the texts of medieval literature. Naturally, what is at issue here is not the term *subject* itself but, rather, the concept it implies. This is why there can be no question of simply rejecting the problem of poetic subjectivity in the Middle Ages on terminological grounds; such a rejection would reduce a fundamental critical and theoretical problem to a question of names. It is a matter, instead, of understanding the poetic "I" and the concept of the self it implies in a sense that is irreducible to the *ego* of modern thought. If, consciously retaining the modern critical usage of the term, we define the literary "subject" solely as that which is signified by the "I" of the poetic text, a number of questions must then be posed. What is the nature of the medieval literary subject, if the first-person pronoun appears in the medieval arts of language not as the stable sign of a *subjectum* and substance but as a term that "determines no nature and properties" (*nullam naturam vel proprietatem determinat*)? Who speaks in medieval vernacular poetry if to say "I," in the tradition of grammatical reflection, is to assume a *persona,* a mask? And who, finally, is the subject of medieval literature, if it is one that does not exist as an actual substance, if it, in a certain sense, *is* not?

The *Roman de la Rose* is exemplary here. For it distinguishes itself, among medieval literary works, as a narrative recounted by an "I" in which the first-person pronoun functions as something other than the sign of a single, actual, and existing individual. This much is inscribed in the very structure of the romance of Guillaume de Lorris and Jean de Meun, which continually explores the simultaneous determinacy and indeterminacy of the single term *je*. By virtue of its bipartition, the romance constitutes a literary text in which the single term *je* is necessarily capable of referring, at the very least, to two distinct poetic voices. As we shall see, this referential duplicity is but the first form of a profound experimentation with the sense and limits of the functions of the poetic "I" throughout the *Roman de la Rose*. It marks the romance, as a whole, as the work of a poetic self of a specific kind: a poetic subject irreducible to many of the notions of subjectivity familiar to us today, whose structure and sense in medieval poetics as a whole remain, to a large degree, to be examined.

II

As a narrative in the first person, the *Roman de la Rose* constitutes a work in which the discourse of the "I" coincides altogether with that of the poetic text. For a consideration of the narrator of the romance, therefore, no textual passage is more decisive than the beginning of the work as a whole, for the lines with which the romance opens are also those in which its "I" first announces itself. Yet the *Roman de la Rose,* as is well known, begins not with an explicit and thematic declaration of its narrator but with a prologue. It suffices to think of the passages that open the romances of Chrétien de Troyes and the discussions of the *generalis modi dispositionis* of the medieval poetic *artes* to recall that, in medieval literary practice and theory alike, the form of the prologue was determined by the most meticulous rhetorical regulation.[26] At first glance the opening of Guillaume de Lorris's poem conforms to the practice recommended in the thirteenth-century *Ars Versificatoria* by Matthew of Vendôme: to begin with a "general proverb, that is, a common saying in which tradition has faith, a common belief to which one may ascribe agreement and in which there lies the uncorrupted integrity of truth" (*generale proverbium, id est communis sententia, cui consuetudo fidem attribuit, opinio communis assensum accomodat, incorruptae veritatis integritas adquiescit*).[27] Guillaume's text, however, begins not with one accepted *sententia* but, rather, with two conflicting assertions, which coincide with the first two couplets of the *Rose*:

> Aucunes genz dient qu'en songes
> n'a se fables non et mençonges;
> mes l'en puet tex songes songier
> qui ne sont mie mençongier.
> (Vv. 1–4)

Some say that there is nothing in dreams but fables and lies, but one may have dreams which are not at all deceitful. (31)

It is worth noting that the subject matter of the two contradictory claims expressed in these lines cannot be classed among any of the literary loci that Matthew, in his *Ars*, draws from the corpus of classical Latin poetry. The first *matiere* of the Rose is not, as Matthew prescribed, *fortuna, calamitas amoris, languore promissionis*. Instead, it is the dream—the figure that, in medieval literature, has been said to mark "a *récit* within a *récit*" and, therefore, to stage a *mise en abîme* of the literary work itself.[28] Although it begins with a "general proverb," Guillaume's romance thus departs from the practice dictated by the rhetorical theory of his time, displacing the formal convention of the *processione generalis sententiae* significantly. The subject matter indicated by the *sententiae* at the start of the poem cannot be classed among the *magnalia* of classical poetry, nor can it be reduced to one of the topics recommended by medieval rhetoricians. Rather, the poetic text indicates in its opening that its *forma tractatus* will be the poem itself, its structure and its sense.

That the romance's opening fiction of the dream is, in fact, simply a fiction of fiction itself is already implicit in the first verses of Guillaume's text. For, by means of the opening verses' paranomastic assimilation of *songes* to *mençonges*,[29] the dream is characterized precisely as a locus of fictions, or, to use the

Old French term, *fables:* "Aucunes genz dient qu'en songes / n'a se *fables* non" (vv. 1–2). The determination of dreaming as confabulation in this passage sets the stage for an association that will recur throughout the two-part romance. The rhyme fellows with which the text's octosyllabic couplets repeatedly bind *songe* and *mensonge,* from *songes/mençonges* at vv. 9853–54 to *mançonge/songe* at vv. 18333–34, *mançonge/songe* at vv. 18463–64 and *songes/mançonges* at vv. 18469–70, merely amplify the prologue's identification of dreaming with invention; they link the dream, through its proximity to falsehood, to literary "fables," which are themselves often perceived as inherently mendatious (*fables / por menteür,* vv. 15186–87; cf. also vv. 2434: *mençonge et fable*), potentially "corruptible" (*corrumpables;* cf. vv. 19951–52) and even "diabolic" (cf. the rhyme words *fables/deables* at vv. 18292–93).[30] The following verses of the prologue, which consider the status of dreams as bearers of truth or falsity, therefore simultaneously concern the status of poetic invention and *fabulare.* As such, they refer proleptically to the poetic dream that has not yet been announced and which will, after the prologue, constitute the body of the *Roman de la Rose.* The *songe-fable* of the prologue, figured as a literary work before the romance itself has assumed the form of a dream, thus announces the poem that has yet to be named. Before the dream of the romance itself begins, the romance precedes itself in its own prologue; it speaks of itself and its character as a *fable,* through the figure of the dream, before it has marked itself as a *narratio fabulae.*

But what, then, is a dream if its structure is that of the literary work? The prologue explains, first of all, that dreams are capable of not being false: "But one may have dreams which are not deceitful" ("mes l'en puet tex songes songier / qui ne sont mie mençongier" [vv. 3–4]) (31). The text must be read carefully here. The poem declares that there are dreams that cannot be reduced to the status of lies, and yet it does not, for that matter, explicitly suggest that dreams may be true as such: later in the prologue we read that "there was nothing in the dream that did not take place just as the dream had told it" (*en ce songe oncques riens n'ot / qui tretot avenu ne soit / si con li songes le recencoit,* vv. 28–30), but in its opening verses the work literally contains no mention of the truth value of the *fable-songe.* The dream is not true but, rather, at the limit, *comes true;* the difference is of the greatest importance. Neither utterly false nor simply true, the work thus occupies the position of dreams in medieval literature and thought, which has been characterized precisely as that of a space "between truth and falsehood."[31] At the same time, its complex structure illustrates one of the most fundamental definitions of the fable known to the authors of the Middle Ages, in which the *fabula* is said to exclude truth and probability alike. "The fable," we read in the *Rhetorica ad Herennium,* "is that which contains neither true nor verisimilar things" (*Fabula est quae neque veras neque veri similes continet res*).[32] The characterization of the *fabula* offered in Cicero's *De Inventione* is almost identical: "the fable is that in which neither true nor verisimilar things are contained" (*Fabula est in qua nec verae nec veri similes res continentur*).[33]

The writers of the twelfth and thirteenth centuries were familiar with a long tradition of medieval thought that maintained that poetic fables, as works of pure fiction, are neither true nor false, neither verisimilar nor illusory. The idea of a poetic production irreducible to truth and falsity alike, in fact, was already expressed by Aristotle, who, as we saw in the preceding chapter, defined rhetorical and poetic utterances as being precisely "neither true nor false" (οὔτε ἀληθὴς οὔτε ψευδής, *neque vera neque falsa*).[34] Such a conception of the literary product appears again in Isidore of Seville's *Etymologiarum,* in the context of an explicit discussion of the status of *fabulae*. Citing Varro,[35] Isidore derives the term *fable* (*fabula*) from the Latin verb "to speak" (*for), suggesting that the fable, as a work of purely linguistic invention, is irreducible to the realm of "facts" (*facta*). According to Isidore, *fabulae,* unlike *factae,* are fictions and are, in principle, neither true nor false (Fabulas *poetae a* fando *nominaverunt, quia non sunt* res factae *sed tantum loquendo fictae*).[36] In a different text Isidore clearly insists that the fabulation of poets is irreducible to truth and falsity:

> *Falsum* ad oratores pertinet, ubi veritas seape ita laeditur, ut quae facta sunt, negentur; *fictum* vero ad poëtas, ubi quae facta non sunt, facta dicantur. Falsum est ergo quod verum non est, fictum quod tantum verisimile est.[37]
>
> The *false* pertains to orators, in whom truth is often wounded, so that they may deny things that happened; the *fictitious,* by contrast, pertains to poets, who claim that things that did not happen happened. The false is therefore what is not true; the fictitious is what is generally verisimilar.

For Isidore the distinction between truth and falsity, which holds for *factae,* is therefore inappropriate for the work of *poëtas. Fabulae,* he maintains, are not *falsae;* as *fictae,* they are not "true" but "verisimilar" and, therefore, essentially irreducible to the opposition between truth and falsity. This conception of literary works remains so influential in the course of the Middle Ages that we find it expressed in the very same terms by Conrad of Hirschau in the twelfth century. "A fable," he writes, in his classification of the types of writing, "is a fictional, not factual, thing" (*Fabula ficta res, non facta*).[38]

The *songe-fable* that is at issue in the beginning of the *Roman de la Rose* may well be of this "fictive" nature, which is situated beyond both facts and their falsification, in the territory of pure invention. When, in a striking abbreviation of the structures of the prologue two thousand lines later in the poem (vv. 2065–74), the narrator does attribute a certain veracity to his tale, asserting that at the end of the romance "the truth" (*la verité*) of his dream will be "entirely revealed" (*toute aperte,* vv. 2071–74), the *verité* of which he speaks is therefore fundamentally different in kind from the *veritas* of the metaphysical tradition; the traditional concept of truth as *adequatio rei et intellectus,* the correspondence of things and thought (or language), has no pertinence at this point.[39] The prologue displaces the entire problem of reality and its distortion, facts and their falsification, by introducing an altogether different opposition: that, namely, between concealment and unconcealment. The entire text of the prologue is constructed around this distinction: covered/uncovered, closed/disclosed, *coverte/aperte,* in Guillaume's words.[40]

> Aucunes genz dient qu'en songes
> n'a se fables non et mençonges;
> mes l'en puet tex songes songier
> qui ne sont mie mençongier
> ainz sont aprés bien aparant,
> si en puis bien traire a garant
> un auctor qui ot non Macrobes,
> qui ne tint pas songes a lobes,
> ançois escrit l'avision
> qui avint au roi Scypion.
> Qui c'oncques cuit ne qui que die
> qu'il est folor et musardie
> de croire que songes aviegne,
> qui se voudra, por fol m'en tiegne,
> quar endroit moi ai ge fiance
> que songes est senefiance
> des biens as genz et des anuiz,
> que li plusor songent de nuiz
> maintes choses covertement
> que l'en voit puis apertement.
> (Vv. 1–20)

> Some say that there is nothing in dreams but fables and lies, but one may have dreams which are not deceitful, whose import becomes quite clear afterward. We may take as witness an author named Macrobius, who did not take dreams as trifles, for he wrote of the vision which came to King Scipio. Whoever thinks or says that to believe in a dream's coming to pass is folly and stupidity may, if he wishes, think me a fool; but, for my part, I am convinced that a dream is the significance of the good and evil that come to men, for most men at night dream many things in a hidden way which may afterward be seen openly. (31)

Here the *songe* is vindicated, through the authoritative citation of Macrobius, as not deceitful (*mie mençongier*) because what it presents in the present becomes, in the future (*aprés*), *bien aparant* (v. 5). What appears at one moment as veiled (*covertement*) thus emerges, at a later time, as unveiled (*apertement*, vv. 19–20). The dream, as Guillaume presents it, has the form of this simultaneously temporal and hermeneutic passage: from the earlier to the later, the closed to the disclosed.

As a fable that reveals itself in being "uncovered," the *songe* of the prologue demands to be read in relation to the notions of *involucrum* and *integumentum* invoked by the philosophers of Chartres to characterize the doctrinal function of classical myth and literature.[41] In its structure as a fiction that implies a movement from the closed to the disclosed and the earlier to the later, Guillaume's dream appears, furthermore, as a development of the fundamental patristic exegetical concept of "figura," which Auerbach reconstructed in a famous essay.[42] In the works of the Church Fathers the term *figura*, together with *umbra, imago*, and *allegoria*, functions to translate the Greek τύπος (type), which appears in Paul's Epistles to characterize the relation of events narrated in the Old Testament to their fulfillment in the time of Christ.[43] As such, *figura* designates a relation of both temporal difference and semiotic fulfillment, by which what once appeared in its mere literality emerges, at a later historical point, in its full metaphorical significance. According to Tertullian, for example, when it is said that Moses gives the name "Joshua" to Oshea (in Num. 13:16), this is but a *figura:* "For he called him 'Jesus.' . . . And we say that this was a figure of things to come" (*et incipit vocare Jesus. . . . Hanc prius dicimus figuram futurorum fuisse*).[44]

The *songe* of the prologue is precisely such a *figura futurorum*, in which it is impossible to separate the temporal difference between the time of the present dream and that *aprés* from the semiotic difference between what appears *covertement* and what appears *apertement*. And yet here the model of *figura* is further complicated; it functions to regulate yet another difference. For in the prologue to the romance the specifically figural distinction, which is both temporal and semiotic, is cast in terms of a difference in the poetic work itself: its beginning and its end. Since it is the romance itself which will constitute the *songe* of which we read in the prologue, the movement by which what is present passes into what is *aprés* and what is *coverte* becomes *aperte* must also be that by which the beginning of the poem itself, in unfolding, reaches its end. Here the double difference that constitutes *figura* in its exegetical sense is thus inscribed in the poetic work; it is inscribed *as* the poetic work, to the degree that the work appears as the fable of a *songe* that dis-closes itself.

The name the text of the prologue gives to this structure is *senefiance*. Dreaming is significance; "Songes est senefiance" (v. 16). The implications of this assertion for the sense of the *Roman de la Rose* as a whole must be registered in all their weight. "Que songes est senefiance" does not simply mean that the work, as a dream, bears significance, referring to "the good and evil that come to men" (*biens as genz et des anuiz,* v. 17) as would an utterance or a set of utterances. The letter of the text, rather, implies a far more radical claim: namely, that the poem, as a dream, "is" the significance of good and evil. As the narration of a dream, the poem, in other words, does not simply possess meaning, as a property that already exists and can be given. Instead, it constitutes it, as it unfolds from its *incipit* to its *explicit,* for it holds within itself the two elements that, in the classical Augustinian theory of the sign, constitute the *signum* as such: that which functions to signify something and that which, in this movement, is thereby signified.[45] In its temporal passage from beginning to end, the work functions as both signifier and signified, the literal and the figural, the *coverte* and the *aperte.*

The narrator of the poem amplifies and further elucidates this structure of "significance" when, at the center of the poem, he presents the trajectory of the romance as a passage that leads from obscurity to clarity and from confusion to the intelligibility of sense:

> Notez ce que ci vois disant,
> d'amors avrez art souffisant.
> Et se vos i trovez riens trouble,
> g'esclarcirai ce qui vos trouble
> quant le songe m'orrez espondre.
> Bien savrez lors d'amors respondre,
> s'il est qui an sache opposer,

> quant le texte m'orrez gloser;
> et savrez lors par cel escrit
> quant que j'avrai devant escrit
> et quant que je bé a escrire.
>   (Vv. 15114–28)

> Take note of what I tell you here. You will have an adequate art of love. And if you have any difficulty, I will clarify what confuses you when you have heard me explain the dream. Then, when you have heard me gloss the text, you will know how to reply about love if someone opposes you. And then you will understand, thanks to this writing, whatever I have written before and whatever I still wish to write. (258)

The significance of the work appears, in this passage, as that of reading. As a dream that progressively discloses its sense, the romance, we read, is not only a "text"; it is also a "gloss," which illuminates its own tale, rendering it intelligible through time.[46] If every gloss marks a "surplus of meaning" (*de . . . sens le surplus metre*), in the terms of the prologue to Marie de France's *Lais*,[47] then here the work must be said to include its own surplus within itself; the poem exceeds itself, "clarifying" (*esclairer*) its own "difficulty" and obscurity (*trouble*) even as it unfolds its tale. "This writing" (*cel escrit*), the romance, is itself by being also its own commentary; it is one, paradoxically, in being two. The significance of the dream can be revealed only because of this simultaneity, in the work, of singularity and duplicity; it can manifest itself precisely because of this poetic identity of sameness and alterity.

It is in this context that we must understand the "allegorical" character of the *Roman de la Rose,* which has so often been invoked and so rarely defined by critics of the work.[48] The romance is not merely allegorical because it has the form of a dream narrative in which an "I" encounters figures who, through *sermocinatio* and sustained metaphors, act as particular individuals while representing abstract concepts. Such stylistic and formal observations, which are surely incontrovertible, only graze the surface of the allegorical and figural dimensions of the poem. As a dream that uncovers its sense in unfolding through time, the work itself has the form of a single, extended *figura;* its literary structure is that of the patristic and medieval "type" (τύπος), in which a historical difference between two points delimits the space in which an event is revealed in its full significance. Before its particular figures, personifications, and their interaction, the work, in this sense, is in its very structure allegorical. It is *allegoria* in the sense that Isidore of Seville gives to the term, for it constitutes a "foreign speech" (*alieniloquium*) in which "one thing is said and another is signified" (*aliud enim sonat, et aliud intelligitur*).[49] At its inception the romance presents itself, above all, as "indicating something else" (ἄλλο ἀγορεύει), and it simultaneously shows the "something else" to which it incessantly points to be nothing other than itself.

The work, then, is a double one. For, according to the specific structure of the *fable* delineated in the prologue, the romance is essentially fractured, as a dream, into its closure and disclosure, which take the form of its beginning and its end. This division does not constitute one trait of the work among others; it is, rather, the defining trait of the romance insofar as it is a dream and, as such, significance (*senefiance*). As a "meaningful" dream, the work itself is more—and less—than itself. It is but the announcement of a work to come, and, at the same time, it is the very work that it announces.

When, after the prologue, the "I" of the poem finally appears in the text, it is, in turn, double. It speaks of *itself*, such that it distinguishes itself from itself as a present self from a past one:

> El vintieme an de mon aage,
> el point qu'Amors prent le paage
> des jones genz, couchier m'aloie
> une nuit, si con je souloie.
> (Vv. 21–24)

In the twentieth year of my life, at the time when Love exacts his tribute from young people, I lay down one night, as usual. (31)

Critics of the *Rose* have often noted the division implicit in this self-recollection. In Badel's terms it lies in the structure of the medieval "autobiographical dream," which can be summarized in the following formula: "*I* recount that *I* dreamed or saw supernatural powers" ("*Je* raconte que *Je* a songé ou vu des puissances surnaturelles").[50] E. B. Vitz has suggested the difference implicit in Guillaume's "I" follows from its position in the "oddly hybrid genre" of autobiography, in which the "'I' who speaks, speaks of himself as if he were another."[51]

Yet this division of the poetic self cannot be fully understood on its own terms. It is, in fact, simply the extension to the "I" of the fracture in signification which the prologue presented as the essential structure of the work as a whole. In its first appearance the "I" doubles itself precisely because, as the voice of the poetic text, it, like the work, bears the constitutive fracture of *senefiance*. This is why the work, as a *songe-fable,* must be considered together with the poetic "I"; the two share a single structure of doubling and differentiation.

The Contingent Subject

The "I," to return to Augustine's terms, functions here as a *signum* in both senses: it is what signifies something (the "I" who refers to *mon aage*) and what is thereby signified (the "I" in his *vintieme an*). It is, in Benveniste's terms, the marker of *discours* and the protagonist of a *histoire,* the subject of enunciation and the subject spoken of in that enunciation.[52] This is perhaps the full sense in which the *Roman de la Rose,* as Zink writes, "marks the final stage of the increasingly close relation between allegory and subjectivity":[53] the allegorical work, which differs from itself, as a *fable* and *songe,* cannot but be recited by an allegorical self, who is himself fractured and double.

No sooner, however, is a second "I" distinguished from the first, as the remembered self from the speaking self, than the second "I" itself is doubled through the invocation of the dream. The initial doubling of the "I" by recollection functions, in this way, to introduce a further fracture in the subject, namely, that between the "I" who dreams and the "I" who is dreamt.

The poetic text thus first introduces the "I" who, after going to bed (*couchier m'aloit*), sees a dream:

> El vintieme an de mon aage,
> el point qu'Amors prent le paage
> des jones genz, couchier m'aloie
> une nuit, si con je souloie
> et me dormoie mout forment,
> et vi un songe en mon dormant
> qui mout fu biaus et mout me plot.
> (Vv. 21–27)

In the twentieth year of my life, at the time when Love exacts his tribute from young people, I lay down one night, as usual, and slept very soundly. During my sleep I saw a very beautiful and pleasing dream. (31)

After describing the sleep of the dreaming "I," however, the text passes to the *songe* itself. The narrative of this dream consists in the depiction of not only a *locus amoenus* in the month of May but also, eventually, an "I" in the dream, who is formally distinct from the "I" who dreams:

> Avis m'iere qu'il estoit mais,
> il y a ja bien .v. anz ou mais
> qu'en may estoie, ce sonjoie,
> el tens enmoreus, plain de joie,
> el tens ou toute rien s'esgaie,
> que l'en ne voit buisson ne haie

> qui en may parer ne se veille
> et covrir de novele fuelle.
> . . . .
> En icelui tens deliteus,
> que toute rien d'amer s'esfroie,
> songai une nuit que j'estoie.
> (Vv. 45-52, 84-86)

I became aware that it was May, five years or more ago; I dreamed that I was filled with joy in May, the amorous month, when everything rejoices, when one sees no bush or hedge that does not wish to adorn itself with new leaves.... And so I dreamed one night that I was in that delicious season when everything is stirred by love. (31-32)

In the line "songai une nuit que j'estoie" the paradox of the doubling in the dream comes fully to light. The dreaming "I," who is merely implied here by the verbal form of *songai,* dreams that "he was" in the "lovely place"; yet, insofar as he dreams of himself, the first "I" must necessarily dream of himself as another. A single grammatical term, *I,* functions here as a placeholder for two irreducible poetic selves.

In its rhetoric the doubling produced by the figure of the dream is the temporal inversion of the doubling carried out by the narrator's self-recollection. As we have seen, the romance proper begins with the self-differentiation of the "I" through memory. It consists, to summarize, in the phrase: "I *remember* that I *was,*" in which the first and second "I," by definition, cannot fully coincide. Given the prophetic structure of the dream, by which what appears in sleep later is *aprés bien aparant,* the doubling of the dream, by contrast, has the form of an anticipation. It can be expressed as follows: "I *dream* that I *will be,*" in which the second "I" necessarily signifies a future self defined in distinction to the first. Such is the rhetorical order that regulates what Zink has called the "chronological disorder" marking the opening of the romance.[54] The anticipation articulated in the dream is the precise temporal inversion of the recollection with which the poem begins; it doubles the doubling of the self in memory and, in this complex movement, constitutes the poetic subject of the romance as divided with respect to the past and divided with respect to the future. In such an anamnesis of a prolepsis, the narrator recollects himself as what he may have been and, at the same time, projects himself as what he may one day be.

It is, therefore, difficult to consider the *Roman de la Rose* an autobiography in any strict sense, in addition to the notable problems that this genre poses for medieval literature in general.[55] At most one may speak, as Emmanuelle Baumgartner has suggested, of a "simulacrum of autobiography,"[56] or, in Claire Nouvet's terms, of an "autobiographical dream. . . . in which I do not see myself but the lyric shape of the self, a shape in which I, you, or anybody, can recognize oneself."[57] With a gesture that announces the *Libro de buen amor* and its singular "I," *yo joan rroyz, / açipreste de fita,* the romance presents its subject as a figure formed—and deformed—in language alone.[58] Nameless, multiplied, simultaneously commemorated and announced, recalled and foreseen, the "I" of Guillaume's text is not one. And where the self is not itself (αὐτός), there can be no writing (γραφεῖν) of a single life (βίος) as such: no "autobiography" in the sense that Philippe Lejeune, for example, gives the term when he defines it as "a retrospective *récit* in prose that a real person makes of his own existence."[59] Not only is the romance neither simply "retrospective" nor "in prose"; it is also not a *récit* in which the "I" can be attributed to a "real person" who speaks of "his own existence." At its very outset the poetic text has already divested the "I" of its self-identity; by the time the narration of the dream begins and we read the words "songai une nuit que j'estoie," the *je* of the text functions to mark a movement of self-differentiation by which the narrator of the poem withdraws from all identity with itself. As the subject of the allegorical work, the "I" of the poem reveals itself to the very degree that it shows itself to be other than itself.

This self-differentiation of the "I" does not end with the text attributed to Guillaume de Lorris. As we shall see, Jean de Meun's continuation and completion of the *Roman de la Rose* brings the allegorical structure of the poetic self to the most extreme point of its development. In Guillaume's romance the "I" marks a potential difference in the narrator, a difference between the self who speaks the discourse of the *incipit* and the self as it may have been or may one day be. Jean de Meun carries this difference of the self from itself one step further. In the second part of the poem the *je* constitutes the sign of a noncoincidence of the subject with himself which is as irreparable as it is fully actual. For in Jean's text the first-person pronoun will be, in the most literal sense, the cipher of a self who ceases to be himself: a subject, as we shall see, who dies and survives himself as another, only to be himself, in turn, displaced and supplanted by a final figure, for whom the text of the poem has no name.

45

III

In the vast majority of the medieval manuscripts of the *Roman de la Rose,* the text of Guillaume's romance was clearly distinguished from that of Jean de Meun's continuation. Placed after a rubric marking the end of the first part of the romance, the opening verses of the continuation would almost always have been immediately identifiable as the work of the poem's second author, long before the text itself explicitly announces the substitution of Guillaume by Jean. The thirteenth- and fourteenth-century manuscripts BN fr 1559, BN fr 1569, BN fr 1567, and BN fr 25926, for example, all clearly indicate the interruption in the text of the romance, either by explicit commentaries and interpolations on the two authors or by typographical marks that signal the end of Guillaume's poem and the start of Jean's.[60] And yet, despite the interruption between the texts of the two poets, Jean's continuation begins precisely where the first poem ended. Referring, by means of an anaphora, to the discourse that preceded it, the syntax of Jean's text establishes a specific relation to Guillaume's romance. At the end of the "first *Rose,*" after the incarceration of Bel Accueil, the narrator of Guillaume's poem speaks:

> Ja mes n'iert rien qui me confort
> se je pert vostre bienveillance,
> car je n'ai mes aillors fiance.
> (Vv. 4026–29)

If I lose your good will, there will never be any comfort for me, since I have no confidence elsewhere. (88)

And Jean's text begins:

> Et si l'ai je perdue, espoir,
> a poi que ne m'en desespoir.
> (Vv. 4029–30)

And perhaps I have lost it; I am ready to despair of it. (91)

The *incipit* ties the continuation to the opening of the romance by recalling the many "losses" that precede it: the "loss of joy" (*la joie que j'ai perdu,* v. 3929), the "loss of hope and expectation" (*je criens ausi avoir perdue / et m'esperance et m'atendue,* vv. 3943–44), and the "loss that is so great and evident" (*ma perte / qui est si grant et si aperte,* vv. 4011–12). It announces, at the same time, the loss that, in the poem, will soon be attributed to the narrator's love:

cele amor fut si eperdue, / qu'el s'en foï, si est perdue (vv. 5363–64). Most immediately, however, the anaphoric direct object in "si *l'*ai je perdue" appears to refer to the *bienveillance* of Guillaume's last verses, as Armand Strubel has indicated:[61] the poetic self with which Jean's poem opens, according to this reading, has lost the faith and confidence to which Guillaume's text refers before its end. The anaphoric relation, in this way, appears as the instrument by which the two parts of the romance are seamlessly bound together.[62]

Such an understanding of the first couplet of Jean's continuation is certainly valid in grammatical terms, yet it is possible to offer a different interpretation of the poetic text. The words "l'ai je perdue," situated after an interruption in the text of the romance and at the start of a continuation, can be read to mark the loss in the continuity of the poem itself. As a syntactic figure that by definition refers to a preceding linguistic segment, the anaphora appears to carry particular weight in this context. It functions to inscribe the loss articulated in the phrase "l'ai je perdue" in the very syntax of the poetic text. Placed after an interruption in discourse, the anaphora cannot function easily; its distance from the anaphorized term, whether it be in the preceding line (*bienveillance*) or in the words that follow it (*espoir*), may well deprive it of a determinate referent. The language of the text thus threatens to alter the function of the anaphora in discourse; for here the very figure that, in ordinary speech, operates as a means of linguistic recuperation and semantic consolidation marks precisely a difficulty—and, at the limit, an impossibility—of reference. As such, the anaphoric, elided pronoun *le* appears as a cipher of the very loss stated in the whole phrase "l'ai je perdue": that of the unity of the romance itself, its form as the work of a single "I."[63]

The rupture with which the text of Jean de Meun's poem opens implies a loss in the narrator himself. Here the correlation between the work and its subject, which we already observed in the *incipit* of Guillaume's poem, remains fully operative. We have seen that, in the first verses of the continuation, Jean's text constitutes itself in relation to the rupture that separates it from the preceding poem, thereby calling attention to an interruption and lack of unity in the romance as a whole. In its appearance in the first scene of the "second *Rose*," Jean's "I," like the romance as a whole, risks being stripped of unity and self-identity; despairing, it suffers a violence that exposes it, ultimately, to its own mortality. The first scene of the continuation thus depicts the "I" in a state in which its every *espoir* shows itself, through a play of *annominatio*, to be merely *desespoir:*

> Et si l'ai je perdue, espoir,
> a poi que ne m'en desespoir.
> Desespoir! Las! je non feré,
> ja ne m'en desesperé,
> quar s'Esperance m'iert faillanz,
> je ne seroie pas vaillanz.
> (Vv. 4029–34)

> And perhaps I have lost it; I am ready to despair of it. Despair! Alas! I shall not do so. I shall never despair of it, for if Hope were to fail me, I should lack valor. (91)

Citing a classical figure of the *trouvères* often invoked in the first part of the romance (see vv. 1833–35; v. 2404; v. 2609; v. 2941; cf. also vv. 4073–74; v. 10466), the narrator declares that his future will bring him only "martyrdom":[64] "Donc n'i a mes fors du soffir / et mon cors a martire offrir" (vv. 4145–46); "So there is nothing to do but suffer and offer my body to martyrdom" (92). And in the most pronounced expression of his despair, the narrator, raising the possibility that he will never reach the goal of his amorous journey, imagines his own death:

> Or aut si com aler pourra,
> face en Amors ce qu'il vourra
> ou d'eschaper ou d'encourir.
> S'il veust, si me lesse mourir.
> N'en vendroie ja mes a chief,
> si sui je mors se ne l'achief,
> ou s'autres pour moi ne l'achieve.
> (Vv. 4165–71)

> So let things go as they can, let the God of Love do as he wishes, whether it be to let me escape, to go on farther, or, if he wishes, to let me die. I shall never come to the end of my task, and I shall die if either I or another for me do not finish it. (93)

The narrator of Jean's text, whom the text of the poem has not yet formally distinguished from that of Guillaume's romance, thus raises the possibility that he may die, never "achieve" his work, and that another, in his place ("pour moi"), may continue it. His suggestion, which formally recalls that of countless medieval scribes, acquires a specific sense in the context of the two-part romance. Here the *je* of the continuation can be read as alluding, albeit implicitly, to the event that precedes it, namely, the interruption of Guillaume's "I" and the fragmentation of the first part of the romance; and it can be understood, at the same time, as indicating the position that it has assumed in effecting the continuation of the poetic text as such. In the form of a dejected conjecture ("n'en vendroie ja mes a chief . . ."), the "I," in this way, inscribes its own position in the order of the poem, as the means of the continuation of a work that, on account of death, was never brought to its end.

The subject of Jean's text is thus constituted, in its first appearance, by its relation to an excess that it cannot master. Its syntax betrays the rupture that its text, as a continuation, cannot conceal; its speech expresses the absence of an object that, through a displacement effected by the anaphora, it cannot identify as such. The poetic "I," in this way, defines itself in terms of the very interruption it should have effaced; it replaces an absent "I" only to raise the possibility that it, too, may fall silent before the end of its work, rendering the discourse it appears to animate merely the "testamant" of a dead author (v. 4188).[65]

Relating itself to the possibility of its disappearance and its subsequent substitution, the "I" of the opening scene of Jean's continuation does not only, however, refer, by metalepsis, to the rupture between the two halves of the entire *Roman de la Rose* which has already taken place. At the same time, it refers, by prolepsis, to the explicit revelation of that rupture over five thousand lines later. Here, in what has been often called the "conjoined midpoint" of the romance as a whole,[66] the figure of Amors reveals the double authorship of the poetic text. The extratextual conditions of the writing of the work, in this scene, are folded into the poetic text itself; the historical genesis of the romance is inscribed, rhetorically, within the very work it would appear to explain. In this passage the text of the work declares what the reader of the poem already knows: that Guillaume de Lorris, after "beginning" his romance (*conmancier le romant,* v. 10519) and failing to bring it to its end, is followed by "Jehans Chopinel," born "seur Laire a Meün" (v. 10537). Jean de Meun, Amors relates, thus "continues" the text of the poem precisely at the point at which Guillaume, interrupted by death, "ceases" to write:

> car quant Guillaumes cessera,
> Jehans le continuera,
> enprés sa mort, que je ne mante.
> (Vv. 10557–59)

For when Guillaume shall cease, Jean will continue it—may I not lie. (188)

In this commentary on the romance within the romance itself, Amors reveals the "I" to be the placeholder for irreducibly different selves, who are named as such by the text of the romance. The text of the "second *Rose*" thus develops, in the most consistent and far-reaching fashion, the structure that, as we have seen, marked the narrator of the "first *Rose*" as such: its doubling and difference from itself. In Jean's text the *je* does not merely appear as the sign of a virtual distinction, as in the self-recollection and self-anticipation of the beginning of Guillaume's poem; it does not solely function, in the rhetoric of the text, to articulate a structural self-differentiation of the poetic self. As the pronoun of two irreducibly different subjects who are named by the text of the poem as such, the "I" now reveals itself as the mark of a fundamental nonidentity; it shows itself, in the most literal sense, as the name of another.

The discourse of Amors, however, implies a further, more far-reaching consequence for the status of the poetic subject of the romance. For, even as Amors discloses that the single "I" of the text refers to two poets, Guillaume and Jean, his words also clearly suggest that his interlocutor, the narrator of the poem, is to be identified with neither of the two. And for a simple reason: both poets appear to be absent from this recollected scene, and they have yet to undertake the composition of their romance. Amors explains to his interlocutor that Guillaume, his "leal serjant" (v. 10509), has still to "begin his romance" (*conmancier le romant*): "doit il conmancier le romant / ou seront mis tuit mi conmant" (vv. 10519–20); "He is to begin the romance in which all my commandments will be set down" (187). Love adds that Jean de Meun, the poet who will continue the future *romant,* is himself still "to be born" (*a naistre,* v. 10578, v. 10588). Amors' entire discourse thus shows itself to be a purely anticipatory one: "I am a prophet" (*je sui prophetes*), Love tells us (v. 10636). Citing the end of Guillaume's text (in vv. 10525–30, which refer to vv. 4023–28), the opening of Jean's continuation (in vv. 10565–66, which refer to vv. 4029–39), and the *explicit* of the romance as a whole (in 10571–72, which refer to vv. 21749–50), Amors announces the precise contours of the *Roman de la Rose* itself, which he presents as a poem that is still to be written:

> et [Guillaume] jusque la le fornira
> ou il a Bel Acueill dira,
> qui languist ore en la prison
> par douleur et par mesprison:
> "Mout sui durement esmaiez
> que entroubliez ne m'aiez,
> si en ai deul et desconfort,

> ja mes n'iert riens qui me confort
> se je per vostre bienveillance,
> car je n'ai mes aillieurs fiance."
> . . . .
> ... quant Guillaumes cessera,
> Jehans le continuera,
> enprés sa mort, que je ne mante,
> anz trespassez plus de .XL.,
> et dira por la mescheance,
> par poor de desesperance
> qu'il n'ait de Bel Acueill perdue
> la bienvoillance avant eüe:
> "Et si l'ai je perdue, espoir,
> a poi que ne m'en desespoir,"
> et toutes les autres paroles,
> quex qu'els soient, sages ou foles,
> jusqu'a tant qu'il avra coillie
> seur la branche vert et foillie
> la tres bele rose vermeille
> et qu'il soit jorz et qu'il s'esveille.
>   (Vv. 10521–30, 10557–72)

> He [Guillaume] will finish it up to the point where he will say to Fair Welcoming, who now languishes, unjustly and in sorrow, in prison: "I am terribly afraid that you may have forgotten me, and I am in sorrow and pain. If I lose your good will, there will never be any comfort for me, since I have no confidence elsewhere.". . . When Guillaume shall cease, Jean will continue it—may I not lie—more than forty years after his death, and because of Fair Welcoming's misfortune, and through the despairing fear that he may have lost the good will that Fair Welcoming had shown him before, he will say, "And perhaps I have lost it. I am ready to despair of it." And he will set down all the other speeches, whatever they may be, wise or foolish, up to the time when he will have cut the beautiful red rose on its green, leafy branch, to the time when it is day and he awakes. (187–88)

Dragonetti has noted the surprise these lines provoke in the reader of the romance, who now discovers that "he has read what has not yet been written."[67] And yet this passage communicates a further, more startling fact: it now appears, inversely, that the work has, even before its existence, already been foreseen and therefore in some sense written. For, in his prophetic certainty of the form of the work to come, Amors appears to possess a familiarity with the text of the poem which could be had only after the completion of the work itself. At once recalling and rewriting the text of Ovid's elegy for Tibullus (*Amores*, 3:9, 7–12 and 15),[68] Love cannot but speak of the romance of Guillaume and Jean as an "art of love" already, in some sense, past; he cites the decisive moments of the entire romance with an accuracy that betrays the knowledge of an already written work.

Here Jean de Meun develops the specific temporal structure of Guillaume's poem in the most radical form. As we have seen, the "first *Rose*" presents itself, through the trope of the dream recollection, as the work of the remembrance of an anticipation. In an *amplificatio* of precisely this temporal structure, the "second *Rose*" now constitutes itself as a poetic text that, paradoxically, is at once before and beyond itself. Preceding itself in the form of prophecy and succeeding itself in the form of citation, the poem appears as its own preface and its own postface. It cites *itself* and, therefore, distinguishes itself from itself; it announces and recollects *itself,* and hence, by definition, cannot fully coincide with itself. In this movement of self-differentiation the text of the poem refers to itself as other than itself: as a work conceived in the *Roman de la Rose* prospectively, before its *incipit,* and retrospectively, from a point beyond its *explicit.*

This scene, therefore, tells a great deal about the identity—or, rather, lack of identity—of the narrator to whom the "I" of the romance refers. As in the strangely belated passages in which Dante's *Commedia* "here registers of necessity" (*di necessità qui si registra*) the name of its protagonist and in which the narrator of Proust's *Recherche* is at last given a single, tentative, first name, the scene of naming in the *Roman de la Rose* is anything but straightforward.[69] The subject of the romance is revealed to have been Guillaume de Lorris, but, then, it is disclosed that Guillaume has died and been survived, in his function as the speaker of the poetic "I," by Jean de Meun. But at this point the narrator appears in yet another guise, as someone other than both Guillaume and Jean—namely, the figure to whom Amors speaks in recollecting and announcing the lives and works of both authors of the future romance. Critics have failed to register the fundamental poetic paradox that is implicit here—namely, that the "I" of the text must be, and yet cannot be, referred to Guillaume de Lorris and Jean de Meun. For in this passage the discourse of the poetic "I" is cited and attributed to the first and to the second authors of the anticipated and recollected *romant;* the narrator of the first part of the poem is said to be Guillaume, and the narrator of the second is identified as Jean. And yet at the same time, because these authors are now mentioned in their absence, as third parties, the speaker who converses with Love in this scene cannot be either Guillaume or Jean; since Amors indicates that the two poets are absent, distanced in space and time, the narrator who learns of them at this point must be distinguished from both. He must constitute a third figure, irreducible to the two authors of the poem.

It is worth pausing, at this point, to pose a simple question: who, then, is the narrator of the *Roman de la Rose?* What literary subject, in other words, is signified by the "I" of the romance? The question now shows itself in all its complexity. As we have seen, the unnamed speaker of the *incipit* of the poem is revealed to have been Guillaume only to be reported dead, after the fact, and survived by another; yet this second poet, Jean, is himself not yet born; and the narrator of the poem, who learns of these two absent poets, then appears as yet a different, nameless figure, which cannot coincide with the "I" of the work of Guillaume and Jean, for that work does not yet exist.

The text of the romance, in this scene, refers the poetic "I" to Guillaume and Jean and, at the same time, renders that reference impossible; it attributes the discourses of the poem to two figures and yet contests the very possibility of such an attribution. The central scene of naming in the *Roman de la Rose*, which critics have long understood as the decisive passage in which the narrator is at last identified, is therefore in truth far more complex than it might appear. It stages a double movement in which identification and the loss of identity, the ascription of names and their withholding, cannot be told apart, a movement in which the constitution of the poetic subject provokes his simultaneous deconstitution as such. In the poetic text the first-person pronoun is the single term that articulates this simultaneous sameness and difference of poetic selves; it is the operator of identity and the loss of identity. As what allows for the attribution of names and, ultimately, ruins them, the "I" shows itself here as the fundamental *persona* of the poem, in the original Latin meaning of the word. It is that which lends a face and a form to what has none, that which, in a continuous play of *metanomasia*, naming and unnaming, gives heteronyms and pseudonyms to what is anonymous. It is that through which the speaker of the poem, in sounding the voices of the many figures of the *Roman de la Rose*, articulates his infinite noncoincidence with himself.

As such, the "I" of the *Roman de la Rose* therefore defines the structure of a specific literary self. If, returning to the critical term from which we began, one calls such a self a "subject," then it is one that is capable of his own difference from itself, that can be otherwise than it is and, in the most extreme case, cease to be altogether. In short: a *contingent subject*, that is itself in being capable, at every moment, of being something other than itself and of not being at all. This is the sense of the "literary subjectivity" articulated in the two-part *Roman de la Rose*. Its figure can only be, like that of the *persona* of the late ancient grammarians, a linguistic function that serves to articulate a position in discourse; its pronoun must be, precisely like that of Abelard, a term that "determines no nature or properties" (*nullam naturam vel proprietatem determinat*). In its bare, indeterminate capacity to be other than it is, such a contingent subject—the subject of the *Roman de la Rose*—is always the placeholder for another subject; and, *a limine,* it is the placeholder for something other than any subject at all.

IV

An important aspect of the *Romance of the Rose*'s revelation of the contingency of the subject remains to be investigated. It concerns the staging of the extraordinary scene at the center of the poem in which the poetic "I," as we have seen, is at once identified and unidentified, rendered definite and indefinite in its simultaneous reference to at least three figures: a dead poet, "Guillaume de Lorriz"; a poet to come, "Jehan de Meün"; and, finally, a poetic figure situated beyond life, death, and survival, in the singular space of the simultaneous recollection and anticipation of the absent, cited *romant.* Why is it the figure of Amors who speaks in this decisive scene, revealing the subject of the poem in his essential capacity to be other than he is? How is one to interpret the fact that the poetic "I" learns of its contingency from Love?

The position and function of Amors, as the figure who unveils the singular status of the poetic subject, could not be of greater importance for the understanding of the order of the work as a whole. And yet this very aspect of Love in the romance seems to have received little attention and, what is worse, given rise to significant misunderstandings in the critical literature on the joint work of Guillaume de Lorris and Jean de Meun. Gianfranco Contini's important essay "Un nodo della cultura medievale: La serie *Roman de la Rose-Fiore-Divina Commedia,*" which advances the Italian philologist's famous argument for the attribution of the anonymous Italian translation of the "first *Rose,*" *Il Fiore,* to Dante, is particularly telling in this regard.[70] Contini distinguishes the two-part romance from the tradition of courtly literature on the grounds that, in the poem of Guillaume and Jean, love appears as "entirely deprived" (*onninamente scevro*) of any element of death. Contini thus opposes the romance to the *Commedia.* The first, he argues, is a work from which death is simply absent; the second, by contrast, is an "extraordinary exploration of death [*Nekya*] in which there is only one character who is not dead, not yet dead, namely, the character who says 'I.'" Considering the differences between the two works in terms that hardly conceal his estimation of the *Roman de la Rose,* Contini writes:

> The most important thing [that distinguishes the *Rose* from the *Commedia*], and I mean this not for Leopardi or Freud but for the Middle Ages, is that in the *Rose* love is not only abstract but also entirely deprived of death. Consider a courtly poet such as Guittone, who writes, "AMORE quanto A MORTE vale a dire," "Amor dogliosa morte si pò dire, Quasi en nomo logica sposizione, Ch'egli è nome lo qual si pò partire En A e MOR, che son due divisione, E MOR si pone MORTE a difinire." Take Federigo dell'Ambra, who says: "AMOR da savi quasi A-MOR s'espone; Guarda s'amore a morte s'apareggia." I believe that the *Roman de la Rose,* by contrast, enjoys the special privilege of being the only large, if not great, work of world literature from which death is absent. To be sure, there are characters who die: for example, Malebouche dies, strangled before having his tongue cut out, but he is an entity who is fictitious, down even to his name; historical characters such as Manfred and Conradin die, to justify Charles d'Anjou; mythological creatures die, such as Narcissus; exemplary beings such as Nero and Virginia die. But the list stops there. If we now consider the *Commedia,* it is all an extraordinary celebration of death, in which there is only one character who is not dead, who is not yet dead, namely, the character who says "I."⁷¹

The question of the complex status of the "I" of the *Commedia,* as the sign of a "living" character, is one that we may set aside in this context (although it is worth recalling that it is a problem explicitly raised by the narrator of the *Commedia* itself, who says, in the paradoxical terms of the end of the *Inferno,* "I did not die, and I did not remain alive" [*Io non mori' e non rimasi vivo*]).⁷² Concerning the "I" of the *Roman de la Rose,* however, our analysis of the poetic text leads us to differ sharply from Contini. Not only is the classic anagrammatic figure to which Contini refers, by which *Amor* appears as *A-Mort,* present in the romance at several points, from vv. 4181–82, *de Bel Acueill enprés ma mort, / qui sanz moi mal fere m'a mort,* to vv. 4737–38, *Ceste a toute vertu s'amort, / mes l'autre met les genz a mort* and vv. 19209–10, *Vet il bien porchaçant sa mort / quant a tex mauvestiez s'amort.*⁷³ More significantly, the central scene of the romance reveals the very subject of the poem to constitute the place of the most radical linguistic experiment with the graphically and phonetically linked, albeit distinct,⁷⁴ figures of *amor* and *a-mort,* in which the lover undergoes—and survives—his death, to be repeatedly substituted, as the speaker of the text, by another. If Contini can claim that in the *Commedia* "there is only one character who is not dead, who is not yet dead, namely, the character who says 'I,'" we may therefore formulate a symmetrically opposed statement with respect to the *Roman de la Rose:* here, by contrast, the one, exemplary character who is indeed dead, who is already absent and yet in some way present in the poem, is precisely the one who says "I." As Contini saw well, death can hardly be considered a topic among others in the romance; instead, it is a force that at once determines and, so to speak, "in-determines" the single figure who recites the language of the poem.

The *Roman de la Rose,* therefore, must be restituted to the very tradition of lyric poetry to which Contini opposed it. The narrator of the romance, who dies and is survived by another, can even be read as an extreme figure of the lyric self of classical and medieval love poetry. For lyric poetry, from its origins in archaic Greece, is nothing if not an attempt, in literary language, to fashion a subject on the threshold of his (or her) own dissolution: a subject "pierced to the bones," as Archilochus says of himself,[75] a piece of "wax,"[76] according to Pindar, "melted" by Eros, in Alkman's terms,[77] "close to death" (τεθνάκην δ' ὀλίγω 'πιδεύς), as Sappho says, "shaking, turning greener than grass," "neither living nor dead."[78] Such is the *malesse* of the amorous, lyric "I" that, as in Catullus' rendition of Sappho's thirty-first fragment, "nothing" remains for him to say, his tongue "faltering" and his eyes being "shrouded in a double night" (*nihil est super mi / lingua sed turpet . . . gemina teguntur lumina nocte*).[79] The first vernacular poets of the Middle Ages draw on this classical tradition, when, inventing modern European literature, they place the experience of a violent desire at the origin of all literary composition. Love, at this point, can no longer function as a particular theme, or *materia,* of which the poet may chose to make use in the *inventio* of his work. As what allows the "finder," the troubadour, to "find" and compose his verse, *Amor,* rather, is the name given by the poets to the state of inspiration in which they become capable of composing their works; it is the fundamental figure by which the troubadours present the genesis of their poetic production. In the text of the first recorded vernacular poet, Guilhem de Peitieus, love thus appears as the indistinct state of a "pure Nothing" (*dreit rien*) in which the poet finds his "verse" (*vers*) and falls prey to an unnamed yet mortal illness:

> Farai un vers de dreit nien,
> non er de mi ni d'autra gen
> . . . .
> Malautz soi e cre mi morir

> I will make a verse of pure nothing; it will not be about me or about anyone else. . . . I am ill, and believe that I am dying [80]

Guilhem's *vers* already articulates what will become a classic motif among the troubadours: that of the poet who speaks to say that, overcome, he does not know what he says. "Escotatz," Raimbaut d'Aurenga sings, "mas no say que s'es, / senhor, so que vueilh comensar . . ." (Listen, but I do not know, Lord, what I wish to begin . . .).[81] "Si ai perdut mon saber," Ponç d'Ortafà tells us,

> qu'a penas sai on m'estau,
> ni sai d'on ven ni on vau,
> ni que•m fauc le jorn ni•l ser;
> e soi d'aital captenensa
> que no velh ni posc dormir,
> ni•m plai viure ni morir
> ni mal ni be no m'agensa.

I have so lost my mind that I barely know where I am; I don't know where I come from or where I'm going, nor what I do by day or by night. And I am in such a state that I neither wake nor sleep; I'm content neither to live nor to die, and neither good nor evil pleases me.[82]

In constituting himself as a poetic "I," the troubadour submits himself, in these texts, to a violence close to death. "Eu sai be," the speaker of a text by Bernart de Ventadorn informs us, "que per amor morrai" (I know well that I shall die of love).[83] "Ai las," we read at the opening of a *cobla tensonada* of Giraut de Borneilh, "com mor!" (Alas, how I die!).[84] But the derangement of the troubadour is such that, in many cases, he cannot say with certainty either that he dies or that he lives. In a poem of Bernart de Ventadorn the lyric self thus finds himself at a threshold between the two: "Ni posc viure ni morir" (I can neither live nor die).[85] And in a Gallego-Portuguese text of the troubadour Bonifacio Calvo, the poetic "I" announces, in a striking gesture, that it is beyond life and death alike: "Ora non moiro, nen uiuo, nen sei / como me uay, ne ren de mi" (Now I am not dying, nor am I living, nor do I know how I am, nor anything else about myself).[86]

Here, as elsewhere, the corpus of troubadour verse determines the form of subsequent Romance lyric poetry. In the songs of the first poets of northern France, the experience of love appears, as in the Provençals, as the immediate cause of the *trouvère*'s self-loss: as Dragonetti has shown in detail, it forces him to *foloier, desver, embriconner*.[87] The appearance of the self as a lover thus marks the possibility of poetry and the impossibility of reason. "Ja n'ameroit nus

57

sagement," we read in Gace Brulé, "no one would ever love wisely."[88] "J'aim trop folement"; "I love too madly."[89] Gace doubts whether the term *madness* (*folie*) is even adequate to his passion:

> Ne faz pas sen ne je n'i voi folie,
> Qu'a force vuil cele ou je n'ai poissance.
> Tant a sor moi amours grant seignorie
> Qu'el me destruit raison et abstinence.

> I am not being reasonable, nor do I see folly in this, for I passionately desire the lady over whom I have no power. Love has such great mastery over me that it destroys my reason and self-control.[90]

Such is the "dispossession necessitated by great love," to cite Dragonetti's phrase.[91] It is, as Alain de Lille writes, "a mad reason, a deranged prudence" (*insipiens ratio, demens prudentia*), or, in the words of the second part of the *Roman de la Rose*, "c'est fos sens, c'est sage folie" (v. 4293),[92] which submits the lover to "martyrdom," to use the classic term that we have already also observed in the two-part romance. Desiring, the subject loses each of the traits that appear to define him as a man, resembling more and more, in the image of Cavalcanti's sonnet, "a man who is outside life," "made of branches, or stones, or wood":

> I'vo come colui ch'è fuor di vita,
> che pare, a chi lo sguarda, ch'omo sia
> fatto di rame o di pietra o di legno,
>
> che si conduca sol per maestria
> e porti ne lo core una ferita
> che sia, com'egli è morto, aperto segna.[93]

> And I, as one beyond life's compass thrown,
> Seem but a thing that's fashioned to design,
> Melted of bronze or carven in tree or stone.
>
> A wound I bear within this heart of mine
> Which by its mastering quality is grown
> To be of that heart's death an open sign.[94]

Carried beyond life and death, "like one beyond life's compass thrown," the speaker is then capable of being a poet: he becomes a bare "thing" (*un che*) that writes and signifies when Love dictates, according to the definition of the Dolce Stil Novo given by Dante in *Purgatorio* XXIV.[95] The poetic self, in this way, is simultaneously constituted and deconstituted; as it steps forward,

The Contingent Subject

in the literary text, it exposes itself to a force that divests it of all substantial identity.

As the figure that articulates the ultimate noncoincidence of the poetic "I" with itself, the character of Amors in the *Roman de la Rose* must be situated in this tradition. Love, in the work of Guillaume and Jean, is what allows the narrator to speak in announcing himself, like the "I" of the lyric poets, as the subject of what he cannot master: a "very grave illness" (*mout pesant maladie*, v. 2874), an "illness of thinking" (*maladie de pensse*, v. 4348), for which he would "rather be dead than alive" (*mieluz voudroie estre moirz que vis*, v. 1333) and on account of which he can say, at once, "this is my death, this is my life" (*ce est ma mort, ce est ma vie*, v. 2888). The madness and *rage* (v. 10218) of his desire makes of him the exemplary figure of the "lovers" of whom Richesse elsewhere speaks, who cannot even be said to "live":

> Vivent? certes non font, ainz meurent
> tant con en tel torment demeurent,
> qu'en ne doit pas apeler vie
> tel rage ne tel desverie.
> (Vv. 10219–22)

Live! Indeed they do not do so; rather they die while they dwell in such torment, for one should not give the name "life" to such madness and folly. (182)

And yet here the motif of what Bernart de Ventadorn calls "death-by-love" (*mort per amor*)[96] is carried to an extreme and unprecedented point. For in the *Roman de la Rose* love is not merely what allows the poet to speak in being exposed to a violence that calls his life into question. In the work of Guillaume and Jean, the figure of Amors, instead, reveals the literary self, which is already fractured by the *senefiance* of the work and further multiplied by the rhetoric of the text, to be already dead, to be announced as another, and, at the same time, to be in some way present in the space of the poem in yet a different, nameless, and unidentified role. The lover who says "I" in the romance, therefore, speaks not merely to say, like the poetic subject of the lyric tradition, "Speaking, I say that I lose myself and that I die." His speech implies a far more radical statement: "Speaking, I say that I lose myself, that I die and that, in this death, I survive myself, always different from myself."

In this sense the narrator of the *Roman de la Rose*, exactly like Pygmalion's statue, is a being who cannot be properly termed either alive or dead: one cannot know if he is "ou vive ou morte" (v. 20896).[97] His speech carries him beyond himself, irreparably dividing himself from himself in the very moment in which it allows him to express himself. And this excess that marks the self with respect to its every form, its every *persona* in the poem, is precisely the work of the god of love, Amors. The "art d'aimer" which, according to Guillaume's text (vv. 37–38), is "tote enclose" in the "Romanz de la Rose" appears to have this singular poetic self as its ultimate product: a self who, in a movement of perpetual identification and loss of identity, constitution and deconstitution, is itself in its capacity both to be someone else and no longer to be at all. For love, in the *Roman de la Rose,* is what allows the narrator to find himself, again and again, as someone other than himself; it is what renders the poetic "I" the cipher of the contingent subject.

V

The contingent subject of the *Roman de la Rose* is not a character simply described in the course of the poem of Guillaume de Lorris and Jean de Meun; nor is it in any sense an object of which the text could be said to speak. Since the romance, from its beginning to its end, takes the form of a first-person discourse, the "I," as we have seen, constitutes the fundamental form through which the poem unfolds. Such is the structural proximity of the two-part romance to medieval lyric poetry, which Zumthor noted in writing that "the 'I' of the *Roman de la Rose* is formally the 'I' of a *pastourelle*" in which the discourse of the poetic *je* cannot be distinguished from that of the text itself and which Sylvia Huot has addressed in her definition of the work as a whole as a "lyrico-narrative composition."[98] In addition to its specific roles at various points in the narration, whenever it appears and comes to light as such, the "I" of the romance therefore has a consistent structural function in the poem. It marks the event of poetic discourse, the very fact that the language of the romance takes place.

Such a claim obliges us to reconsider the significance of the poetic subject of the *Roman de la Rose.* For, if in a work in the first person the "I" refers not to a particular individual in the poem but the mere existence of the text as such, then the poetic subject who is signified by this pronoun occupies a specific and fundamental position in the romance: it constitutes nothing less than the fundamental figure for the language of the poem itself. The fact that the text of the romance appears in the form of a subject that maintains itself, at every moment, in relation to the possibility of its being otherwise and no longer being means that the work itself, in taking place, holds itself in relation

The Contingent Subject

to the possibility of its being otherwise than it is and not being at all; it means that in the poem speech appears, through the form of a subjectivity, in its irreducible potentiality to be otherwise than it is and simply not to be. The contingency of the poetic subject, in other words, marks the contingency of the language of the work, its irreducible capacity to take place otherwise than it does and not to take place at all.

In the *Roman de la Rose* the figure of such a capacity appears in exemplary terms in Nature's discourse on the necessity of change and corruption in the sublunary world. Here we read of a mythological creature that, in a cycle of perpetual self-destruction and self-survival, constitutes itself as infinitely capable of being different from itself:

> Toujorz est il uns seus phenix;
> et vit, ainceis qu'il soit feniz,
> par.V.C. ans; au darrenier
> si fet un feu grant et plenier
> d'espices et s'i boute e s'art.
> Ainsinc fet de son cors esart.
> Mes por ce qu'il sa fourme garde,
> de sa poudre, conment qu'il s'arde,
> uns autres phenix an revient,
> ou cil meïsmes, se devient
> (Vv. 15947–62)

There is always a single phoenix that lives, up until its end, for five hundred years. At the last it makes a large, full fire of spices where it sits down and is burned. Thus it brings about the destruction of its own body. Yet since it keeps its form, however it may burn, from its ashes there comes a different phoenix—or perhaps the very same one. (271)[99]

Not only does the "burning" (*s'arder*) of the mythical bird in this passage recall the consuming passion of the narrator, which the text repeatedly characterizes by the very same term (see v. 4356, *s'art et se delite;* v. 13016, *mieuz s'arde*).[100] On account of its poetic subject, the two-part romance itself can be read as precisely such a phoenix. The work, in its organization and in the rhetoric of its language, can be said to erect the "great and full fire" (*feu grant et plenier*) in which it "destroys its own body" (*fet de son cors esart*) by showing itself to be capable of a form other than the one it has, in fact, assumed. In Jean's passage on the phoenix, in which the language of the text gathers together the expressions *s'arder* and *s'arter* (to burn), *ars* and *art* (art), and *faire esart* (to destroy),[101] the word *esart* must therefore be heard not only in its relation to the

61

middle Latin terms *exsarire, "to clear away,"[102] and *exardere*, "to burn."[103] It must also be read, at the same time, in a sense that is suggested by the paranomasia of the poetic text alone: as *es-art*, in which the prefix *es-* (from the Latin *ex-*) functions, in accordance with its two senses in Old French, as both intensive and privative.[104] Because it originates in a subject who is always different from himself, the language of the romance, in its literal "ardour," "fet es-art" of its own design; it reaches the final point of its art in undoing, "ex-arting" and "de-arting," itself. The life of the work, like that of the phoenix, consists in the double movement of this "es-art": in the simultaneous intensification and privation, development and elimination, of its own form. In its very *ars* the work consumes itself (*s'art, s'arde*); in its own rhetoric it unravels the figures of its *texere*. Destroying its actual form, the poem thus fulfills itself: it reveals itself in its capacity to be otherwise than it is.

Such is the paradoxical structure of the two-part *Roman de la Rose*. By virtue of constituting itself as the work of a poetic self that does not coincide with itself, it, too, is in a fundamental sense always "uns autres" and yet "toujorz . . . uns seus." Whenever the work appears as other than it is, as a fractured, doubled, anticipated, and recollected work, it is therefore simply itself, just as the phoenix, in presenting itself as *uns autres*, is in fact still *uns seus phenix*. "Uns autres phenix an revient, / ou cil meïmes": here, where "the very same" (*cil meïsmes*) is placed in apposition to the "other" (*uns autres*), where the subject of the phrase is itself in being other than itself, it is impossible to distinguish between difference and sameness, alterity and identity, death and life. Yet in this absolute indistinction of interruption and continuity, destruction and preservation, a *fourme conmune* (v. 15965) remains; someone or something undergoes and survives the violence of the *feu grant et plenier*, to be incessantly reborn, "thus resuscitated" (*ainsinc resoucite*, v. 15956) as both another and the same. In the *Roman de la Rose* the mark of this *fourme* is the pronoun *I*, the indeterminate *persona* through which the discourse of the poem unfolds. And the one this "I" signifies, the artisan of the *art* and *esart* of the *Rose*, is the one continually identified and unidentified, constituted and deconstituted, in the text of the poem. He is the lover revealed by the language of the *Roman de la Rose*, the lover who, in the space of the poem, shows himself in his capacity to be someone other than himself and, at the limit, not to be at all: the contingent subject.

3 *Fortune,*
or
The Contingent Figure

I

Form is not the only element of the *Roman de la Rose* defined by the power of mutability and metamorphosis that the medieval philosophers and theologians called "contingency." The capacity to be otherwise marks what is perhaps the most fundamental register of the work's language, which defines the poem as an allegorical romance: that of its figures. One rhetorical *persona* in particular is exemplary here, by virtue of functioning, at crucial moments in both parts of the romance, to present a capacity of incessant alteration. That figure is Fortune. Presiding over those "facts" (*fet*) which "are most fearful, for they are not stable" (*sunt trop doutable, / por ce qu'il ne sunt pas estable,* vv. 5321–22), Fortune appears in the poem as a figure capable of rendering all things different from themselves, transforming at once "the lowest" into "the highest" and "the highest" into "the lowest" (vv. 3953–63). But, for this very reason, the very nature of Fortune's form—Fortune's "figure"—remains entirely to be clarified. If the allegorical figure can be said to constitute a *persona ficta,* in the terms of the classical and medieval rhetoricians, a "constructed mask" or "person," then to what mask or person can a force of perpetual differentiation give rise? What figure, in every sense, can embody the radical indeterminacy and "in-distinction" that defines the nature of contingency? These questions concern the sense and limits of the technique of personification which ties the *Roman de la Rose,* as an "allegorical drama," to the tradition of Prudentius' *Psychomachia;* as such, they necessarily involve the figural language of the romance as a whole. They can be addressed and answered only through a detailed analysis of the mythological, literary, and philosophical functions of the personification of Fortune in the *Roman de la Rose.*

The fullest development of the figure of Fortune is to be found in the second part of the romance, in which Jean de Meun, recalling a figure mentioned only once in the first half of the work (vv. 3953–63), dedicates over two thousand lines to the description, analysis, and judgment of Fortune by Reason (vv. 4673–6870).[1] As we have seen, Jean begins the narrative of his continuation at the very point at which Guillaume's poem ends, amplifying the scene in which the lover despairs of ever reaching the rose. The kiss granted the narrator by Venus has, at this point, produced the most dire consequences: Jalousie, in indignation, has built his fortress, enlisted Danger, Honte, and Male Bouche to guard it and the Vieille to keep watch over Bel Acueil, who is imprisoned in its tower. It is at this point that Reason descends from her own tower to console the protagonist, proposing, with apparent simplicity, to impart "knowledge" (*connoissance*) of love. "Now I want you to know love," she explains to the narrator:

> Mes or veill que tu le connoisses,
> qui tant an as beü d'angoisses
> que touz an iés desfigurez.
> Nus las, chetis, maleürez
> ne peut fes enprandre greigneur.
> Bon fet connoistre son seigneur,
> et se cetui bien connoissoies,
> legierement issir pourroies
> de la prison ou tant anpires.
> (Vv. 4233–41)

Now I want you to understand him, you who have drunk so much bitterness as to have been completely disfigured by it. No unhappy wretch can support a greater load. It is a good thing to know one's lord; if you knew this one well, you could escape easily from the prison where you are so unhappy. (94)

Reason's "will" (*or veill . . .*, v. 4233) is clear: to "educate" (*educare*) the narrator in every sense, leading him from "anguish" to "knowledge" (according to the rhyme of *angoisse* and *connoisse* which links vv. 4233–34). Holding a long discourse (vv. 4191–7199) on desire, she intends to speak the truth about erotic love, her words operating in accordance with the two "authoritative" functions, *enseigner* and *aprendre*, which she later claims for her speech and for correct speech in general:

> Et ce que ci t'ai recité
> peuz trouver en auctorité,
> car Platon lisoit en s'escole
> que donee nous fu parole
> por fere noz volairs entendre,
> por enseignier et por aprendre.
> (Vv. 7067–72)

> You can find what I have here recounted to you in an authority, for Plato taught in his school that speech was given us to make our wishes known, for teaching, and for learning. (135)

So far Lady Reason could be said to occupy here the same role as she did in the first part of the romance. As before, she seeks now to dissuade the lover from pursuing his amorous search for the rose by speaking against the "folly" (*folie*, v. 3045) of love and the "sickness of thought" (*maladie de pensee*, v. 4348) it implies; as in the first part of the poem, her speech constitutes an extended "chastisement" (*chastiment*, v. 3057) of the project to reach the rose that ultimately provokes the lover's outrage, confirming his resolution to continue on his journey and announcing the reappearance of the figure of Ami. But the two discourses of Reason cannot be simply assimilated; the passage in the "second *Rose*," which consists of over two thousand lines (vv. 4199–7198), is more than a repetition of the hundred-line section of the "first" (vv. 2955–3082). In Jean's text Reason's discourse, while still directed against the two, anagrammatically linked figures of the *rose* and *eros*,[2] appears to have an immediate target that is not mentioned as such in the first part of the poem. Here Reason, whose teaching draws on a series of classical, late ancient, and medieval *auctores*,[3] articulates her discourse on Love as a polemic against a single, unexpected figure: Fortune.

It is certainly possible to consider the presence of this new topic of Reason's second *sermon* (v. 4599) on desire as a straightforward example of the structural confusion of which Ernest Langlois, together with so many other critics of the romance, accuses Jean de Meun's poem. According to such a reading, the fact that Reason enters into a long and detailed discussion of Fortune when she is meant to speak on love merely illustrates Jean's consistent tendency to "digress . . . with long parentheses, which take so much time that one forgets the principal idea";[4] it simply shows, as Armand Strubel argues in his recent edition of the text, that Jean has "forgotten his point of departure," having unwittingly replaced a discourse on Love with one on Fortune.[5] Here it is possible, however, to offer a different reading of Jean's text. The link between love and fortune is, in fact, first of all affirmed by Reason herself, who, at the start of her apparent digression, defines erotic love, in distinction to other forms of affection, precisely as "the love that comes from Fortune": *c'est l'amor,* she says, *qui vient de Fortune* (v. 4753). According to the letter of Reason's phrase, love thus owes its very possibility to the existence of fortune: fortune is that which allows there to be such a thing as *amors* at all. If one recalls that the *Roman de la Rose* defines itself as the work in which *l'art d'Amors est tote enclose* (vv. 37–38), this tie between love and fortune appears to be of crucial importance for the sense of the work as a whole. It implies that Fortune, as the figure for the origin of *Amors,* occupies a decisive structural position in the love poem of Guillaume de Lorris and Jean de Meun.

Who or what, then, is Fortune in the *Roman de la Rose?* We are confronted here, as so often in the study of medieval literary works, with a figure whose sense can be fully elucidated only on the basis of an examination of its place in the classical mythological and literary traditions. To a large extent this place is inscribed in the lexical and semantic form of the term *fortune* itself. As has often been noted, the Latin name *Fortuna,* from which the Old French *Fortune* derives, is formed adjectivally from *fors,* just as *Portunus* is constructed from *portus* and *Neptunus* from an unknown expression.[6] A trace of this formation is in a certain sense still discernible in the linguistic practice of early Roman authors, who refer to the goddess of fortune as *Fors Fortuna* and, when using the two terms in isolation, treat them as essentially synonymous.[7] Nineteenth-century philologists and historians of religion already observed that the name *Fortuna,* therefore, is originally derived from the Indo-European root **bher-,* "to bring," "to bear," and "to carry," which is represented by the Greek φέρω and the Latin *fero.*[8] Scholars are less certain of the original form of the deity to whom the name refers, and Georges Dumézil's judgment that "the origins of Fortune are unknown" still holds today.[9] At most it is possible to say that, in Rome, Fortune did not belong to the class of Roman deities, the *di indigetes,*[10] and that, at the time of the first recorded mentions of her cults, she seems not to have had a long tradition in the religious life of Latium.[11] The few documents we possess from this period indicate that, in the Rome of the early Republic, Fortune was a "maternal divinity of fertility" (hence her subsequent form as *Fortuna muliebris*),[12] a *numina,* as the Pauly-Wissowa *Real-Encyclopädie* tells us, whose name connoted first of all "what arrives" (*das Kommende*) and "what is sent" (*die Schickung*).[13]

Later in the Republic, when the influence of Hellenic culture made itself felt on Rome, the Latin goddess was gradually assimilated to the Greek τύχη,

The Contingent Figure

the deity of luck and chance,[14] and *Fortuna* then came to assume the form with which we are familiar today, as the patron divinity of fortuitous and accidental events. The works of the classical Roman writers bear witness to this new meaning of the term and figure of *fortuna*.[15] It has been noted that, already in Plautus and Terence, "the use of *fortuna* and its compounds in the ordinary sense of luck or chance is constant."[16] In Cicero *fortuna* is likewise assimilated to *casus* and defined, together with *fors,* as that by which a thing takes place in one way while being essentially capable of having taken place otherwise (*quid est . . . aliud fors, quid fortuna, quid casus, quid eventus, nisi cum sic aliquid cecidit, sic evenit, ut uel aliter cadere atque evenire potuerit?*).[17] Hence the mythological figure of the goddess, in the works of the classical Roman writers, as a deity who is herself unstable and perpetually changing. In a passage of Ovid's *Ex Ponto* Fortune appears as "a goddess who is not stable" (*dea non stabilis*);[18] in a text of his *Tristia* we read that "fleeting Fortune wanders with doubting steps" (*passibus ambiguis Fortuna volubilis errat*).[19] We encounter this very figure, presented in striking terms, in the second book of the *Historia naturalia,* in which the elder Pliny suggests that *Fortuna,* in her later form as the goddess of chance, has become the perpetual concern of humanity:

> Toto quippe mundo et omnibus locis omnibusque horis omnium vocibus Fortuna sola invocatur ac nominatur, una accusatur, rea una agitur, una cogituatur, sola laudatur, sola arguitur et cum conviciis colitur, volubilis . . . que, a plerisque vero et caeca existimata, vaga, inconstans, incerta, varia, indignorumque fautrix. Huic omnia expensa, huic feruntur accepta, et in tota ratione mortalium sola utramque paginam facit.[20]

> In the whole world, in all places and at all times, Fortune is the only divinity invoked and named by everyone. She is the only goddess who is accused and the only one thought to be guilty; she is the one in our thoughts, the only one praised, the only one who is blamed and reproached. Humanity believes Fortune, changeable as she is, to be blind, wandering, inconstant, uncertain and variable, the protectress of the unjust. We attribute all our losses and all our gains to her, for she alone carries responsibility, deciding on all adversity and prosperity.

The divinity of which Pliny writes has its counterpart, in the domain of philosophy, in the concept of "fortune" to be found in the works of the Roman statesmen and thinkers. Here the notion of *fortuna* functions to subsume those events that, to invoke the classic terms of the *Historia naturalia,* are themselves "inconstant, uncertain and variable" on account of their fortuitousness. As such, fortune appears as what is essentially foreign to all anticipation, calculation, and, consequently, reason. In a classical text Cicero even defines *fortuna* as what, among all things, is by nature most "opposed to *ratio*" (*contrarium rationi*):

> Nihil enim est tam contrarium rationi et constantiae quam fortuna; ut mihi ne in deum quidem cadere videatur, ut sciat quid casu et fortuito futurum sit. Si enim scit, certe illud eveniet. Sin certe eveniet, nulla fortuna est. Est autem fortuna. Rerum igitur fortuitarum nulla praesensio est.[21]

> For nothing is as opposed to reason and constancy as fortune, so much so that it seems to me that even a god cannot have knowledge of things that are to happen by chance and fortune. For if he knows them, then they take place with certainty; and if they take place with certainty, then there is no fortune. But there is fortune. There can, therefore, be no prescience of fortuitous things.

Fortune, in this passage, is defined as what constitutes an insurmountable barrier to the operation of reason as such. Since they are by definition "fortuitous," Cicero writes, events that take place by fortune are necessarily not necessary and, therefore, in their lack of all "constancy" (*constantia*), beyond the province of regularity and rationalization. Fortune thus confronts all *ratio* with a double impossibility. If the chance event cannot be known, then reason cannot master it. Yet, inversely, if it can indeed be known, such an event is then not truly a chance event; it conforms, instead, to the principles of reason and therefore confirms, once again, that the object of rational intellection cannot be fortuitous. In each case fortune, in its form as fortuitousness, sets a decisive limit to *ratio;* it is what reason, in its form as the apprehension of what is stable and regular, cannot accommodate.

It is to this later, Hellenized sense of *fortuna fortuitarum rerum* which the medieval poets and thinkers refer in their discussions of fortune. The definitions of the term and notion of *fortuna* which one finds among the *auctores* of the Middle Ages demonstrate as much. Whereas the classical Roman sources register, albeit implicitly, the historical etymon of the term *fortune,* defining it as what is "carried," "borne," or "brought" by *fors* (*quid . . . ferat fors, ut fors tulerit*),[22] medieval writers, by contrast, have recourse to a different explanation that ties the word *fortuna* to chance, accidentality, and luck by directly linking it, by means of derivation, to the term *fortuito.* St. Augustine's treatment of the matter is exemplary in this regard. "Praesit *fortuitis* vocerturque *fortuna,*" he writes;[23] "*fortuito* accidit hominibus . . . unde etiam *fortuna* nominatur"; "definitio illa *fortunae* . . . quod a *fortuitis* etiam nomen accepit"; "(causae) *fortu-*

itae, unde etiam *fortuna* nomen accepit."[24] In his *Etymologiarum sive Originum* Isidore of Seville proposes the same historical and semantic definition of the term:

> Fortunam a fortuitis nomen habere dicunt, quasi deam quandam res humanas variis casibus et fortuitis inlundentem; unde et caecam appellant, eo quod passim in quoslibet insurrens sine ullo examine meritorum, et ad bonos et ad malos venit.
>
> Fortune's name is said to derive from what is "fortuitous," as if she were a goddess who toyed with human things according to chance events. This is why she is called blind, since she approaches the good and the bad alike, whispering things to them without concern for their merit.[25]

Such derivations of the term *fortune,* of course, have little scientific or philological value; they are, in every sense, *figurae etymologicae.* Yet, for this very reason, they register with the utmost clarity the single trait that, for a tradition of thought which has its origins in late antiquity, defines the divinity of fortune: its link to what is "fortuitous," to what is uncertain and unstable on account of being merely accidental.

It is hardly surprising, therefore, that in the *Roman de la Rose* the figure of Reason polemicizes at such length against Fortune. Indeed, Reason's hostile identification of Fortune as *la perverse* (cf. vv. 4815, 4863, 6135, and 6804) may even be read as a simple reformulation and elaboration, in the terms of an allegorical narrative, of the Ciceronian *sententia* we examined earlier, according to which *fortuna* is by definition *contrarium rationi.*[26] But the most significant trait of the romance's deployment of the figures of Reason and Fortune lies elsewhere. It consists in the way in which the opposition of fortune and reason, as we have seen, functions to articulate a relation that is fundamental to the structure of the romance and whose sense remains to be explained: that between Reason and Amors, reason and love. As the figure for that from which "*amor* comes" and as the immediate subject of the romance's longest discourse on love, Fortune is the privileged figure by which to examine the relationship between reason and love in the *art d'amors* that is the *Roman de la Rose.* Fortune illustrates that which ties love to reason and, through it, to knowledge, speech, and rhetoric. At the same time, Fortune, as we shall see, reveals that which, in the work of Guillaume de Lorris and Jean de Meun, sunders love and reason altogether: that element in love which reason cannot tolerate, that which, in the amorous journey of the poetic subject, lies forever beyond the grasp of *ratio* and all its forms.

II

Transformed from *Fors Fortuna* into a divinity of pure chance, the Fortuna of late antiquity and the Middle Ages implies a paradox. It consists in the synthesis of the two fundamentally irreducible traits that, as we have seen, characterize the figure of Fortune in the Roman world. On the one hand, Fortuna is tied to the activity of carrying, bearing, and bringing on account of the semantic value inscribed in the etymology of her name; on the other, she assumes the form of a deity of accidents, instability, and chance by virtue of her subsequent form as the Roman equivalent of the Greek τύχη. As a consequence of this double heredity, Fortuna is constituted as a deity who bears fruits that are essentially marked by the instability and mutability from which they originate. Fortune thus appears to bestow gifts that, in their own fortuitousness and inconstancy, are no sooner given than they are taken away. Such is the duplicitous form that Fortuna, as the bearer of what is inconstant, must assume: when she offers, she truly takes, and when she takes, inversely, she ultimately gives.

This paradox of Fortune is expressed in exemplary terms in the second book of *De Consolatione Philosophiae,* in which the figure of Philosophy seeks to convince the literary subject of the work to avoid the "many tricks of that monster" (*multiformes illius prodigii fucos*), Fortuna.[27] In terms that will become canonical in the Middle Ages and to which Jean de Meun will refer in the most explicit fashion, Lady Philosophy announces that she will reveal a "marvel" (*mirum*) about Fortune, an enigma of which it is not easy to speak:

> Mirum est quod dicere gestio, eoque sententiam verbis explicare vix queo. Etenim plus hominibus reor adversam quam prosperam prodesse fortunam. Illa enim semper specie felicitatis cum videtur blanda, mentitur; haec semper vera est, cum se instabilem mutatinone demonstrat. Illa fallit, haec instruit, illa mendacium specie bonorum mentes fruentium ligat, haec cognitione fragilis felicitatis absolvit. Itaque illam videas ventosam, fluentem suique semper ignaram, hanc sobriam succinctamque et ipsius adversitatis exercitatione prudentem. Postremo felix a cero bono devios blanditiis trahit, adversa plerumque ad vera bona reduces unco retrahit.

> What I want to tell you is something wonderful, which makes it very difficult for me to put it into words. For I think that ill fortune is better for men than good. Fortune always cheats when she seems to smile, with the appearance of happiness, but is always truthful when she shows herself to be inconstant by changing. The first kind of fortune deceives, the second instructs; the one binds the minds of those who enjoy goods that cheatingly only seem to be good, the other frees them with the knowledge of the

fragility of mortal happiness. So you can see that the one is inconstant, always running hither and thither, uncertain of herself; and the other is steady, well prepared and—with the practice of adversity itself—wise. Lastly, when fortune is apparently felicitous, she leads men astray by her blandishments, wandering from the true good; when she is adverse, she commonly draws them back, as it were with a hook, towards it.[28]

The *mirum* of which Philosophy speaks consists of the fact that what Fortune brings is not what it seems; the true outcome of Fortune's gift, indeed, is in each case precisely the contrary of what it appears to be. The classical distinction between the two types of fortune, *fortuna mala* and *fortuna bona*,[29] is thus radically complicated; *fortuna bona* shows itself to be *mala* and *fortuna mala* to be *bona*. Prosperity "lies" (*mentitur*), misfortune, by contrast, "discloses" (*demonstrat*); a good state "deceives" (*fallit*), a bad state "teaches" (*instruit*); wealth "binds" (*ligat*) its possessor, poverty "frees" (*absolvit*) him; the one, in its "inconstancy" (*ventositas*), leads "away from the good" (*a vero trahit*), the other, in its "sobriety," leads back toward it (*ad vera bona retrahit*).

Such is the movement of inversion which the divinity of chance and mutability, for Boethius, necessarily implies. Fortuna, in the *De Consolatione*, reveals herself as she truly is to the degree to which she exposes herself, through her gifts, as what she appears not to be; she unveils herself in showing herself and what she bestows *modo negativo*. The "hook" (*unctus*) that regulates this constant exchange of opposing predicates, therefore, traces the outline of a figure of discourse which is defined by its interlacing of two inverse movements: the chiasmus. It is thanks to the chiasmus that, in matters of Fortune, prosperity ends in adversity and adversity, in turn, ends in prosperity; it is by virtue of this figure that Fortune ultimately leads those it materially debases to moral elevation and those it materially elevates to moral debasement. As that which allows for the reciprocal inversion and conversion of the forms of *fortuna*, the chiasmus is the linguistic figure of the paradox of fortune.

This much, at least, is suggested by Jean de Meun in his own rendition of *De Consolatione Philosophiae, Le Livres de Confort de Philosophie*.[30] In the text of the second book of Jean's Old French translation of Boethius, the chiasmus we have observed, by which *fortuna mala* becomes *fortuna bona* and *fortuna bona*, *fortuna mala*, is inscribed in the very syntax of the Boethian text. Whereas the Latin original, in its explication of the paradoxical outcome of good and bad fortune, reads "illa fallit, haec instruit," the Old French text, radically simplifying and abbreviating the sense of the original Latin, articulates the comparison in a different form: "L'amiable les deçoit; la contreire les enseigne."[31]

> Mirum est quod dicere gestio, eoque sententiam verbis explicare vix queo. Etenim plus hominibus reor adversam quam prosperam prodesse fortunam. Illa enim semper specie felicitatis cum videtur blanda, mentitur; haec semper vera est, cum se instabilem mutatinone demonstrat. Illa fallit, haec instruit. [Latin version]32
>
> C'est merveille que je veuil dire et, pour ce, en puis je a paine desploier la sentence par paroles. Car je croi que fortune contraire, felonnesse et povre, profite plus aus hommes que fortune amiable, debonnaire et riche. Car l'amiable, quant elle apert debonnaire et digne par semblance de beneurté, elle ment touz jours; la contraire est touz jours veraie quant elle monstre par sa muance qu'elle n'est pas estable. L'amiable les deçoit; la contraire les enseigne. [Old French version]33
>
> What I want to tell you is something wonderful, which makes it very difficult for me to put it into words. For I think that ill fortune is better for men than good. Fortune always cheats when she seems to smile, with the appearance of happiness, but is always truthful when she shows herself to be inconstant by changing. The first kind of fortune deceives; the second instructs.34

Here Jean's text systematically substitutes the demonstrative forms employed by Boethius (*illa . . . haec*) for the nominal subjects to which they anaphorically refer, in such a way that, when it is time to render the Latin phrase *illa fallit, haec instruit,* the translation must differ significantly in form from the original. Had Jean translated the preceding segment differently, he could very well have rendered the Latin phrase *illa fallit, haec instruit,* by a phrase such as *cele les deçoit, ceste les enseigne,* employing the Old French pronominal equivalents of *haec* and *illa*.35 Instead, he must opt for a different formulation, *l'amiable les deçoit; la contraire les enseigne,* in which the positive terms and negative terms are arranged in a syntactic form in which their chiasmatic structure emerges with unprecedented clarity: *ABBA*. The *mirum,* or rather *merveille,* of which the figure of Philosophy speaks is thus inscribed in the language of the text, which follows the form by which the positive leads to the negative and the negative to the positive. The paradox of Fortune, at this point, comes fully to light: the inconstant divinity who reveals herself through what she bears and gives is, at all times, the contrary of what she seems.

It is in the light of this paradox and its formulation that we must consider the decisive scene in the second half of the *Roman de la Rose* in which the figure of Reason announces that she will inform the poetic subject of the true nature of Fortune. Here Reason begins her discourse on Fortune as follows:

> Et puis qu'a Fortune venons,
> quant de s'amor sermon tenons,

> dire t'en veill fiere merveille,
> n'onc, ce croi, n'oïs sa pareille.
> Ne sai se tu le porras croire,
> toutevois est ce chose voire
> et si la treuve l'en escrite:
> que mieuz vaut au genz et profite
> Fortune perverse et contraire
> que la mole et la debonaire
> (Vv. 4807–16)

And now that we come to Fortune when we hold a discourse about love, I should like to tell you a great marvel of which you have not, I believe, ever heard the like. I do not know if you will be able to believe it, but it is nevertheless true, and one may find it written: perverse, contrary Fortune is worth more and profits men more than does pleasant and agreeable Fortune. (102)

It is not difficult to discern the link that binds the *merveille* (v. 4809) of which Reason speaks here to the *mirum* of Fortune in Boethius, for which Jean also employs the word *merveille* in his translation of *De Consolatione*. The distinction between *Fortune perverse et contraire* and *[Fortune] mole et debonaire* (vv. 4816–17), moreover, clearly recalls the opposition in the text of *Le Livre de la Consolacion* between *fortune contraire, felonnesse et povre* and *fortune amiable, debonnaire et riche*, which, as we have seen, translates and amplifies Boethius' Latin distinction between *fortunam adversam* and *fortunam prosperam*.[36] Reason's discourse on Fortune thus seems to be, as the personification herself informs us, simply a reformulation of what is "written" (*escrite*, v. 4813) in the *auctores;* and the writing at issue appears to be the same *De Confort* explicitly cited in the text only a little later (v. 5007).

If one examines the passage closely, however, it appears that Jean has done more than merely "translate" or "paraphrase" Boethius, as Langlois, in his *Origines et sources du Roman de la Rose,* maintains;[37] more is at play in this discourse of Reason than material "drawn," as Félix Lecoy suggests, from the second book of *De Consolatione Philosophiae*.[38] In its rhetoric the poetic text now carries the double movement that is implicit in the chiasmatic structure of Fortune's gifts a step beyond the Boethian tradition. With a subtle, yet significant departure from the text of *De Consolatione,* Jean now presents the two symmetrical lines of Fortune, by which the *contraire* leads to wisdom and the *aimable* to ignorance, as a single movement. Developing Guillaume's reference to the late ancient and medieval figure of the "wheel of Fortune" (*roe de Fortune, rotae Fortunae*),[39] Jean figures the two currents of the Boethian Fortuna as the spinning of one wheel, which at once reveals good fortune to be bad and bad fortune to be good. The gesture by which Fortune bestows her *joiaus, anneurs,* and *richeces* (vv. 4824–25) appears first of all as the act by which the divinity places her subject at the height of her wheel. Elevated on the wheel, the apparently lucky ones are thus duped and, mistaking the true nature of their condition, lowered by their ignorance even before Fortune takes back what she only seemed to give:

> el leur promest estableté
> en estat de muableté,
> et touz les pest de gloire veine
> en la beneürté mundaine,
> quant seur sa roe les fet estre:
> lors cuident estre si haut mestre
> et leur estas si fers voair
> qu'il n'en puissent ja mes choair
> . . . .
> Et tout est flaterie et guile,
> si con cil aprés le savroient
> se touz leur biens perduz avoient,
> qu'il n'eüssent ou recouvrer
> (Vv. 4827–34, 4850–53)

[Fortune] promises them stability in a condition of mutability; and when she places them on her wheel, she feeds them all on vain glory in worldly prosperity. Then they believe themselves such great rulers and see their estates as so secure that they can never fall from them. . . . But it is all flattery and guile, as these dupes would know if they had lost all their good fortune and had no means of recovery. (103)

Displaced from the top to the bottom of the wheel, the unfortunate ones, by contrast, conversely rise to the point of recognizing the futility of all faith in Fortune:

> Mes la contraire et la perverse,
> quant de leur granz estaz les verse
> et les tumbe, au tor de la roe,
> du sonmet envers an la boe,
> et leur assiet, conme marrastre,
> au queur un doulereus emplastre
> destrempé, non pas de vin aigre,
> mes de povreté lasse et maigre,
> ceste moustre qu'el est veroie

> et que nus fier ne se doie
> en la beneürté Fortune,
> qu'il n'i a seürté nis une
>
> (Vv. 4863-74)

> But when contrary, perverse Fortune turns them from their high estate and tumbles them around the wheel from the summit toward the mire; when, like a mother-in-law, she places on their hearts a painful plaster moistened, not with vinegar, but with unhappy, meager poverty; then she shows that she is sincere and that no one should trust himself to prosperous Fortune, in whom there is no security whatever. (103)

It is important to note the distance that separates this presentation of the paradox of Fortune from its locus classicus in Boethius. Whereas in the text of the *De Consolatione,* Fortune's wheel is mentioned only once, without being associated in any particular way with the characteristic *mirum* of the deity,[40] in the romance the spinning of the *roe* functions as the exemplary figure of Fortune's *merveille.* Boethius' *dictum* that Fortune "deceives" and "lowers" (*fallere*) those it seems to elevate is thus radically literalized: Fortune, in Jean's text, appears as the one who causes the fortunate to fall, on her wheel, from the top to the bottom, *du sonmet envers an la boe* (v. 4866). As what, in a single, perpetual movement, thus lowers the elevated and elevates the lowly, the wheel functions in a new sense, as the emblem of the "marvelous" ambiguity of Fortune's gifts to humanity. The activity of Fortune appears as nothing other than that of a *roe*, which, in its continuous revolution, renders everything it bears different from itself. It is in this sense that, as far as Fortune is concerned, *il n'i a seürté nis une* (v. 4874): there is no place that Fortune does not displace, since fortune, figured by the spinning wheel, consists precisely in a movement of simultaneous placing and displacing.

This is why Fortune must ultimately take back whatever she gives. Since whoever finds himself on the *roe de Fortune* is, by definition, consigned to the course of its perpetually circular movement, it follows that good fortune in itself entails bad fortune and that bad fortune, in turn, immediately entails good fortune. At this point, however, the paradox of Fortune shows itself, through the figure of the wheel, in yet another form: as a poetic figuration of the very "paradox of contingency" we examined, in chapter 1, in the medieval accounts of the nature of possibility. We saw that Abelard, in his glosses on *De interpretatione* in the *Logica Ingredientibus,* defines "possible things" as "those things that exist when they do not exist and do not exist when they exist, and that are naturally capable of turning over into either of the two by virtue of the ease of their nature" (*Possibilia enim sunt esse, cum non sint, et non esse, cum sint, et ita in utrumque partem facilitate naturae verti possunt*).[41] According to the letter of this definition, if a thing is contingent, or "possible," then for it to be capable of something is for it also to be incapable of it; for a contingent thing to be incapable of something, conversely, is for it also to be capable of it. This is why Abelard, with a striking formulation, can state that possible things "exist when they do not exist and do not exist when they exist": the contradictory unity of existence and nonexistence, being in a certain way and being otherwise, constitutes the very essence of contingency. In each case what is contingent can always be otherwise than it is; when a contingent thing exists in a certain way, it is necessarily at the same time capable of existing otherwise and not at all. The paradox implied by Fortune's wheel in Jean's text is no different. It consists, as we have seen, in the *merveille* that to be at the *sonmet de la roe* is to be potentially *an la boe* and that to be *an la boe,* in turn, is to be virtually at the *sonmet.* Whoever is capable of receiving *fortuna prosperam* is necessarily capable of receiving *fortuna adversam;* whoever is placed in a certain position on the wheel is necessarily capable of being displaced. Such is the precise sense in which Fortune functions here as a figure for contingency. Fortune bestows gifts that are *contingentes* in the technical sense of the medieval philosophers; for they are capable, at every moment, of revealing themselves, *facilitate naturae,* as "their opposite," showing themselves, through the literal *vertere* of the wheel, to be other than themselves.

Reason is quick to draw the severe consequence that this contingency of Fortune implies for *les mortiex hommes:* it is impossible to take anything that Fortune gives. Since all fortune, by definition, is unstable, what fortune offers to humankind cannot constitute a stable good, and it cannot, for that reason, be possessed. Nothing that is lacking by nature, Reason explains, can be filled by fortune:

> Ne Fortune ne pueut pas fere,
> tant soit aus homes debonere,
> que nules des choses leur saient,
> conment que conquises les aient,
> dont Nature les fet estranges
> (Vv. 5285–89)

No matter how agreeable Fortune is to men, she cannot give them possession of things which Nature has made foreign to them, no matter how these things have been acquired. (109)

The Contingent Figure

While the goods of Reason are those "inside," *dedanz* (v. 5301), their possessor, those of Fortune appear, by virtue of an etymological figure that implicitly refers to the original form of *Fors Fortuna,* as merely "external" or "foreign," *forain* (v. 5307). Whereas Reason offers things that can be interiorized and so appropriated, Fortune "scatters" (*esparpille,* v. 5314) the very fruit she bears.[42] "Sages" prize Reason's goods; "madmen" alone cherish that which Fortune appears to give:

> Car sachiez que toutes vos choses
> sunt en vos meïsmes encloses.
> Tuit autre bien sunt de Fortune,
> qui les esparpille et aüne
> et tost et done a son voloir,
> dom les fols fet rire et doloir.
> Mes riens que Fortune feroit
> nus sages hom ne priseroit;
> ne nou feroit lié ne dolant
> li tourz de sa roe volant,
> car tuit si fet sunt trop doutable,
> por ce qu'il ne sunt pas estable
> (Vv. 5311–22)

For know that all your possessions are enclosed within yourself. Every other good belongs to Fortune, who disperses and collects them, gives and takes them away as she pleases and with them makes fools laugh and weep. But nothing Fortune did would entrap a wise man nor would the revolution of her turning wheel bind him or make him sorrowful. All her deeds are too fearsome, for they are not stable. (110)

The instability of the figure thus extends itself to that which she seems to offer. Fortune no sooner "disperses" (*esparpille*) her apparent "goods" (*bien*) than she "gathers," "collects," and "assembles" (*aüne*) them, no doubt to scatter them once again, according to the circular movement of her continuously turning wheel. As what is perpetually submitted to *li tourz de sa roe volant,* the "goods" of fortune, like the goddess, are marked as *trop doutable / par ce qu'il ne sunt pas estable* (vv. 5321–22) and, therefore, incapable of being possessed: they are given only insofar as they are taken and taken, in turn, only insofar as they are given. Irreducibly *forain,* such goods cannot, by definition, be "enclosed" and "incorporated" (*en vos meïsmes encloses*); they cannot even be considered as goods, as long as goods are understood, in the traditional sense, as things that may be possessed. "Altogether different goods" (*tuit autre bien*), the things that Fortune offers are, by virtue of their very nature, strictly unappropriable.

This is why Reason takes such care to warn the narrator against Fortune, the personification of "constant mutation" (*mutabilitas constantia*).⁴³ Whoever takes from her and whoever gives to her, whoever receives from her and whoever is bereft by her, has already entered into the movement of perpetual inversion, alteration, and differentiation figured by *li tourz de sa roe volant* (v. 5319). He has already abandoned his one true possession, self-possession, by irreparably exposing himself to what he cannot master; he already numbers among the class of *fols* who, consigned to what they cannot make their own, are made "to laugh and to suffer" (*rire et doloir*, v. 5316) by another. His condition is that expressed by the romance's narrator, who can explain himself only by literally calling his self into question: "Mon queur? Ja n'est il mes a moi" (v. 6887). Condemned by Jean's Reason as by Boethius' Philosophy before her, such a subject has consigned himself to Fortune. He has subjected himself wholly to the power of the divinity who undoes what she does and who *is,* in essence, nothing but this undoing; and he, too, as a consequence, is undone.

III

At this point it becomes possible to measure the full significance of the figure of Fortune in the *Roman de la Rose* in the context of thirteenth-century thought. That Jean de Meun himself was familiar with the faculties of theology and philosophy of his time was one of the central theses of Gérard Paré's classic study, *Les idées et les lettres au XIIIe siècle: Le Roman de la rose.*⁴⁴ Daniel Poirion maintained a similar position when he wrote that "Jean de Meun's allusions to the quarrels of the university of Paris prove . . . that he knows its intellectual climate well."⁴⁵ In *Der scholastische Wortschatz bei Jean de Meun: Die Artes Liberales* Gisela Hilder demonstrated, on purely philological grounds, that such conceptions of Jean de Meun's knowledge of Scholastic philosophy were fundamentally correct.⁴⁶ Hilder's careful lexicographic research proved that Jean de Meun, as she wrote, "knew and worked through not only literary, but also academic works of the twelfth and thirteenth centuries with far greater breadth than previous studies of his sources have shown."⁴⁷ Yet, despite the consensus of a number of scholars that the writing of the second part of the poem was undertaken in full awareness of the academic intellectual life of late-thirteenth-century Paris, many of the most important aspects of the romance have yet to be considered in their philosophical context. The figure of Fortune, as we shall see, is one of these aspects; its full significance in the poem can only be determined through an analysis of its relation to the concept of fortune as it was received, debated, and defined in the philosophy of the second half of the thirteenth century.

Every consideration of the concept of fortune in thirteenth-century thought must begin with the observation that the word *fortuna* is simply the Latin term used by the translators of Aristotle for the word τύχη, "luck" or "chance," which the Philosopher defines in the fourth, fifth, and sixth chapters of book B of the *Physics*. As such, "fortune" constitutes a philosophical notion that is irreducible to the classical literary and mythological figures we have already examined; it can be defined and articulated only with the aid of the complex physical and metaphysical conceptual armaments of thirteenth-century philosophy. *Fortuna* functions as a *terminus technicus* of the philosophy of nature which, from the middle of the thirteenth century onward, is taught and discussed in the faculties of Paris on the basis of the Latin *Physica*.[48] When a philosopher such as Siger of Brabant, for example, considers "Utrum aliquid sit a casu et fortuna" and "Utrum fortuna sit causa," his treatment of the matter, while in many respects original, necessarily entails an analysis of and confrontation with the Aristotelian text *in littera*.[49] By the second half of the thirteenth century the text of the *Physica*, whether followed or rejected, constituted the fundamental source for all reflection on chance and fortune in the sublunary world.

What, in this context, is fortune? The classical Aristotelian definition of *fortuna* is to be found in the fifth chapter of book B of the *Physics*. In the original, as in its oldest medieval Latin translation and its modern English form, it reads as follows:

δῆλον ἄρα ὅτι ἡ τύχη αἰτία κατὰ συμβεβηκὸς ἐν τοῖς κατὰ προαίρεσιν τῶν ἕνεκά του.[50]

Manifestum est ergo quod fortuna causa sit secundum accidens in his quae in minori sunt secundum propositum eorum qaue propter hoc sunt.

It is clear, then, that fortune is a cause, considered as an accident, in those causes of actions that are directed toward an end by choice.

According to the text of the *Physics*, *fortuna* therefore arises in the domain of choice and action (*secundum propositum eorum quae propter hoc sunt*); it is a specifically human matter. Aristotle thus distinguishes it from mere chance (τὸ αὐτόματον, which the Latins render as *casus*), which, he writes, arises in the case of animals and inanimate things.[51] If a stone happens to fall by accident, for example, it may well be an instance of *casus*, but it cannot be a matter of *fortuna*. Fortune can occur only where, in the causes of human actions directed toward definite ends, an accident comes to light as such.

As accidents, the events that take place by virtue of fortune surely refer, beyond the sphere of human actions, to the singular mode of Being (or non-Being, as Pierre Aubenque suggests)[52] which Aristotle characterizes as accidentality (ὂν κατὰ συμβεβηκός, *esse per accidens*);[53] and it is therefore no doubt the case, as Rémi Brague notes, that "it is because of the 'by accident' in things that there can be fortune."[54] But in fortune the accidentality of nature appears in a form that is tied to human action alone, that is, the accidental cause, *causa secundum accidens*.[55] In the treatise on fortune Aristotle distinguishes causation "by accident" (κατὰ συμβεβηκός, *secundum accidens*) from causation "by itself" or "absolutely" (καθ' αὐτό, *secundum seipsam*):

> Sicut enim et quod est, aliud quod per seipsum est, aliud autem secundum accidens, sic et causam contingit esse: ut domus quidem per seipsam causa et aedificativa, secundum accidens autem album aut musicam. Per se quidem igitur causa finita est, secundum accidens autem infinita: infinita enim uni accidunt.[56]

> A thing is as it is and what it is. But in one way it is as it is by itself (καθ' αὐτό) and in a different way it is as it is by accident (κατὰ συμβεβηκός); and the latter too can happen as a cause. Thus, for a house, the builder is the absolute cause of the building; that the builder is pale or cultivated is an accidental cause. That which is by itself is determinate (ὡρισμένον); that which is by accident is indeterminate (ἀόριστοω). For that which happens to a thing can be infinite (ἄπειρα γὰρ ἄν τῷ ἑνί συμβαίη).

Whereas a cause that is "by itself" or "absolute" (*secundum seipsam*) can be defined and determined (being ὡρισμένον, *finita*), an accidental cause (*secundam accidens*) is thus indefinite and indeterminate (ἀόριστον, *infinita*). What happens within human action as accidental cannot, therefore, be calculated; it is quite literally "in-finite" (ἄπειρον, *infinitum*). Such is the paradoxical sense of the Aristotelian definition of *fortune* as a cause that, in taking place among absolute causes, is by definition purely accidental. *Fortuna* is defined as a *causa per accidens* only to be rendered undefinable, as that which is by nature "infinite"; it is determined, in the physical and ethical world, precisely as "what takes place as indeterminate" (ἀόριστον τὸ ἀπὸ τύχης γινόμενον).[57]

In its Aristotelian definition fortune is therefore essentially irreducible to all knowledge in the strict sense. What holds for accidentality in general must necessarily hold for *fortuna*, which "takes place by accident": it "appears to lie close to what is not" (ἐλλύς τι τοῦ μὴ οὗτος)[58] and cannot, for this reason, become the object of science. Aristotle's texts are clear on this point: "a science of the accidental is not even possible," we read in the *Metaphysics*.[59] "For all science is of that which is always or for the most part, but the accidental is of neither of these two classes."⁶⁰ "That there is no science of the accidental," Aristotle insists, "is obvious."⁶¹ Here Aristotle concurs with the doctrine that one ancient text attributes to Anaxagoras, Democritus, and the Stoics, according to which fortune is by nature "a cause inscrutable to the reason of man" (ἄδηλον αἰτίαν ἀνθρωπίνῳ λογισμῷ).⁶²

Toward the end of this discussion of fortune, Aristotle summarizes his reflections with a striking statement. Given its nature as an accidental cause that, for the reasons we have seen, is necessarily indeterminate and infinite, fortune, Aristotle writes, can be defined as what falls outside the domain of reason altogether. Fortune, we read, is thus not a matter of logic but extra-logic or, more exactly, para-logic; it is, in Aristotle's words, "something para-logical" (τι παράλογος) or, according to the Latin text of the *Physics,* "beyond reason" (*extra ratione*):

> Et fortunam dicitur esse aliquid extra ratione, recte est. Ratio enim aut est eorum quae semper sunt, aut eorum quae sunt frequenter: fortuna autem in his quae fiunt praeter haec. Quare quoniam infinitae quae sic causae sunt, et fortuna infinita est.
>
> And it is thus correct to say that fortune is beyond reason [τι παράλογος]. For reason concerns itself with what is always or without exception, but fortune's place in what exists is beyond reason. And since the causes of such things are indeterminate, fortune too is indeterminate.⁶³

Necessarily in excess of reason, fortune appears as what takes place in causes and things and yet, at the same time, does not coincide with them; it is the singular element, in everything that is determined and defined by human activity, which remains necessarily indeterminate and undefinable, forever present in what is caused by human beings in the form of existing "beside," "outside," or "beyond" it.

The philosophers of the thirteenth century did not fail to emphasize the singular physical and metaphysical status that fortune, in such a context, necessarily assumes. In his *Commentarium in Physicorum* St. Thomas Aquinas, for example, begins his exposition of the Aristotelian doctrine of *fortuna* by noting the typological distinction between causes we have examined here: causes that, on the one hand, are "absolute" (*per se*) and hence "finite and determined" (*finitae et determinatae*) and which, on the other, are "accidental" (*per accidens*) and therefore "infinite and indeterminate" (*infinitae et indeterminatae*).⁶⁴ Following the movement of the *Physics,* Thomas then offers the following commentary on the Aristotelian definition of fortune as what is *extra ratione:*

> Dicit ergo primo quod recte dicitur fortunam esse sine ratione: quia ratiocinari non possumus nisi de his quae sunt semper vel frequenter; fortuna autem est extra utrumque. Et ideo, quia causae tales . . . sunt per accidens et infinitae et sine ratione.
>
> First he says that fortune is rightly said to be without reason. For we can reason only with what either always exists or exists for the most part; but fortune lies beyond both. Such, therefore, are the causes that are accidental, indeterminate and without reason.[65]

Seeking to clarify the sense of the Aristotelian definition of *fortune* as an accident that is *extra ratione*, Thomas has recourse in this passage to a formulation that is altogether his own. With an expression that at once conforms to Aristotle's thought and yet is absent from the text of the *Physics* itself, Thomas writes that *fortuna* is, by definition, *sine ratione*, "without reason," literally groundless. The fundamental paradox implicit in Aristotle's definition of *fortune* thus emerges with striking clarity: fortune now appears as a cause that by its very nature has no reason, as a ground, in other words, that is itself groundless.

One of the examples Thomas offers of fortune is particularly significant in this respect. *Fortuna,* he writes, is to be found in such cases as when a man, digging a hole to plant a tree, accidentally discovers a treasure (*utpote si fossurae sepulcri adiungatur per accidens inventio thesauri*).[66] The example cannot be found anywhere in the text of the *Physics,* but Thomas is not the first to cite it in a discussion of the Aristotelian doctrine of fortune. Before him, Boethius had already related a similar story to explain the nature of fortune and chance. In the fifth book of *De Consolatione Philosophiae,* Philosophy, explicitly referring to Aristotle's *Physics,* analyzes the nature of chance (the term in this passage is *casus*) by means of a variation on the same example: "it is as if a man digging in the ground in order to till his field were to find he had dug up a quantity of gold" (*ut si quis colendi agri causa fodiens humum defossi auri pondus inveniat*).[67] What is the origin of this story, which appears in the medieval philosophers as a classic example of fortune?

There is only one passage in the Aristotelian *corpus* that contains a similar example. It is to be found in the fifth book of the *Metaphysics,* in a discussion of the nature of accidentality which contains an explicit reference to fortune (τὸ τυχόν), which William of Moerbeke renders by means of the Latin term *contingens*. The text at issue reads as follows:

> Accidens dicitur quod inest alicui et uerum est dicere, non tamen ex necessitate nec secundum magis, puta iam aliquis fodiens plante fossam the-

saurum inueniat. Hoc igitur accidens fodiendi fossam, inuenire thesaurum; nec enim ex necessitate hoc ex hoc aut post hoc, nec ut secundum magis si quis plantat inueniat thesaurum. Et musicus utique quis erit albus; sed quoniam nec ex necessitate nec ut secundum magis hoc fit, accidens ipsum dicimus. Quare quoniam est existens aliquid et alicui, et horum quedam et alicui et quandoque quodcumque extiterit quidem, sed non quia hoc aut nunc aut hic, accidens erit. Nec est aliqua causa determinata accidentis sed contingens; hoc autem indeterminatum. . . . Euenit quidem et est accidens, at non in quantum ipsum sed in quantum alterum.⁶⁸

An accident is said to be that which is in something and can be truly said, but neither of necessity or for the most part, as, for example, if someone in digging a hole for a plant found treasure. The finding of the treasure is an accident for the man who digs the hole. For neither does the one come of necessity from the other or after the other, nor, if a man plants, does he for the most part find treasure. And a cultured man may be pale; but since this does not happen of necessity or for the most part, it is said to be an accident. Since there are attributes and subjects, and certain attributes are in certain subjects in a particular place and at a particular time, any attribute that is in a subject, but not for being what it is at this time or in this place, will therefore be said to be accident. There is thus no definite cause for an accident, but only a contingent one; and it is therefore indeterminate (οὐδὲ δὴ ἄτιον ὡρισμένον οὐδὲν τοῦ συμβεβηκότος ἀλλὰ τὸ τυχόν. τοῦτο δ' ἀόριστον). . . . For the accident takes place and exists not as itself but as something different (γένονε μὲν δὴ καὶ ἔστι τὸ συμβεβηκός, ἀλλ' οὐχ ᾗ αὐτὸ ἀλλ' ᾗ ἕτερον).

If one recalls the Aristotelian definition of fortune as "a cause, considered as an accident, in those actions that are directed toward an end," the pertinence of this text to the treatise on fortune becomes clear, and the reasons for which Boethius and Thomas refer to it in their discussions of the nature of fortune appear entirely comprehensible. As what takes place by accident in the human world, fortune is precisely what happens "neither necessarily, nor for the most part" (*nec ex necessitate nec secundum magis*); it is, by definition, implicated in the very *euenire* that is at issue in this passage. As Albert the Great writes in the passage of his *Metaphysica* that refers to this discussion of accidentality, what is at issue in the story of the man who accidentally discovers a treasure is that which happens *forte sive fortuito*.⁶⁹

Aristotle's discussion of the accidental discovery of the hidden treasure in the *Metaphysics,* therefore, is of great importance for an understanding of fortune. It allows for the distinction between "accidental cause" and "absolute cause," whose importance we have traced in the *Physics* and its medieval commentaries, to be elaborated in terms of a further difference that concerns the very existence of fortune. For the opposition between *causa per se* and *causa per accidens* now appears as a fundamental difference between two modes of taking place, *euenire: euenire in quantum se,* on the one hand, and *euenire in quantum alterum,* on the other. The final sentence of the passage quoted earlier, which concerns the "event" of the accident and hence also of fortune, must be heard in all its significance in this context. *Euenit quidem et est accidens, at non in quantum ipsum sed in quantum alterum* (γένονε καὶ ἔστι τὸ συμβεβηκός, ἀλλ' οὐχ ᾗ ἄλλα᾽ ᾗ ἕτερον): in its form the Latin translation, unlike many of the modern English versions,[70] does not shy away from the radical and perplexing thesis that Aristotle clearly states—namely, that the accident does not take place as itself but as something different. But what does it mean for something to "take place not as itself but as something different," *euenire non in quantum ipsum sed in quantum alterum?* Aristotle's example helps to explain the sense of his statement. The man who digs into the earth to plant his tree does not encounter the treasure *as* a treasure. Insofar as he digs into the earth, he can only perceive the treasure as an obstacle to his task, which is to dig a hole. To the degree that he finds the treasure *as* a treasure, therefore, the man has found something he did not expect; he has discovered something other than what he meant to find. In finding the treasure, the man perceives what lies beneath him in a way he did not anticipate; he encounters it not as itself but, as Aristotle writes, as another, *in quantum alterum.* And this—the revelation of something not as itself but another—is what Aristotle calls fortune.[71]

The *Physics*, in this passage, thus reveals the specific mode of existence of fortune. As what occurs by accident, Fortune is what exists not as itself but as another; it is what takes place, distinguishing itself from itself, simultaneously as itself and as "something different." Insofar as it "is" at all, fortune is thus different from itself; its *esse per se,* paradoxically, is an *esse per accidens,* since for it to be *seipsum* is for it to be *in quantum alterum.* It is worth pausing to consider the paradoxical structure of this existence, which bears an essential affinity to contingency and its aporia: for it to be itself, it must be different from itself; for it to appear as such, it must present itself as something other than itself. Such is the final sense of this essentially human phenomenon, the singular "cause, considered as an accident, in those causes of actions that are directed toward an end by choice." Fortune is what, in those causes of actions that are directed toward an end by choice, opens all human activity and production to its own difference from itself, in-determining and in-defining it; it is what, as an "accidental cause," exposes all human causation to what exceeds anticipation, calculation, and reason, being by nature para-logical, *extra* and *sine ratione*.

The definition and elaboration of the concept of fortune in thirteenth-century philosophy makes it possible to clarify the paradox that accompanies the form and actions of the allegorical figure in the *Roman de la Rose*. In Jean de Meun's poetic appropriation and transformation of Boethius, as we saw, when Fortune gives she ultimately takes, and when she takes, conversely, she truly gives, in such a way that everything the divinity offers shows itself as essentially unappropriable. It is now possible to offer an explanation for the paradoxical form by which Fortune, in the poetic text, appears to render her actions different from themselves and her gifts impossible to possess: all of Fortune's gestures, whether acts of giving or of taking, are something other than themselves, because Fortune functions here as the figural form of the concept of *fortuna* in thirteenth-century philosophy, that is, what takes place as different from itself. Jean de Meun's figure of Fortune, in this sense, constitutes a precise transposition, into the field of poetic invention, of the physical and metaphysical notion of *fortuna* developed by the medieval philosophers: τύχη-*fortuna*, that which takes place not as itself but as another. The medieval philosophical concept of *fortuna*, which subsumes what takes place in the human world as other than itself, thus becomes the *Fortune* of the *Roman de la Rose*, the poetic figure who always appears as different from herself and whose gifts, taking place *forte sive fortuito*, cannot be transformed into stable goods that may be possessed. It is this simultaneously philosophical and poetic *inventio* that is at play in Fortune's paradoxical acts and gifts; and it is this *inventio*, we shall now see, which determines the form that the figure of Fortune, as a *persona ficta* in the rhetorical sense, assumes in the text of the poem.

IV

It is possible, at this point, to reformulate our initial question, considering it in a new light. If Fortune, in the *Roman de la Rose*, is indeed the cipher of what takes place not as itself but as something different, what kind of figure can she then constitute in the text of the poem? As Guillaume de Lorris and Jean de Meun present her, Fortune is first of all a figure spoken of by another figure, Reason; in this sense the poets follow the practice of *De Consolatione Philosophiae*, in which Fortune appears only in the discourse of Lady Philosophy. Fortune "herself," in the romance as in *De Consolatione*, is silent. When she appears in the work, Fortune is thus only ever present by virtue of another;

and, as a result, she may only ever be present in it *as* another, in a form as different from her own as she herself is different from those who speak of her. The romance, in its dramatic organization and *dispositio,* thus already registers what will be the fundamental trait of the figure as it appears in Reason's following description: that it is nothing if not different from itself.

At first glance, to be sure, the figure of Fortune appears as a simple product of what modern critics generally call "personification."[72] In the terms of classical and medieval rhetorical theory, the character thus owes its existence to *sermocinatio,* the figure of thought by which discourse is organized through the attribution of speech to a number of characters, or *personae;* it constitutes an example of the movement by which, according to the *Rhetorica ad Herennium,* "language is assigned to some character that is in conformity with his function" (*alicui personae sermo adtribuitur et is exponitur cum ratione dignitatis*).[73] More exactly, Fortune, like the other abstract entities of the poem, appears to be an example of what the Greek rhetoricians called προσωποποιΐα, Quintilian *fictio personae,*[74] Cicero *personarum ficta inductio,*[75] and the *Ad Herennium conformatio:* the "fabrication" (ποιεῖν, *fingere*) of a "mask" and, according to the metonymy we noted in the preceding chapter, "dramatic role" or "character." We seem to be confronted, in this case, with the figure Quintilian referred to as that "by which we fashion body and speech" (*et corpora et verba fingimus*) and which the anonymous author of the *Ad Herennium* defined, as follows, in terms that were to become canonical in the Middle Ages:

> cum aliqua que non adest persona configitur quasi adsit, aut cum res muta aut informis fit eloquens, et forma ei et oratio adtribuitur ad dignitatem ad-commodata aut actio quedam.

> that by which someone who is absent is depicted as if he were present, or by which a speechless or formless thing is rendered articulate, and a definite form and speech are attributed to him in conformity with his character.[76]

As an *abstractum agens,* Lady Fortune therefore appears to fall into the class of *personae fictae* defined here; she seems to constitute a simple case of a "formless and speechless" entity that has been transformed, through the figural language of the poetic text, into a "character" gifted with a determinate form and language.

Yet with Fortune things are, once again, not what they seem. As the figure of instability, change and self-differentiation, she cannot have a self-consistent form; defined as a "goddess who is not stable" (*dea non stabilis*),[77] a being in "constant mutation" (*constantia mutabilis*),[78] and "a thing that is not stable, but errant and changeable" (*chose qui n'est estable, / conme foloianz et movable*)

(vv. 6085–86), Fortune cannot assume a shape that is definite and unitary. If she is, as it first seems, indeed the product of προσωποποιΐα and *fictio personae*, then her *persona*—her πρόσωπον, mask, and "face"—threatens not to be one. Already in Boethius, the classical doubling of *fortuna* into *fortuna bona* and *fortuna mala*, *fortuna prospera* and *fortuna adversa*, entails a fundamental fracture in Fortune's own appearance: she becomes, from the opening of the *De Consolatione*,[79] a creature of two faces, whose *vultus* is later characterized as *ambiguus*.[80] Boethius' depiction of the Janus-like goddess, as Pierre Courcelle has shown, has a history that is consistent and well documented in the early medieval Latin tradition,[81] one that no doubt extends to Alain de Lille's *Anticlaudianus*, in which Fortune is said to have a *vultus ambiguus* that is "partly living" and "partly dying" (*pars vultus vivit . . . pars moritur*).[82] The iconographical tradition of the *Consolatio*, in any case, demonstrates as much: one finds Fortune presented, often beside her wheel, as a being of two faces, one smiling, the other one frowning, one bright, the other obscure.[83] This tradition of representation, in which Fortune appears precisely as what resists any stable depiction, is equally well represented in the French literary tradition, most notably from the time of the *Roman de la Rose* onward.[84] Gervais de Bus presents the divinity of chance as a being of two faces in the *Roman de Fauvel*;[85] Pierre Michault depicts her, in "La dance aux Aveugles," with "visage biparty," "car l'une partie et droite moytié estoyt noire comme charbon et l'autre partie blanche comme croye";[86] Guillaume de Machaut relates that, in pagan antiquity, the goddess was believed "to have two faces" (*deulz faces*), *l'une de joie et de leesce, / l'autre moustroit en sa colour / Signifiance de doulour*.[87] If it is possible to speak, with reference to these works, of a "personification" of Fortune, then the *persona ficta* at issue is therefore of a specific kind. It is a face fashioned in the literary text to be immediately multiplied, divided from itself, and stripped of identity as such.

The figure of Fortune in the *Roman de la Rose* constitutes a radical yet consistent development of this tradition. The text of the romance subjects the figure of Fortune, as "a thing that is not stable, but errant and changeable" (*chose qui n'est estable, / conme foloianz et movable*, vv. 6085–86), to the force of the instability it is to present. In her *mansion* (v. 6088) Fortune appears in the text as a creature who, in the absence of any fixed and proper shape, must mechanically construct and assume whatever form she apears to have:

> quant el veut estre honoree,
> si se tret en la part doree

> de sa meson et la sojorne:
> lors pare son cors et atorne,
> et se vest, conme une reïne,
> de grant robe qui li treïne,
> de toute diverses ouleurs,
> de mout desguisees couleurs
> qui sunt es saies et es laines
> selonc les herbes et les graines
> et selonc autre choses maintes
> don les draperies sunt taintes
> don toutes riches genz se vestent
> qui por honeurs avoir s'aprestent.
> (Vv. 6089–102)

When she wants to be honored, she withdraws into the golden part of her house and dwells there. Then she apparels herself and adorns her body and, like a queen, clothes herself in long dresses that trail behind her, with many different perfumes and with highly varied colors, dresses made of silks and woolens, with patterns of plants and grains and many other things with which are colored the cloths in which rich people dress when they prepare themselves to receive honors. (121)

Here the text speaks not of the appearance of Fortune but, rather, of the constitution of that appearance; and what is presented in this passage is not the form of the divinity but, instead, the very formation of that form. Before describing Fortune as *honoree*, the poem thus describes her will to be such (*elle veut estre honoree*, v. 6089); before situating the goddess in her *part doree*, it traces the movement by which she reaches it at all (*si se tret en la part doree / de sa meson et la sojorne*, vv. 6090–91). The scene shows the very act of covering and veiling by which Lady Fortune, instead of becoming a queen, appears "as" if she were one: *el se vest, conme une reïne, / de grant robe qui li treïne* ... (vv. 6093–94). It is not the guise of the figure which is at issue here but, rather, its *disguisees couleurs* (v. 6096),[88] in both of the two contradictory senses implied by the Old French term *desguise*: the undoing of an original guise (a "dis-guise") and the assumption of a new and different guise (a "disguise").[89] "Ainsinc," we read, "Fortune se desguise."

Newly covered, Fortune then discovers herself:

> Aisinc Fortune se desguise,
> mes bien te di qu'ele ne prise
> tretouz cels du monde un festu
> quant voit son cors ainsinc vestu,

> ainz est tant orgueilleuse et fiere
> qu'i n'est orguieuz qui s'i aYere;
> car quant el voit ses granz richeces,
> ses granz honeurs, ses granz nobleces,
> de si tres grant folie habunde
> qu'el ne croit pas qu'il ait u munde
> home ne fame qui la vaille,
> conment que la chose amprés aille.
>   (Vv. 6103–14)

Fortune thus disguises herself. But I tell you indeed that she would not give a thing for anyone in the world when she sees her body dressed like that; she is so proud and haughty that there is no pride to be compared with hers. For when she sees her great riches, her great honors and glories, she is so full of her overweening folly that she does not believe, no matter how things may go afterward, that there is anywhere in the world a man or woman worth as much as she. (121)

Fortune, transformed into something other than what she was, now appears to observe herself for the first time; and the narration of the romance, as a consequence, passes into the first proper *descriptio* of the figure to be found in Jean's text. But the instability and self-differentiation that, as we have seen, mark the form of Fortune do not now come to an end. For in the very gesture by which Fortune, having clothed herself as if she were a queen, seeks to perceive herself as she is, she cannot but distinguish herself from herself; and, in the very moment in which the poem appears to describe the figure of Fortune as she is, it therefore divides her in two. Fortune now sees *herself* and, as a result, perceives herself as another: she "sees her body thus clothed" (*voit son cors ainsinc vestu*, v. 6106), she "sees her great wealth" (*voit ses granz richeces*, v. 6109) and, as a result, can judge herself, as if she herself were a third party, with respect to the men and women of the world (*el ne croit pas qu'il ait u munde / home ne fame qui la vaille, / conment que la chose amprés aille*, vv. 6112–14).

In the text of the poem the self-differentiation implied by Fortune's self-contemplation is the structural prelude to a further, more significant doubling in her form; it anticipates Fortune's fracture, in her own *mansion*, into two figures who are in every respect opposed and irreconcilable. As soon as Fortune beholds herself, in the sense we have seen, she moves, reeling and "rolling" (*roant*) like her wheel, into a different room and a different state:

> Puis va tant roant par sa sale
> qu'el entre en la partie sale,

> foible, decrevee et crolant,
> o toute sa roe volant.
> Lors va çoupant et jus se boute
> ausinc con s'el n'i veïst goute;
> et quant iluec se voit cheüe,
> sa chiere et son habit remue,
> et si se desnue et desrobe
> qu'el est orfeline de robe
> et semble qu'el n'ait riens vaillant,
> tant li vont tuit bien defaillant.
> Et quant el voit la meschaance,
> si quiert honteuse chevichance
> et se vet au bordel cropir,
> pleine de deul et de sopir.
> La pleure a lermes espandues
> les granz honeurs qu'el a perdues
> et les deliz ou ele estoit
> quant des granz robes se vestoit
> (Vv. 6115–34)

Then she goes along, with her whole wheel flying, roaming through her hall until she comes to the part that is dirty, weak, cracked, and shaking. She goes stumbling along and throws herself to the ground as if she had seen nothing there; and when she sees herself fallen there, she changes her countenance and her clothing; she bares and undresses herself until she is stripped of her clothing, and she is so lacking in every good thing that it seems that she has nothing worth anything. And when she sees her misfortune, she seeks a shameful way out and, full of sorrow and sighing, goes to stagnate in a whorehouse. There, with lavish tears, she weeps over the great honors that she has lost and the delights in which she lived when she was dressed in magnificent robes. (122)

Here Fortune is struck with the very force of inversion she figures. She "throws herself down" (*jus se boute,* v. 6119), from the heights of her wealth, to the state of one who is fallen (*cheüe,* v. 6121). Before, when she was "as a queen" (*conme une reïne,* v. 6093), she contemplated her own luxury; now, by contrast, it is as if she could not see: *con se'l n'i veïst goute* (v. 6120). The very *persona* the text had fashioned thus undoes itself: the figure "changes" (or "exchanges," *remue*) its own body (v. 6122), "strips" (*desnue*) and "unclothes" (*desrobe,* v. 6124) the very "clothes" (*robe,* v. 6124) in which it had covered itself one scene before. The "wealth" (*richeses*) and "nobility" (*nobleces,* vv. 6109–10) of Fortune thus turn to poverty; if before it seemed that "none of the men and women in the world" equaled her worth (*el ne croit pas qu'il ait u munde / home ne fame qui la vaille,* vv. 6112–13), now, according to a perfectly symmetrical figure, it appears that she possesses "nothing of worth" (*qu'el n'ait riens vaillant,* 6125). Fortune's imperious pride thus turns to despair, and her face, which once registered her "great honours" and "great nobility" (*granz honeurs, ses granz nobleces,* v. 6110), shows itself to express only "mourning and regret" (*deul et sopir,* v. 6130). With the transformation of each of her traits into its opposite, Fortune reveals herself now as what she was not before: her tears are in exact proportion to the goods she has lost ([*el*] *pleure a larmes espandues / les granz honeurs qu'el a perdus,* vv. 6131–32).

If one considers Fortune as a figure in the technical sense as a *fictio personae, conformatio,* or *prosopopeia,* a radical consequence must therefore be drawn from her perpetually changing form. As a figure who assumes one form only to take on its symmetrical opposite, Fortune has no single, self-identical mask, πρόσωπον or *persona:* "now she is clear; now she is dark" (*or est clere, or est obscure,* v. 4769). Fortune, as we have seen, is no sooner given a face, in the text of the poem, than she is literally defaced as such. But, then, she cannot constitute a personification, or *persona ficta,* in any rigorous sense: by her very nature Fortune constitutes at the very least two opposed *personae fictae* and, therefore, *stricto sensu* none. This is why she is of such importance in the order of the poem. For, as a figure whose form is ceaselessly composed, decomposed, and recomposed in the text of the poem, Fortune exposes the most fundamental mechanism of allegorical personification: the "making of a face," *personae fictio,* and πρόσωπον ποιεῖν. This is the sense of this singular *conformatio,* for which the classical and medieval term *deformatio* is perhaps more apt:[90] in appearing in the text as the figure of a continuous metamorphosis, Fortune brings to light the fundamental operation by which language, in figural discourse, allows *personae* to be lent to—and, consequently, also taken from— what is by definition faceless.

The account that the poetic text offers of the abode of Fortune is, in this sense, exemplary. The *Roman de la Rose* situates Fortune's dwelling in a landscape that is itself traversed by the very instability and mutation that marks her figure. Appropriating Alain de Lille's description of the Isle of Fortune in book 7 and 8 of the *Anticlaudianus,*[91] Jean de Meun presents the proper place of the allegorical *persona* as a site that "retains no form, but rather mutates and reforms itself":

> Une roche est en mer seanz,
> bien parfont, el mileu leanz,
> qui seur la mer en haut se lance,
> contre cui la mer groce et tance.
> Li flot la hurtent et debatent,
> qui tourjourz a lui se conbatent,
> et maintes foiz tant i cotissent
> que toute en mer l'ensevelissent;
> ancune foiz se redespuelle
> de l'eve qui toute la muelle
> si con li floz ariers se tire,
> donc saut en l'air et si respire.
> Met el ne retient nule forme,
> ainceis se tresmue et reforme
> et se desguise et se treschange;
> tourjors se vest de forme estrange
> (Vv. 5891–906)

There is a rock placed in the depths of the sea, in its center, projecting on high above it, against which the sea growls and struggles. The waves, continually fighting it, beat against it, worry it, and many times dash against it so strongly that it is entirely engulfed; again it sheds the water which has drenched it, the waves draw back, and it rises again into the air and breathes. It does not keep any one shape; it alters and changes itself, always appearing in strange forms. (118)

Here the power of alteration and differentiation inscribed in the figure of Fortune extends, metonymically, to the site of her dwelling. Just as the figure of Fortune, considered in its technical sense as *fictio personae* or *conformatio*, is not one, so the landscape in which the allegorical *persona* is situated differs, by its very nature, from itself. "Contradiction," as Paré writes, is thus "permanently installed in the residence of Fortune."[92] "Formed" only to be then "deformed" (*deforme*), "disguised" (*desguise*), "mutated" (*tresmue*), and "changed" (*trechange*), the *forme estrange* of the isle is none other than the singular form—and non-form—of the figure of Fortune itself. It is the form of rhetorical self-contradiction, in which everything, as Alain de Lille writes in the *Anticlaudianus*, appears, *per antifrasim*, as the contrary of itself.[93] "La roche," we read, "porte un bois doutable" (v. 5917):

> La sunt li geneste geant,
> et pin et cedre nain seant:
> chascun arbre ainsinc se defforme,

> si prent l'un de l'autre la forme.
> La tient sa feulle toute flestre
> li loriers, qui verz devroit estre;
> et seiche i redevient l'olive,
> qui doit estre enpreignant et vive:
> sauce, qui brahaign estre doivent,
> i fleurissent et fruit reçoivent;
> contre la vigne estrive l'orme
> et li tost du resin la forme.
> Li roussigneus a tart i chante
> mes mout i bret, mout s' i demante
> li chahuans o sa grant hure,
> prophetes de malaventure,
> hideus messagier de douleur
>
> (Vv. 5931–47)

There is a strange wood on the rock. . . . There the broom plants are giant, while pine and cedar, their growth arrested, are dwarf. Every tree thus deforms itself; one takes the shape of another. The laurel, which should be green, has tarnished leaves; the olive in its turn dries up when it should be fecund and living; the willows, which should be sterile, flower and bear fruit; the elm strives against the vine and steals the form of the grapevine. There the nightingale rarely sings, but the screech-owl with his great beard, the prophet of misfortune and hideous messenger of sorrow, cries out and raves. (119)

Submitted to the rule of Fortune, the *bois* appears as the contrary of itself. According to the principle that what enters into the field of Fortune's power "deforms itself; one takes the shape of another" (*se defforme, / si prent l'un de l'autre la forme,* vv. 5933–34), here what is by nature small is large, even as what should be large, by contrast, is small; what should die lives on, and what should be fertile is sterile; what should sing is silent, and what should be silent is all too loud. It is an "inverted world,"[94] in which, as in Chrétien de Troyes's *Cligès,* "all things thus go backwards" (*ci vont les choses a envers*):[95] everything occurs not as itself but as its opposite.

In this sense the terrain of Fortune, like the figure itself, occurs in the poetic text precisely as *fortuna* takes place according to the philosophy of the thirteenth century: "not as itself but as something different" (*non in quantum ispum sed in quantum alterum*). The paradoxical dwelling, like its mistress, therefore marks the limit of all stable figuration. For just as the *persona* of Fortune, for the reasons we have seen, constitutes two opposing *personae* and hence exceeds the form of the *fictio personae*, so that which lives on the isle of Fortune, on account of its incessant mutability and self-differentiation, cannot be represented by any determinate shape. Figured as what defigures itself, what lives in the landscape of fortune cannot assume a unitary, stable form, for it is by definition what, in the words of the text, "deforms itself"; it is the figure of inconstancy, accidentality, and indeterminacy and cannot, therefore, be characterized by any single mode of appearance. The *impossibile* of the isle of Fortune, in this sense, is simply the possibility of figuration itself; what is truly "impossible" in this "series of impossible things"[96] is for Fortune and everything she touches to assume a stable form. Yet in the text this impossibility of representation does not function as a barrier to the unfolding of the language of poetry; it does not merely indicate the failure of literary discourse before fortune and its force. Instead, the *impossibile* of Fortune's *bois*, like Fortune herself, now undergoes a final inversion and, transformed into its contrary, opens onto a poetic *possibile* in an altogether different sense. In this metamorphosis beyond form and figure, in this movement of incessant formation and deformation, what emerges in the *Roman de la Rose* is simply the bare *possibile* of literary discourse itself, its capacity to lend and to take away, to compose and decompose, the figures of its own rhetoric; what now comes to light, in the text of the romance, is therefore the very accidentality, indeterminacy, and indefinition—the contingency—of poetic language as such.

V

Toward the end of her discourse Reason advances a thesis that condenses her preceding discussion and, at the same time, carries it to what is perhaps the most extreme point of its development. *Fortune,* she explains, *does not exist.* The proposition is classical in form; it recalls, among other *dicta,* the declaration with which Augustine's teacher Lactantius sought to liquidate the matter, writing that "fortune in itself is nothing" (*Fortuna ergo per se nihil est*).[97] As such, Reason's claim is founded on the fundamental metaphysical and theological principle that Being, defined as the form of what is stable and present, cannot in any sense be attributed to what in itself is unstable, disorderly, and irreducible to all presence.[98] In Reason's words, which refer explicitly to the texts of the *auctores,*[99] fortune thus is not an actual "power" or "potentiality" (*puissance,* v. 6261) but merely a "disorder" (*desordenance,* v. 6262), that is, a "weakness" (*feblece,* v. 6263) and "absence" (*defaut,* v. 6263) of true existence:

> Si n'apele je pas puissance
> poair mal ne desordenance,
> car l'escriture dit, e bien,
> que toute poissance est de bien,
> ne nus a bien fere ne faut
> for par feblece et par defaut.
> Et qui seroit bien cler voianz,
> il verroit que mal est noianz,
> car ainsinc le dit l'escriture
> (Vv. 6261–69)

I do not give the name of power to evil or unregulated power, for it is written, and it is well written, that all power comes from the good and that no man fails to do good except through weakness and omission; and he who understood clearly would see that evil is nothing, for so it is written. (124)

Fortune, in its definition as indefinite, is therefore in the strict sense "nothing" (or "Nothing"); it is but a "lack," "absence," or "loss," a *defaut* in what can properly be said to be. As what appears to exist but is nothing more, fortune is likened to the "shadow" (*ombre,* v. 6283) of evil. It is a "lack of light" in which what appears is nothing but the "pure absence" (*pur defaut,* v. 6288) of a present good:

> si con li ombres ne pose
> en l'air occurci nule chose
> fors defaillance de lumiere,
> tretout en autele maniere,
> en creature ou bien defaut,
> mal n'i met riens fors pur defaut
> de bonté.
> (Vv. 6283–89)

Just as the shadow places nothing in the air that is darkened except a lack of light, so in similar way, in a creature in whom good is absent, evil puts nothing except the pure absence of good. (124)

Classed as a type of "evil" (*mal*) on account of the instability, inconstancy, and disorder it necessarily implies, fortune thus appears in Reason's discourse as lacking all substantial existence. The movement of perpetual metamorphosis that we have traced throughout the discussion of fortune finds its ultimate ground—or, rather, non-ground—in this *pur defaut*: fortune, in the text of the poem, appears as what is lacking in identity because it is, in the most fundamental metaphysical sense, what is deprived of all being. The continual self-differentiation of fortune, which provokes what is composed to be decomposed and what is figured to be defigured, shows itself now as what it is: the "strange and alien form" (*forme estrange,* v. 5906) in which a "nothing," a *pur defaut* and *defaillance,* appears in the language of poetry.

In the end Reason's project—to impart a sure "knowledge" (*connoissance;* cf. vv. 4233–41) of fortune—thus undoes itself. Just as accidents, for Aristotle, cannot give rise to any science in the strict sense, so a "shadow" cannot constitute the object of rational apprehension. No *ratio* can be given for what, by definition, exists *sine ratione.* A "pure nothing" (*pur defaut*), Fortune cannot engender knowledge; on the contrary, she can only, in Reason's own words, "trouble" it (*ele trouble . . . connoissance,* v. 4861), deranging the faculty of intellection that seeks to grasp it. It is a point that Lady Reason registers when she explains to the narrator that even she could not recount "all the turns" of Fortune's wheel:

> De Fortune la semilleuse
> et de sa roe perilleuse
> touz les tourz conter ne porraie.
> (Vv. 6825–27)

I could not count all the turns of wily Fortune and of her perilous wheel. (132)

In this significant avowal Reason, brought to the end of her discourse, admits her incapacity of telling "all," saying "everything," about Fortune. The voice of constancy thus registers, despite itself, the inconstancy it cannot master; it ultimately indicates the "nothing" that, at once itself and not itself, existing and not existing, necessary exceeds it.

The silent and ventriloquized figure that Reason introduces into the dramatis personae of the *Roman de la Rose,* therefore, is a singular one. As the embodiment of what does not exist and, therefore, cannot be figured, Fortune appears to mark the limit of all allegorical depiction—all figuration—as such. At the same time, however, it is necessary to formulate a further principle, which is in some sense the inverse of the one just stated: precisely because she is the embodiment of what, on account of not existing, can *only* be figured, Fortune constitutes an allegorical figure that is in every sense exemplary. In showing herself to have no proper face, form, or figure, Fortune reveals herself as what must be lent a face, given a form and figure, since she herself—as a mere shadow—has none; in exposing herself, through a movement of perpetual inversion and mutation, as formless, Fortune marks the very mechanisms of figuration by which poetic language gives a shape, through rhetoric, to what by definition can have no form. The figure of Fortune is a properly poetic one, in other words, because it constitutes a figure for nothing and for no one; its significance lies in the fact that it carries the very structure of figural personification to its limits, at which, in a simultaneous formation and deformation, there emerges a "void" that exists in language alone.

It is possible, at this point, to specify the exact sense in which Lady Fortune can be said to constitute the fundamental figure of contingency in the *Roman de la Rose*. The *genetivus* in the syntagm, "the figure of contingency," must be heard as simultaneously *objectivus* and *subjectivus*. It must be understood as objective, for Fortune functions throughout Reason's discourse as a figure for contingency, representing, through her wheel, her figure, and her dwelling place, the very capacity of self-differentiation which the medieval philosophers term *contingentia*. But it must also be grasped as subjective, for, at the same time, the figure of Fortune is irreparably exposed to the very inconstancy and alteration it would depict; it itself is marked, in its taking place, as contingent. At once a figure for contingency and a contingent figure, Fortune is therefore the exemplary *persona ficta*, in the *Roman de la Rose,* for the poetics of contingency at work in the romance of Guillaume de Lorris and Jean de Meun as a whole. We saw, in the preceding chapter, that the "I" of the two-part romance constitutes the fundamental structure through which the language of the poem shows itself, in the form of a subjectivity, to be capable of taking place and not taking place. Our study of the figure of Fortune allows us to deepen our analysis of the specific *ars poetica* of the work, through the articulation of a further claim: namely, that Fortune constitutes the exemplary form in which the language of the poem appears, in its figural discourse, as contingent.

At this point it becomes possible fully to understand why, in the longest discussion of erotic love in the *Roman de la Rose,* the poetic text speaks above all of fortune. As we saw in the last chapter, in the romance love constitutes the locus of an experience of absolute contingency, in that the figure of Amors functions to reveal the poetic subject's constitutive capacity to be different from itself and not to be at all. As the exemplary allegorical *persona* for what is unstable and undoes itself, Lady Fortune is the emblem of this contingency; she functions, in the romance as a whole, as a figural construction of the element in love that constitutes and deconstitutes the identity of the narrator of the poem. This is perhaps the final sense in which erotic love, in the words of the text, is truly "l'amor qui vient de Fortune" (v. 4753). Fortune is the "origin" of *amor* in the sense that it constitutes the absolute contingency from which the experience of erotic love arises; it is the element of uncertainty and instability to which the lover has always already surrendered himself. Reason's discussion of erotic love must take the form of a description of fortune because fortune is the figure for the dimension to which the poetic self, by means of his love, is irreparably consigned: a power of differentiation, alteration, and metamorphosis whose force is so great that it cannot even be understood in the terms of identity and existence, being conceivable only as a shadow, or "absence," in the ordered world.[100]

As the accidental, indeterminate, and undefined power to which the lover is necessarily subjected, fortune is simultaneously the element in love which Reason cannot bear; it is the element in love which, in its constant mutation, is not only "opposed to reason" (*contrarium rationi*), as Cicero suggests, but also "outside" or "beside reason" (τι παράλογος, *extra ratione*), in Aristotle's phrase, and, at the limit, altogether "without reason" (*sine ratione*), as Thomas writes. Fortune is that to which the lover abandons himself in the moment in which he falls prey to what can be neither mastered nor appropriated; it is that which, paradoxically both itself and the contrary of itself, marks everything it touches with its own mutability and metamorphosis. Nothing but a shadow, a "lack," and a literal "fault," *defaut* and *defaillance*, fortune is the essential void—the contingency—at the center of desire, whose origin forever escapes the narrator's grasp:

> Certes il defaut en moi donques,
> si ne sai je pas don ce vient
> ne ja ne savrai, se devient.
> (Vv. 4162–64)

The fault then lies certainly in me, and I do not know where it comes from, nor, perhaps, shall I ever know. (93)

The fault in the speaker is the mark of his subjection at once to desire and to fortune. It is the cipher of the shadow to which the narrator, like Narcissus, is consigned by virtue of his desire: a force all the more effective for being "without anything of its own" (*nihil habet ista sui*),[101] which withdraws the poetic self from the domain of possession and self-possession, transforming him into the nameless, unidentifiable "I" of the poem.

It is hardly a surprise, therefore, that, when Fortune appears in the poem with a wheel, she is not simply presented, as in the classical poets, beside her *rota*,[102] nor is she herself on her own wheel, as in certain medieval iconographical representations.[103] Instead, in the romance the wheel of fortune func-

The Contingent Figure

tions to present the place of the lover and, therefore, to figure the singular situation of the narrator of the poem. When the text of Guillaume's poem first mentions fortune's wheel, it leaves no doubts as to the figure inscribed at its center:

> Ele a une roe qui torne
> et, quant ele veut, ele met
> le plus bas amont ou somet,
> et celui que est sor la roe
> reverse a un tor en la boue.
> Et je sui cil qui est versez!
> (Vv. 3958–63)

She has a wheel that turns and, when she wishes, she raises the lowest up to the summit and with a turn plunges the one who was on top of the wheel into the mud. And I am the one who is turned over! (87)

The "one who is turned over" (*cil qui est versez,* v. 3963) on the wheel of fortune, exposed to the contingency of love, is the nameless narrator of the *Roman de la Rose*. And, since the discourse of the narrator is simply the discourse of the poetic text, the language of the poem, at this point, must also be said to be exposed to the essential contingency that defines the lover's fate. In appearing as the speech of its protagonist, the discourse of the poem too, like *cil qui est versez,* is submitted to what it cannot master and cannot make its own. For here language, in the incessant movement of its simultaneous figuration and disfiguration, formation and deformation, is displaced from its traditional position as the bearer of meaning; it ceases to function, according to Reason's Augustinian formulation, in the service of "understanding" (*entendre*) and "teaching" (*aprendre,* vv. 7071–72).[104] Like its own subject, the discourse of the text is exposed to a "volubility" (*volubilitas*) beyond all order and form; as a result, it too, like its "I," is in-determined and in-defined. It shows itself, in a sense that is at once close and irreducible to that of the first troubadour, as a *vers de dreit nien,* a "verse of pure nothing," a romance, we might say, of *riens fors pur defaut* (v. 6287), "nothing other than pure lack." The language of the romance is opened, in this way, to its own contingency: to that dimension, within its form and order, which exceeds whatever causation, decision, and intention it may articulate. It can no longer be distinguished from the fortune of which it would speak, for it itself now takes place, *forte sive fortuito,* "not as itself but as something different." Exceeding reason, its forms, and the figures of its rhetoric, language now reveals itself, simply, as poetry.

4 | *Through the Looking-Glass*
The Knowledge of Contingency

I

Toward the end of the *Roman de la Rose* Nature, encouraged by Genius, gives her "confession" (v. 16696), which the narrator of the romance, in turn, recounts "word for word, just as she said it" (*mot a mot, si conme el l'a dite,* v. 16698).[1] Nature's first subject, the "beautiful form" (*bele fourme,* v. 16702) of creation, leads her to consider the "beautiful golden chain" (*la bele chaene doree,* v. 16756) which binds the four elements of the world, the "cold and hot and dry and moist" (*froit et chaut et sec et moeste,* v. 16931).[2] The balance between them, Nature explains, is delicate. Their slightest displacement results in the death of sublunary beings; even the harmonious alteration of the four elements may cause creaturely life to end (vv. 16946–52). Among human beings, however, the cause of death may also lie beyond the realm of physical occurrences. A decision of the will, not Nature, ended the life of Empedocles, for example, when he decided to leap into Mount Etna, "in order to show that those who fear death are indeed of weak mind" (*por montrer que bien sunt failli / cil qui mort veulent redouter,* 286; vv. 17016–17); and Origen, not the order of the elements, was responsible for the violence he suffered when he decided to cut off his testicles "so that he could serve the religious ladies with devotion and so that there would be no suspicion that he might ever lie with them" (*por servir en devotion / les dames de religion / si que nus soupeçon n'eüst / que gesir avec eus peüst,* 286; vv. 17025–28). Death, like all human occurrences, thus appears as the immediate result of one of two forms of causation, which remain irreducibly distinct. Although inevitable among sublunary creatures, the end of life, once determined by the golden chain of nature, can always also be "hastened for some other reason" (*par autre cas haste*, 285; v. 16953) by the acts of men.

Discussing the terrain of life within her control, Nature thus also indicates a dimension within the physical order which exceeds all natural necessity as such: human action. But the text's invocation of this dimension is not simple; it is immediately followed, in Nature's discourse, by the expression of uncertainty as to its very existence. Calling into question the autonomy of human action in the very moment in which she first invokes it, Nature suggests that apparently unforeseen acts may in fact be predicted and, therefore, necessary. "Fate" seems to rule out the very possibility of there being, in human action, such a thing as possibility:

> Si dit l'en que les destinees
> leur orent tex morz destinees
> et tel eür leur ont meü
> des lors qu'ils furent conceü,
> et qu'il pristrent leur nacions
> en teles constellacions
> que par droite neccessité,
> sanz autre possibilité,
> (c'est san poair de l'eschever),
> conbien qu'il leur doie grever,
> leur convient tel mort recevoir.
> (Vv. 17029–39)

It is said that the fates had decreed such deaths for them and had set up such destinies from the times when they were conceived. And since they took their births under such constellations that by strict necessity, without any other possibility (that is, without being able to avoid it), they must accept such a death, however much it should grieve them. (286)

Nature is quick to reject such a view, denying the reality of the *droite neccessité* claimed by those who would ascribe all occurrences to the destinies (*destinees*) decreed by fate. By means of "good teaching" (*par doctrine*, v. 17047), "by clean, pure nourishment" (*par nourreture nete et fine*, v. 17048) "by following good company" (*par sivre bone compagnie*, v. 17049), and "by certain medicines" (*par aucunes medicines*, v. 17051), men may alter the course of events, such that "it will be otherwise" (*qu'il soit autrement*, v. 17054). The capacity to be "otherwise" (*autrement*) is precisely what is at issue here, for it constitutes the essence of an event not determined by the forces of nature. Human action shows itself as indeterminate—as unconstrained by nature—precisely in ensuring that events "happen otherwise, since they may well be otherwise than they are" (*Lors ira la chose autrement, / car autrement peut il bien estre*, vv. 17062–63).

The fate and destiny of which Nature speaks, therefore, do not appear to pose any serious threat to human action. Indeed, in the text of the poem they function to anticipate a far greater challenge to the freedom of the will, whose nature is not physical and astronomical but, rather, metaphysical and theological. Nature raises the problem of divine omniscience, which appears to render the apparent indeterminacy of human action wholly determinate:

> Mais de sodre la question
> conment predestinacion et la divine prescience,
> plaine de toute porveance,
> peut estre o volanté delivre,
> fort est a lais genz a descrivre.
>
> (Vv. 17071–75)

But to solve the question of how predestination and divine foreknowledge, full of all providence, can exist with free will is a difficult thing to explain to lay people. (287)

The *question* to which Nature refers here, which cannot easily be explained to the "laity," the *lais genz*,[3] is a Scholastic *quaestio* in the full sense of the term. *Predestinacion, prescience,* and *porveance*—like the modal expressions Nature has already employed in her discussion of fate, *neccessité* and *possibilité*—are lexical forms that translate a series of *termini technici* of thirteenth-century philosophy and theology.[4] They allow the poetic text of the *Roman de la Rose* to articulate the theological form of the problem we have already encountered in medieval philosophy of language and logic: that of the relation of the divine faculty of knowledge to "future contingents," events that "can take place and not take place" and which, to the human intellect, appear to be essentially indeterminate.

Nature, at this point in the romance, undertakes precisely the task she deems most difficult: to offer instruction in the problem, *amprandre la chose* (v. 17077), "describing" (*descrivre*, v. 17076) the problem of contingency. *Description* is to be taken here in the full sense of the Old French term *descrivre*, which, in distinction to the modern English form, implies not so much a mere depiction or representation as an active *de-scrivre*, a practice of "writing out," from the Latin *describere*.⁵ When Nature sets out to "solve the question" (*sodre la question*), the text of the poem does not simply recount the debates that surrounded the problem of the conflict of divine omniscience and human freedom; it "de-scribes" them in "trans-scribing" them, transforming them in inscribing them in the context of the poem as a whole. Folded into the text of the *Roman de la Rose,* the *question* of future contingents does not retain the form and sense it had among the doctors of the *scholae.* "Described" over the course of almost eight hundred lines (vv. 17071–844), the problem of contingency, in its theological, ethical, and logical implications, acquires a new form. It is incorporated into the poem; it becomes a central topical and argumentative element in the romance; and its significance, as a result, can be determined only on the basis of a critical confrontation with the literary text.

Despite its importance in the text of the poem, Nature's discussion of future contingents has elicited neither chapters in books on the *Roman de la Rose* nor even scholarly articles, the only exception being Gérard Paré's discussion of it in his 1947 work, *Les idées et les lettres aux XIIIe siècle: Le Roman de la Rose,*⁶ to which Faith Lyons added a number of pertinent remarks in a set of notes published in 1973.⁷ The critics and scholars of the *Roman de la Rose* have traditionally understood Nature's discussion of free will and divine omniscience as a "description" in the simplest sense of the word: a summary representation of the doctrines of free will and divine omniscience to be found in the works of the *auctores* of late antiquity. Such a description would appear to call for neither analysis nor even summary, being altogether transparent in its reference to philosophical and literary antecedents. It is especially telling, in this context, that Hilder's often helpful study of Jean de Meun's "scholastic vocabulary" omits from its index virtually all of the technical terms invoked in Nature's discussion of contingency, thus failing to register not only fundamental theological concepts at issue here, such as *predestinacion, prescience,* and *ydees* (see v. 17451), as well as expressions for the modal categories, such as *possibilité* and *neccessité,* but even such unusual lexical formations as the substantives *possible* and *necessaire,* "the possible" and "the necessary" (see vv. 17195–96).⁸

The text's discussion of contingency, therefore, has remained almost entirely without critical commentary; since the end of the nineteenth century, the belief that Jean de Meun's text constitutes a straightforward, albeit vulgar, reworking of Boethius' treatment of the matter in the *De Consolatione Philosophiae,* has gone unchallenged. Since Ernest Langlois identified book 5 of the *De Consolatione* as the principal source of Nature's speech in 1890,⁹ writing in the notes to his edition that the "entire chapter on divine foreknowledge and free will is borrowed from Boethius,"[10] the opinion of the editors, translators, and scholars of the poem has been unanimous. "The argumentation of the poem," we read in Félix Lecoy's notes to his edition, "is essentially borrowed from Book V of Boethius' *De Consolatione*, which discusses the same subject and which was, furthermore, the classical text on this matter."[11] Lecoy certainly admits that Jean de Meun "takes certain freedoms" with respect to the Boethian model; but he adds, immediately afterward, that, "if the truth be told, it must be said that these liberties generally result in simplifications of Boethius' thought."[12] The more recent readers of the romance have concurred with this judgment. The passage on freedom and foreknowledge, Daniel Poirion writes in the one paragraph that he dedicates to it in his 1973 study of the romance, shows the "the ease with which our poet translates, adapts, and summarizes" the Boethian doctrines on the subject.[13] In his 1992 edition and translation of the poem, Armand Strubel sets aside the entire problem of Nature's discussion, writing, in a phrase reminiscent of Lecoy, that Jean de Meun "borrows from Book V of the *Consolation*, simplifying it."[14] Lecoy had observed that, in this passage, Jean's text is at times "somewhat unclear in it details," yet the details, for Lecoy, did not demand close attention;[15] and, with a symmetrical gesture, Strubel notes that Jean makes use of certain "logical subtleties" absent from Boethius, yet the "subtleties" do not appear to complicate in any way the status of the passage as a "borrowing" from the author of *De Consolatione*.

The critical literature on the *Roman de la Rose* has thus succeeded in effectively avoiding any critical confrontation with this extended discourse in the poem, even while it has indicated several points at which the text of the romance cannot be reduced to a mere borrowing. The eight hundred lines in which Nature discusses the *quaestio* of the reconciliation of divine knowledge and the contingency of human action thus shrink to microscopic proportions; they appear as yet another example of Jean de Meun's compulsion to include everything, no matter how irrelevant, in his *summa* of medieval learning. Like Reason's discussion of Fortune, which we examined in the last chapter, Nature's treatment of contingency appears as a "digression," one that, in this case, need not even be read as such. Strubel's comments on this passage, as on the figure of Fortune in the text, are representative of the critical consensus. "Here," he writes, in his note to the beginning of Nature's discussion, "the allegorical drama is once again completely forgotten, for the sake of a heavily didactic exposition; even the pretext and artifice of the lament disappear from sight—as does, moreover, the goal of 'amatory' instruction."[16]

The Knowledge of Contingency

On this matter, however, the judgment of the scholars remains essentially unfounded. Nature's discussion of divine foreknowledge and free will demands to be read attentively, considered in detail with respect to the philosophical and theological tradition, and situated in the trajectory of the romance as a whole. The so-called digression on the freedom of the will, which provoked Gérard Paré to speak of "pure Scholasticism" in poetic form,[17] marks perhaps the most extended chapter of the *Roman de la Rose* in which Jean de Meun invokes and develops a subject drawn from the faculties of theology and philosophy of his time; and, as such, it constitutes a crucial passage—and, perhaps, the crucial passage—for any attempt to determine the relation of the romance to thirteenth-century thought. But there is a further reason for which we must confront this chapter in the two-part romance. It lies in the simple fact that the subject matter of this discussion is none other than the central theological and epistemological *quaestio de futuris contingentibus,* which constituted one of the central medieval forms of the exploration of the problem we have seen to be essential to the romance, namely, the status of what can both "be and not be." Dismissed for over a century as of minimal importance to the true "allegorical drama" of the work, Nature's discourse on *divine presciance,* for these reasons, is of the greatest significance for understanding the *Roman de la Rose*. It reveals the full extent to which the romance is engaged with thirteenth-century philosophy, and it shows, furthermore, that this engagement is deepest precisely concerning the issue of the theological, ethical, and linguistic status of contingency.

When it is considered in relation to the poetics of contingency of the romance as a whole, Nature's discussion of divine knowledge and human freedom cannot but appear in a fundamentally new light. It marks the point in the romance in which the text investigates a fundamental dimension of its own form—contingency—as a *quaestio* that is at once literary and philosophical; it constitutes the passage in the narrative of the two-part "art of love" in which the text addresses the contingency of its own construction as an argumentative topic to be explored in simultaneously poetic and speculative terms. Here we must therefore consider the discussion with great care. What is the precise form of the *question* broached by Nature, and what is its poetic function in the *Roman de la Rose?* These questions can be answered only by a close study of the "description"—and transformation—of the philosophical and theological problem of contingency in the text of the poem.

II

Raising the *question* of the relation between the divine intellect and the freedom of the will, Nature cites and recites the classical treatments of the problem of contingency, making explicit reference to the *auctoritates* with which our consideration of the poetics of contingency began. As the reader will recall, the concept of contingency finds its first formulation in the domain of logic and the philosophy of language and, in particular, in Aristotle's *De Interpretatione*. With a philosophical decision that determines the fundamental form of the medieval reflection on the nature of language, Aristotle, as we saw in chapter 1, conceives of the elements of speech as the signs of impressions on the soul, which he derives in turn from things; and he defines the canonical form of the conjunction of linguistic terms as the predicative assertion, which "states one thing about another thing" (τι κατά τινός, *alicuis de aliquo*).[18] The assertion is then considered as true when it corresponds to the things that it signifies and as false, by contrast, when it does not. It is in this context that Aristotle raises the difficult question of "future and singular matters" that can both take place and not take place. By virtue of not having the form of present beings, such contingent events cannot be spoken of truly, for they cannot present themselves as stable beings which terms might signify; and, for that very reason, they can also not be spoken of falsely, since there can be noncorrespondence only where, in principle, there can also be correspondence.

It is this irreducibility of contingent events to truth and falsity alike that Nature, in her discussion of divine omniscience, raises as a genuine question. How, she asks her interlocutor, is one to speak of a being that can both be and not be a *chose possible* (v. 17175)?

> S'aucuns l'avoit devant veüe
> et deïst: tel chose sera
> ne riens ne l'an destournera,
> n'avroit il pas dit verité?
> (Vv. 17178–81)

If anyone had foreseen it, and said, "Such a thing will be, and nothing will deflect it," wouldn't he have said the truth? (288)

The answer seems clear: the event did indeed take place, and the statement that predicted it appears, as a result, necessarily to have been true, even before the time of its occurrence. But Nature immediately draws the unacceptable consequence that such a position implies:

> Donc seroit ce neccessité,
> car il s'ansuit, se chose est vaire,
> donques est ele neccessaire,
> par la convertibilité
> de voir et de neccessité.
> (Vv. 17182–86)

> Thus this would be necessity. For it follows, from the convertibility of truth and necessity, that if a thing is true, then it is necessary. (288)

Nature reasons here according to the Aristotelian and Boethian principle that we have already encountered: *veritas propositionis sequitur necessitem rei*, "the truth of the statement follows from the necessity of the thing."[19] If it can be spoken of truly or falsely, Nature concludes, the *chose possible* was destined to happen as it did. In an untranslatable paranomastic play on *force* and *efforcer*, the text reads: *don convient il qu'el soit a force / quant necessité s'an efforce* (vv. 17187–88); "it must perforce be when forced by necessity" (288). In such a case, however, the *chose possible* loses its defining trait: precisely its *possibilité*, its capacity both to take place and not to take place. Drawing on the Scholastic notion of *convertibilitas*, Nature thus invokes the *convertibilité* of truth and necessity.[20] Since what is true must be so and what is necessary cannot but be true, necessity and truth imply each other; as predicates, they are "convertible," in the terms of the medieval doctors, for in any given statement the two terms may be substituted for each other without necessitating any change in sense. To ensure the contingency of the *chose possible*, Nature is thus obliged to deny that the speech that bears on it is indeed true or false; she must reject the position according to which he who predicted a contingent event had *dit verité*. The text of the poem is inevitably led, in this way, implicitly to trace the contours of the same "language of contingency" whose development we have traced in medieval philosophy: a language that, while retaining the form of meaningful speech, the statement, cannot, and must not, operate according to such a form.

The principal subject of Nature's discussion, however, is not the linguistic problem of contingency. It is, instead, the epistemological and theological issue to which the logical problem of contingency gives rise—namely, the question of how future contingents stand with respect to the divine intellect, *conme[nt] il sunt en sa sciance* (v. 17100). Speech and thought prove themselves, in this matter, to be in practice inextricable yet in principle distinguishable; the difficult topic of the language of contingency implies that of the knowledge of contingency, although the two are nevertheless formally distinct. The question that motivated the linguistic dimension of the problematic, from Aristotle to the logicians of the Middle Ages, can be formulated in the following terms: how is it possible to speak of future contingents? The query to which the figure of Nature, like so many medieval theologians, seeks to respond can instead be expressed in the question: how is it possible to know—and, above all, for God to know—future contingents?

The formulation of the problem of the knowledge of contingency was, in a certain sense, inevitable. As we saw, Boethius resolved the question of the truth value of statements bearing on future contingents by arguing that they, strictly speaking, bear neither truth nor falsity but, rather, "indefinite truth or indefinite falsity" (*indefinitam veritatem vel falsitatem*).[21] The solution succeeds in ensuring the indeterminacy of the future and the freedom of the will without compromising the principle of noncontradiction, according to which no two contradictory statements may be either both true or both false. But it does so at the expense of what has been called a "temporalization" of truth:[22] the truth value of the statement concerning contingency is considered indeterminate because of its specific temporal index—namely, its pertinence to an event in the future. But what of a divinity who is by definition omniscient, with respect to whom it can make no sense to invoke the distinctions constitutive of the human experience of time? Whatever its antecedents in the logical debates of Hellenistic philosophy may be, the issue first emerges in its full theological and ethical dimensions in the patristic period of the Church. Sketched by Augustine, the "first philosopher of the will,"[23] the problem is clearly and fully expressed by Boethius, who discusses it in the concluding book of the *De Consolatione Philosophiae.* Here the narrator, turning to Lady Philosophy, explains that he is "confused" by a "strong doubt": "it seems," he says, "much too conflicting and contradictory that God foreknows all things and that there is any free will."[24] On the one hand, the perfection of the divine intellect appears to extinguish all possibility in human action: "for if he foresees all and cannot in any way be mistaken, then that must necessarily happen which in his providence he foresees will be."[25] But, on the other hand, if the will is unconstrained and altogether unexpected, the consequence appears equally impious: in God "there will no longer be firm foreknowledge of the future, but rather uncertain opinion, which I judge impious to believe."[26] Such is the double impossibility to which the narrator of *De Consolatione,* for perhaps the first time in the history of Western thought, gives expression. The certainty of freedom seems to ban the possibility of divine foreknowledge, for foreknowledge would abolish the indeterminacy constitutive of the will; yet the faith in divine

The Knowledge of Contingency

omniscience, in turn, appears to exclude the irreducible contingency of human action, since contingency would compromise the perfection of the divine intellect.

The problem of the reconciliation of divine omniscience with contingency was so widely debated in the centuries following Boethius that, in the second half of the eleventh century, Anselm of Canterbury can call it a *quaestio famosissima*,[27] when he refers to it in passing in his treatment of a related issue in *De Casu Diaboli*, the foreknowledge of evil angels. But the "father of Scholasticism" does not treat the problem of the knowledge of contingency as an issue raised and resolved by the *auctoritates*, for he devotes a treatise of his own to the same subject, *De Concordia Praescientia et Praedestinationis et Gratiae Dei cum Libero Arbitrio*.[28] Anselm's work opens with an exemplary formulation of the problem:

> Videntur quidem praescientia dei et liberum arbitrium repugnari, quoniam ea quae deus praescit, necesse est esse futura, et quae per liberum arbitrium fiunt, nulla necessitate proveniunt. Sed si repugnant, impossibile est simul et esse praescientiam dei quae omnia praevidet, et aliquid fieri per libertatem arbitrii.[29]

> It seems that God's foreknowledge and the free will are opposed, since that which God foreknows must happen, and those things that take place by means of the free will do not follow from any necessity. But if the two are indeed opposed, then it is impossible to maintain the existence both of God's foreknowledge, which foresees everything, and of things that happen by means of the free will.

What concerns Anselm here is precisely the sense of the *simul*, the "both," which appears to join divine knowledge and the will at the price of a logical impossibility. Foreknowledge and freedom would seem to define two classes of objects, classes that remain irreducible by virtue of their temporal determinations: in one case, objects eternally determined in the mind of God and, in the other, objects indeterminate to man by virtue of having not yet happened. And yet the treatise makes clear that, despite their differences, the two members of both classes must coincide for the sake of theology and ethics. The issue that confronts Anselm is how to conceive of this coincidence: the simultaneity, *simul esse*, of human action insofar as it is known, eternally and temporally, by the divine and human faculties of intellection alike.

With the rise of systematic theology in the twelfth-century, the *quaestio* discussed by Anselm achieved a prominence greater than any it had had in the works of the Church Fathers. The *Sententiae* of Peter Lombard, whose final edition can be dated between 1155 and 1157,[30] were instrumental in this matter. In the first book of his *summa* of Christian theology, which is devoted to the nature of God, Lombard sets himself the task of considering divine "knowledge, foreknowledge, and providence" immediately after examining the nature of the Trinity.[31] Once he has analyzed the nature of divine *scientia,* of which *praescientia* is but a specification, Lombard develops the problem Anselm had formulated in his effort to conceive of the "simultaneity" of foreknowledge and freedom by investigating the possible senses in which God's knowledge can be said to be related to contingent events. Citing and systematically redistributing the doctrines of the Church Fathers, Peter thus considers "whether there could be divine knowledge or foreknowledge or disposition or predestination if there were no future things" (*utrum scientia vel praescientia vel dispositio vel praedestinatio potuerit esse in Deo si nulla fuissent futura*),[32] "whether divine knowledge or foreknowledge is the cause of things, or things are the cause of foreknowledge" (*an scientia vel praescientia sit causa rerum, vel res sint causa praedescientia*),[33] and "whether it is possible for divine knowledge to increase or decrease, or be altered in some other way" (*utrum scientia Dei possit augeri vel minui, vel aliquo modo mutari*).[34] In each case the Lombard seeks to define divine knowledge in its relation to "singular and future matters" in such a way that the determinacy of its own necessary activity in no way contests the indeterminacy of its contingent objects.

There is little need to reassert the centrality of Lombard's *Sententiae* to the development of Scholastic theology in the later twelfth and thirteenth centuries. "*The* sourcebook of theology" for the later Middle Ages,[35] the *Sententiae* constitute the fundamental work commented upon by every theologian of the new universities. In the thirteenth century Lombard's treatment of divine foreknowledge and its relation to freedom, which are analyzed for the first time with the aid of material drawn from the newly translated works of Aristotelian philosophy, ensures the presence of the *quaestio de futuris contingentibus* in the intellectual life of the *scholae*.[36] At the same time, however, the issue of contingency became the subject of the most heated controversy. It is significant that on March 7, 1277, when Étienne Tempier brands 217 propositions as heretical in what has been called the "greatest condemnation of the Middle Ages,"[37] those bearing on contingency are well represented among them. The longest and most detailed heretical article listed in the *collectio errorum* concerns precisely the question of whether "the first cause has knowledge of future contingents."[38] The text of the condemnation demonstrates that the matter was delicate. On the one hand, in theology the denial of divine foreknowledge merited excommunication;[39] but, on the other hand, in ethics the refusal to admit the existence of free action was deemed equally impious.[40] Any attempt to consider the problem of the knowledge of contingency had to avoid this double danger and, therefore, to answer to a double, apparently contradictory, demand: that thought maintain the determinacy of contingency with respect to divine knowledge and, at the same time, its indeterminacy with respect to human action.

Raising the *question* of the accord between *presciance* and *volonté,* the text of the *Roman de la Rose* thus broaches one of the most widely debated, controversial, and theologically charged issues of medieval theology and philosophy. In doing so, the poem does not simply record, repeat, or—what is worse—"simplify" the matter, as the critics of the romance have all too summarily claimed.[41] Exploring the problem of the knowledge of contingency for literary ends, the poem recasts it in its own terms, those of poetry; in the development of each step of its argument, it exploits the *famosissima quaestio* and transforms its sense, ultimately referring it, as we shall see, to the form and structure of the *Roman de la Rose* itself.

III

Critics have so often insisted that the discussion of contingency in the *Roman de la Rose* is the result of a lack of narrative order that the internal structure of the discussion itself has hardly been considered. In the distribution of its arguments, the passage, however, is logically and rigorously constructed. Like the *summae* and *commentarii* of the thirteenth century, it proceeds by means of the successive advancement, analysis, and refutation of propositions drawn from biblical, patristic, theological, and philosophical sources. Here arguments are articulated as in the philosophical exercises of reading practiced in the universities: the *auctores* are cited "not to complete, but to contradict each other," according to the methodological principle that the positions proposed must be *non solum diversa sed adversa.*[42] Nature's discussion may be effectively decomposed into four distinct moments organized according to the position, examination, and resolution of the question. The passage thus begins with the articulation of the problem: the reconciliation of *presciance* and *volonté,* divine knowledge and human action, or, more simply, necessity and contingency. A first answer is set forth, which suggests the dominance of necessity over contingency. It is composed of two separate propositions, each of which is refuted. A second answer is then proposed, which, in exact contrast to the first, now suggests the dominance of contingency over necessity. The second answer, like the first, has the form of two distinct propositions, each of which is subjected to analysis and ultimately rejected. A third solution to the *question* is finally proposed; it alone allows for the integral resolution of foreknowledge and freedom, the divine and the human, necessity and contingency.

The text of the poem first registers the importance of the reconciliation of *sciance* and *volonté* by presenting it as the object not simply of a discussion but also a demand. Nature clearly indicates that the existence of an accord between necessity and contingency is not in question: "il est voirs, que qu'il leur samble, / qu' eus s'antreseuffrent bien ansamble" (vv. 17081–82); "It is true, however it may seem to the laity, that the two accord very well together" (287). Not the truth of the reconciliation, but its nature and structure, will be the subject of Nature's discussion. There must be an *antreseuffrement,* an "accord" or "reconciliation," of the two terms at issue. The consequences of any other possibility would be too grave to be admissible:

> autrement cil qui bien feroient
> ja loier avoir n'an devroient,
> ne cil qui de pechier se peine
> ja mes n'an devroit avoir peine,
> se tex estoit la verité
> que tout fust par neccessité;
> car cil qui bien fere vourroit,
> autrement vouloir nou pourroit,
> ne cil qui le mal vorroit fere
> ne s'an pourrait mie retrere:
> voissist ou non, il le feroit
> puis que destiné li seroit.
>
> (Vv. 17083–94)

Otherwise those who did good would never be rewarded for it, while those who took trouble to sin should never have any punishment, if it were true that everything occurred by necessity. He who wanted to do good could not wish otherwise, and he who wanted to do evil could not help himself. Whether he wished to or not, he would do it, since it would be his destiny. (287)

Were there no accord between necessity and contingency, the will would have no ground; its effects would be determined in advance, and the very possibility of divine recompense, as well as retribution, would be eliminated. But once she has demonstrated the necessity of its existence, albeit negatively, Nature

The Knowledge of Contingency

must still define the form of the *antreseuffrement* without which human action and divine judgment would have no sense. The recognition of an ethical as well as theological imperative—that foreknowledge and freedom be reconciled—constitutes only the condition for Nature to "dispute the matter" itself (*disputer de la matiere*, v. 17096).

Nature's initial proposal appears, at first glance, to be orthodox in form. It consists in the claim that, being perfect, God cannot but be omniscient, his knowledge extending to all human actions, no matter how singular. Divine prescience, here literally rendered and decomposed into a "knowing before" (*prae-scientia*), would embrace all events:

> Dex n'est mie deceüz
> des fez qu'il a devant seüz:
> donc avandront il san doutance
> si conme il sunt en sa sciance;
> mes il set quant il avandront,
> conment et quel chief il tandront.
> (Vv. 17097–102)

> God is not deceived by the deeds that he has known before; and they undoubtedly will happen just as they exist in his knowledge. But he knows when they will happen, how and what result they will work toward. (287)

Were God to have such a *sciance*, however, the characteristic forms of human action would cease to exist as such; their outcomes already determined in the mind of God, deeds could no longer be considered in terms of virtue or vice.

> Qui bien regarder i vorroit,
> il ne seroit vertuz ne vices;
> ne sacrefier en galices,
> ne Dieu prier riens ne vaudroit,
> quant vices et vertuz faudroit.
> (Vv. 17138–42)

> If one wanted to consider the matter well, there would be neither virtue nor vice; and the celebration of the mass in the chalice of suffering and prayers to God would be worth nothing as long as vice and virtue were lacking. (288)

But Nature's first proposition, if true, would not only abolish the possibility of human action. It would also set an implacable limit to God's own power:

> Ou se Diex joustice fesoit,
> con vices et vertuz ne soit,

> il ne seroit pas droituriers,
> ainz clameroit les usuriers,
> les larrons et les murtriers quites;
> et les bons et les ypocrites,
> touz peseroit a pois onni.
> (Vv. 17143–49)

Or if God did justice, in the absence of vice and virtue, it would not be just; instead, he would declare usurers, thieves, and murderers acquitted. He would weigh all, the good and the hypocrites, with an equal weight. (288)

Grace by works, as a result, would be impossible: *Nus ne pouvroit recouver / la grace Dieu par bien ouvrer* (vv. 17155–56). But such an ethical impossibility is but the consequence of a far graver theological incapacity: God would not reward and punish, for he *could not* do so. Precisely because he would know all things "before" their occurrence, determining the time, manner, and result of all human actions, God would be unable to *fere joustice*. The first proposition advanced by Nature, in this way, refutes itself on its own terms. The argument in favor of omniscience ultimately limits the very omnipotence it would appear to assert, and, as a result, it must be rejected.

Like the first thesis advanced by Nature for the dominance of necessity over contingency, the second, if true, would *quasser franche volanté* (v. 17173), "shatter free will" (288), sealing the triumph of the *destinees* over every *chose possible*. But, while the first may be described as theological, to the extent to which it concerns the divine faculty of knowledge, the second, by contrast, is logical in character. It involves the linguistic form of contingency, and it is here that Nature poses the question that we have already cited concerning the expression of things considered to be possible:

> S'aucuns l'avoit devant veüe
> et deïst: tel chose sera
> ne riens ne l'an destournera,
> n'avroit il pas dit verité?
> Donc seroit ce neccesité,
> car il s'ansuit, se chose est vaire,
> donques est ele neccessaire,
> par la convertibilité
> de voir et de neccessité.
> Don convient il qu'el soit a force,
> quant necessité s'an efforce.
> (Vv. 17178–88)

> If anyone had foreseen it and said, "Such a thing will be, and nothing will deflect it," wouldn't he have told the truth? Thus this would be necessity. For it follows, from the convertibility of truth and necessity, that if a thing is true, then it is necessary. Hence a thing must perforce be when it is forced by necessity. (288)

The truth of prediction would appear to imply the necessity of what is predicted, and the *chose possible,* once predicted, would therefore appear to be in fact a *chose neccessaire.*

Nature, however, immediately indicates that such reasoning is flawed. Whoever announces a future contingent, she tells the narrator, "says something that is true but not, for that matter, necessary" (*il diroit chose vaire, / mes non pas por ce necessaire*) (vv. 17191–92). Without calling into question the "convertibility" of truth and necessity, Nature introduces a modal distinction that reduces the proposition at issue to "not being worth a wimple":

> car conment qu'il l'ait ainz veüe
> la chose n'est pas avenue
> par necessaire avenemant,
> mes par possible seulemant;
> car s'il est qui bien i regart,
> c'est necessitez en regart,
> et non pas nécessité simple,
> si que ce ne vaut une guimple.
> (Vv. 17193–200)

> For although he may have foreseen it, the thing happened not by means of a necessary occurrence, but by means of a possible one alone. If one looks closely, this is necessity in retrospect, not simple necessity, which means that this argument is not worth a wimple. (288–89)

The two types of necessity to which Nature refers here, *necessitez en regart* (necessity in retrospect) and *nécessité simple* (simple necessity) have been traditionally rendered by modern translators of the *Roman de la Rose* as "conditional necessity" and "absolute necessity."[43] The decision can hardly be considered an error, for that fundamental logical distinction is indeed at issue in this passage. But, in clarifying the terms of the text, the modern translators of the poem obscure the lexical difficulty that makes itself felt here; they efface the linguistic problem with which Jean de Meun is confronted in this passage as he seeks to incorporate technical terms of Aristotelian modal logic in the vernacular language of poetry.[44] *Necessitez en regart,* "retrospective necessity," here translates the modal category known to Boethius as *necessitas conditionis*,[45] to Anselm of Canterbury as *necessitas consequens* or *sequens*,[46] Albert the Great as *necessitas consequentiae*,[47] and Bonaventure as *necessitas respective*;[48] *necessité simple*, by contrast, renders what the same philosophers of the Middle Ages, respectively, called *necessitas simplex* or *absoluta, antecedens,* and *consequentis. Necessité en regart*, therefore, defines a retrospective necessity that holds once a certain condition has been stipulated, such as that formulated in the sentence "if you speak, then you necessarily speak." *Necessité simple*, on the other hand, defines an absolute necessity that so to speak precedes that of which it is predicated, as when God, creating the heavens, decreed that their movement would be necessary.[49] When Nature speaks of the necessity proper to a true prediction, stating that *c'est necessitez en regart / et non pas necessité simple* (vv. 17198–99), she therefore summarizes, in two verses, a classical logical argument against determinism—namely, that, although a thing must indeed be said to be necessary once it is as it is, such a necessity is merely "conditional," *en regart,* and cannot be said to imply any determinism.

Not limiting herself to arguments drawn from logic alone, Nature adduces a further, ethical reason for the impossibility of any dominance of necessity over contingency. Were human activity to be altogether necessary, *destine / et par force determiné* (vv. 17215–16), she explains,

> Por conseill, por euvre de mains
> ja n'an seroit ne plus ne mains,
> ne mieux ne pis n'an porroit estre,
> fust chose nee ou chose a nestre,
> fust chose fete ou chose a fere,
> fust chose a dire ou chose a tere.
> Nus d'aprandre mestier n'avroit,
> sanz estuide des arz savroit
> quan qu'il savra s'il s'estudie
> par grant travaill toute sa vie.
>   (Vv. 17217–26)

There would never be more or less, and there could not be any better or worse, because of any advice or manual labor, whether it was a thing born or to be born, done or to be done, something to be said or something to keep silent about. No one would need to study; he would know without study whatever arts he will know if he studies with great labor for his whole life. (289)

The Knowledge of Contingency

While Nature's first argument against the doctrine that the truth of prediction eliminates contingency was formal and logical, her second is thus practical. It suggests that the contingency of human action must be maintained for the sake of a series of fundamental ethical oppositions: *plus / mains, mieux / pis, chose fete / a fere, chose a dire / chose a tere*. It constitutes Nature's final rejection of the second proposition cited in favor of necessity, and, as such, it marks the end of the first part of Nature's discussion of the *antreseuffrement* of divine foreknowledge and human freedom.

The theological and philosophical thesis that Nature now formulates follows logically from the course of her discussion. It consists of an uncompromising vindication of the existence and effective power of free will in human action:

> donc doit l'an plainement nier
> que les euvres d'humanité
> aviegnent par necessité;
> ainz font bien ou mal franchement
> par leur vouloir tant seulement;
> n'il n'est riens for eus, au voir dire,
> qui tel vouloir leur face eslire
> que prandre ou lessier nou poïssent,
> se de reson user vossissent.
> (Vv. 17228–36)

One must therefore deny completely that the works of humanity happen by necessity. Instead people do good or evil freely through their will alone. To tell the truth, there is nothing outside of themselves that may make their will choose in such a way that they cannot take or leave it, if they wished to use their reason. (289)

If human actions, however, are indeed determined by *rien for eus*, "nothing outside themselves," then the subject at issue changes decisively; the contingency of the free will, not the necessity of divine foreknowledge, becomes the starting point from which to articulate the *antreseuffrement* sought by the text. It is at this point that Nature, definitively abandoning her first attempt to resolve the debate, turns to examine the second set of answers to the problem, which, in contrast to the first, seeks to ensure the dominance of contingency over necessity. It is this second chapter of Nature's discourse, therefore, which we too must now consider, as we draw close to what the text of the romance calls "le neu de la question" (v. 17253).

IV

At the start of the second half of her discussion, Nature indicates that she is not the first to seek to vindicate the contingency of human action in the face of the necessity of divine knowledge. A long tradition of theological and philosophical reflection, both before and after the advent of Christianity, aimed to ensure the independence of freedom from all forms of physical and metaphysical necessity. Nature situates her discourse in the context of this tradition, as she attributes a first proposition in favor of contingency to "many" before her "who have wanted to trouble themselves":

> Maint se voudrent a ce pener,
> et distrent par sentence fine
> que la presciance divine
> ne met point de necessité
> seur les euvres d'humanité;
> car bien se vont apercevant,
> por ce que Dex les set devant,
> ne s'ansuit il pas qu'els aviegnent
> par force ne que tex fins tiegnent;
> mes por ce qu'eles avendront
> et tel chief ou tel fin tendront,
> por ce les set ainz Diex, ce dient.
> (Vv. 17240–51)

Many have wanted to trouble themselves and have said, in a distilled judgment, that divine foreknowledge lays no necessity whatsoever on the works of humanity. They go around pointing out that because God knows them beforehand, it does not follow that the works of men are forced to take place or that they hold to such ends. But because they will happen and will have this or that result, therefore, they say, God knows them beforehand. (289)

The proposition advanced by the anonymous many to whom Nature refers here concerns the very issue raised by Peter Lombard in the second chapter of the thirty-eighth distinction of his *Sententiae:* "whether [divine] knowledge is the cause of things, or things are the cause of providence" (*an scientiae sit causa rerum, vel res sint causa praescientiae*).[50] The many to whom Nature refers here decide resolutely in favor of the second option. Inverting the determinist thesis, according to which divine foreknowledge is the cause of human actions, they maintain that "future events . . . are the cause of God's foreknowledge," *li fet qui sunt a venir . . . causent an Dieu sa presciance* (vv. 17256, 17258).

The many, Nature explains, making use of a Boethian expression, thus "untie the knot of the question badly" (*mauvaisement deslient / le neu de ceste question,* vv. 17252–53).[51] They show themselves to be guilty of advancing a claim dismissed as "preposterous" in *De Consolatione Philosophiae,* namely, that "the cause of eternal foreknowledge is the occurrence of temporal things."[52] Implicitly contesting the omnipotence and perfection of God, they "enfeeble" (*afoibloier,* v. 17264) the divine faculty of knowledge by rendering it dependent, for its operation, on contingent events determined by the human will. Nature is thus obliged to reject the proposition as "painful to relate and even sinful to think":

> Don ne vaut riens ceste reponse
> qui la Dieu presciance ensconse
> et repont sa grant porveance
> souz les tenebres d'ignorance,
> qui n'a poair, tant est certeine,
> d'aprendre riens par euvre humeine;
> et s'el le poait, san doutance,
> ce li vandroit de non poissance,
> qui rest douleur a recenser
> et pechié neïs du penser.
> (Vv. 17273–82)

This reply then, which hides God's foreknowledge and conceals his great providence under the shadows of ignorance, is worth nothing. This much is certain: his providence can learn nothing from the works of humanity; and if it could, such a characteristic would surely come from impotence. Such an idea remains painful to relate and even sinful to consider. (289–90)

The attempt to secure the relative autonomy of divine knowledge and free will, in this case, thus ends by accomplishing the opposite. No longer compelled by foreknowledge, human action becomes its very cause; but, by that very token, the divine intellect loses its necessity and its perfection, becoming an "impotent" effect of the will. Were the proposition to be true, it would therefore be altogether impossible to speak of any *antreseuffrement* of foreknowledge and free will; in its absolutely unpredictable contingency, the will, instead, would ruin the very faculty with which it ought to be reconciled.

At this point Nature formulates a second proposition on the *question.* Like the first, it aims to maintain the contingency of the will despite the necessity of foreknowledge; but, unlike it, it appears not to limit in any way the perfection of the divine faculty of knowledge. Those who hold it, Nature relates, doubt neither the freedom of human action nor the necessity by which God knows all events, past and future. But they specify that such knowledge of contingency is by its nature accompanied by a "light addition" (*addicion legiere,* vv. 17291) which altogether transforms its sense. Although hardly "obscure," as Lecoy called it,[53] the argument of the text is subtle, and the passage must be cited here in its entirety:

> Li autre autrement an santirent,
> et selonc leur sens respondirent
> et s'acorderent bien san faille
> que des choses, conmant qu'il aille,
> qui vont par volanté delivre,
> si conme election les livre,
> set Diex quan qu'il an avandra
> et quel fin chascune tandra,
> par une addicion legiere,
> c'est a savoir en tel maniere
> conme ele sunt a avenir;
> et veulent par ce soutenir
> qu'il n'i a pas necessité,
> ainz vont par possibilité,
> si qu'il set quel fin el feront
> et s'el seront ou ne seront;
> tout ce set il bien de chascune
> que de II. vaies tandra l'une:
> cest ira par negacion,
> ceste par affirmacion,
> non pas si termineemant
> qu'el n'aviegne, espoir, autremant;
> car bien peut autrement venir,
> se frans voulairs s'i veust tenir.
> (Vv. 17283–306)

Others felt otherwise about it and replied according to their ideas; they certainly agreed that however it may happen with things that go by free will, just as choice gives them out, God knows whatever will happen with them and toward what end each one will tend, by a small addition, that is, the manner in which they will happen. With this argument they want to uphold the idea that there is no necessity, but that things happen according to possibility. Thus God knows what ends things will come to and whether they will take place or not. He knows all this, that everything will hold to one of two ways. One thing will happen by negation, another by affirmation, but not so determinately that it may not perhaps turn out otherwise, for if free will wants to insist, it may turn out otherwise. (290)

The *addicion legiere* that necessarily accompanies the knowledge of contingent things thus consists in *savoir en tel maniere / ele sunt a avenir,* "knowing in what manner they are to happen" (vv. 17292–93). The divine mind, according to this proposition, knows the specific modal status of every event; it registers whether a thing occurs by necessity or by possibility, *par necessité* (v. 17295) or *par possibilité* (v. 17296). If the object is contingent, the divine intellect then knows "if it will be or not be" (v. 17298), that is, which of "the two paths," occurrence or nonoccurrence, it will "take" (v. 17300). But, the advocates of this answer add, before the time of the event itself, this knowledge cannot be "determinate" (*termine*), "for it could still happen otherwise" (v. 17309). The knowledge of contingency, like the truth of its expression, would thus be structurally indefinite; it would be marked by the very indeterminacy of its object.

Nature, as always, clearly indicates the heretical doctrine implicit in such a position. *Mes,* she asks, immediately after summarizing the idea, *conmant osa nus ce dire?* "But how did anyone dare to say such a thing?" (v. 17307).

> Conmant osa tant Dieu despire
> qu'il li dona tel presciance
> qu'il n'an set riens fors an doutance,
> quant il n'an peut apercevoir
> determinablemant le voir?
> (Vv. 17308–12)

How did he dare despise God so much as to give him the kind of foreknowledge with which he knows nothing except in a doubtful way, when he cannot perceive the truth determinately? (290)

The *legiere addicion,* in this case, subtracts from that to which it is added. Cognizant of the "manner" of each thing's occurrence, God is said to know *le possible* in its very possibility; but, therefore, he cannot be said to know it *termineement,* "determinately" (v. 17303), and his *savoir* thus shows itself to be, in truth, a mere *doutance* (v. 17310). Without determinacy, divine foreknowledge thus ceases to be itself; stripped of its absolute certainty, it becomes, in Nature's words, an *opinion decevable* (v. 17370). Nature, as a result, once again rejects the very proposition she advanced.

At this point in the argument of the text, however, the solution is close at hand. Having formulated, considered, and refuted two propositions that would destroy the contingency of the will and two that would ruin the necessity of foreknowledge, Nature now advances a final thesis that succeeds in ensuring the *antreseuffrement* that she seeks:

> Li autre alerent autre voie,
> et maint ancor a ce se tienent,
> qu'il dient des fez qui avienent
> ça jus par possibilité
> qu'il vont tuit par necessité
> quant a Dieu, non pas autrement;
> car il set termineement
> de tourjorz et san nule faille,
> conment que de franc voloir aille
> les choses ainz que fetes saient,
> quelconques fins que eles aient,
> et par sciance necessaire.
>   (Vv. 17322–33)

> Still others have gone by a different path and many still hold to this idea. They say of the deeds that take place by possibility here on earth that they all come by necessity as far as God is concerned, but not otherwise. For however it may be with free will, he knows things determinately, forever, without any mistake, before they have taken place, whatever ends they may have, and he knows all this through necessary knowledge. (290)

The "different path" at last furnishes an answer to the theological and epistemological problem of contingency. The final resolution of the matter consists in defining contingency as the object of a double apprehension, which at last resolves the question of how to understand the identity (*simul esse*) and difference of free will and necessary foreknowledge. On the one hand, the contingent event appears to men in its occurrence *par possibilité* (v. 17325) and, therefore, as indeterminate by nature; on the other, it appears to God *par necessité* (v. 17326) and hence as "forever, without any mistake," the object of a fully "determinate" (*termine*) knowledge. Nature thus follows the principle invoked by Boethius to solve the same question in *De Consolatione Philosophiae*: "everything which is known is grasped not according to its own power but rather according to the capability of those who know it" (*omne enim quod cognoscitur non secundum sui vim sed secundum cognoscientium potius comprehenditur facultatem*).[54] Contingency functions here, as in a prominent tradition of medieval Aristotelian philosophy,[55] as a *discrimen* that articulates the fundamental difference between the structures of the human intellect and the divine mind. What is future (*a avenir*) for men is always already determinate (*termine*) for God; what exceeds the realm of knowledge and truth, *quant aus homes* (v. 17341), is the object of flawless intellection, *quant a Dieu* (v. 17327).

Divine foreknowledge, therefore, exerts no compulsion on human action: *contraignance pas n'i fet / ne quant a soi ne quant aus homes* (vv. 17340–41), "God lays no constraint upon them, either as far as he or they are concerned" (290). Nature announces that she will recount a "rough example" (*gros example*, 17363) to illustrate the matter to the "lay people who do not understand writing" (*genz lais qui n'antandent letre*, v. 17364; 291), since they will surely demand a "a rough thing, without any subtlety of a gloss" (*grose chose, / sanz grant soutiveté de glose*, vv. 17365–66; 291). Take a man, she reasons, who freely (*par franc vouloir*, v. 17367) decides to commit, or not to commit, an act. Take, then, a second man, who knows of the first man's activity or, alternately, abstention from activity. Whether it preceded the man's deed or followed it, the second man's knowledge would in itself impose on it neither "necessity nor compulsion" (*necessité ne contraignance*, v. 17379). God's *sciance*, Nature informs her interlocutor, likewise remains without influence on the contingent events that number among its objects. "More nobly and altogether determinately" (*plus noblement / et tout determinablement*, vv.17391–92) than any human knowledge, it views everything that exists in the perfect presence of its own eternity:

> Tout ce voit Diex apertement
> devant ses euz presantement,
> et toutes les condicions
> des fez et des antancions.
> (Vv. 17421–24)

God sees all this clearly, in its presence before his eyes, along with all the conditions of deeds and intentions. (292)

The concept of eternity, already traced by Augustine,[56] defined in precise, canonical terms by Boethius, and widely invoked in the theology of the twelfth and thirteenth centuries,[57] intervenes here to allow for the demarcation of the divine and human mind. The entire course of *fez, antancions*, and *condicions*, which men experience in temporal succession, appear before God "in their presence" (*presantement*), placed "before" (*devant*) the incessant contemplation of his eyes. Later in the romance, Nature explains that, in "a moment of eternity," God intuits the entire "threefold temporality" of humanity:

> Dieu qui voit en sa presence
> la trible temporalité
> souz un momant d'eternité.
> (Vv. 19044–46)

God, who, in his presence, sees threefold temporality in a single moment of eternity. (315)

Such a vision, we read, at another point, knows neither future nor past:

> il n'a futur ne preterit
> car se bien la verité sant,
> tuit li trois tens i sunt presant.
> (Vv. 19986–88)

It has neither future nor past, for if they are true, all three times are present there. (329)

The very events on which the human will, in its irreducible contingency, has decided and will decide upon thus appear to the divine intellect in a perpetual *nunc stans:* in an "intemporal knowledge of everything, in which no temporal difference may be posited," as Albert the Great writes in one of his treatments of the matter.[58]

After its carefully constructed discussion, its propositions and counter-propositions, its proposals and refutations, the poem would thus seem to resolve the issue through the invocation of a classical solution. So it would seem—were the text not to complicate the terms of the discussion, introducing a poetic figure that transforms the sense of the *question* altogether, displacing it from the terrain of theology to that of poetics, and dislocating the terms of the discussion, as we shall presently see, to a point at which they refer, above all, to the form of the *Roman de la Rose* itself.

V

When one examines the text of the poem closely, the resolution proposed by Nature shows itself to be more complex that it might seem. It concludes the discussion of the *question,* as we have seen, through a presentation of the doctrine of the eternity of the divine mind. But it simultaneously introduces an altogether unexpected figure: a *mirouers pardurables,* an "everlasting mirror." Nature explains the perfection of the divine intellect in the following terms:

> Riens ne se peut de lui garder,
> ja tant ne savra retarder,
> car ja chose n'iert si lonctiegne
> que Dex devant sai ne la tiegne
> ausinc con s'ele fust presante:
> demeurt .X anz ou .XX ou .XXX.,
> voire .V.C., voire .C. mile,
> soit a fere a champ ou a vile,
> soit honeste ou desavenant,
> si la voit Dex des maintenant
> ausinc con s'el fust avenue,
> et de tourjorz l'a il veüe
> par demonstrance veritable
> a son mirouer pardurable,
> que nus fors li ne set polir,
> san riens a franc voloir tolir.
>
> (Vv. 17425–40)

Nothing can be kept from him, no matter how one may try to delay; for there will never be a thing so far away that God may not hold it before him as if it were present. Let ten years go by, or twenty or thirty, even five hundred or a hundred thousand, and whether the event occurs in the country or the city, whether it is honest or something that one should not do, still God sees it from this very moment as if it had taken place. And he has seen it always in true detail in his eternal mirror, which no one, except him, can polish, and which takes nothing away from free will. (292)

It is worth pausing to consider the significance of the striking figure introduced in this passage. It cannot be found in the classical works on contingency of which Jean de Meun made use, such as the *De Consolatione Philosophiae;* nor does it number among the terms and images employed by the theologians and philosophers who treated the question of free will and divine omniscience in the twelfth and thirteenth centuries. Yet its function, at this point, is decisive. Divine knowledge is both perfect and yet without any force of constraint on its objects, we read, precisely because its operation is that of a mirror that reflects, without determining, that which lies before it. Paul's canonical dictum (1 Cor. 13:12) on knowledge, mirrors, and human perception is thus altogether inverted: here it is not man but God who looks "through a glass" (*per speculum*) and, for that very reason, sees its objects not "darkly" (*in aenigmate*) but "openly" (*apertement,* v. 17421) and in perfect presence (*presantement,* v. 17422).[59]

Although unanticipated, the *mirouers pardurables* therefore proves crucial here. Unlike the story of the two men which illustrated the mutual independence of knowledge and its object, the "mirror" of which we read is not identified by the text as a *gros example*. It cannot be said merely to function in the service of doctrinal exposition, as an *integumentum* of a theological truth to which it is inessential. Nature, in this context, does not shy away from assertions of strict identity. Referring to the mirror, she explains, in terms all the more striking for their simplicity, that *c'est la predestinacion, / c'est la presciance divine*, "it [i. e., the mirror] *is* predestination, and it *is* divine foreknowledge":

> Cil mirouers c'est il meïsmes,
> de cui conmancement preïsmes.
> An cest biau mirouer poli,
> qu'il tient et tint tourjorz o li,
> ou tout voit quan qu'il avandra
> et tourjorz presant le tandra,
> voit il ou les ames iront
> qui leaument le serviront,
> et de ceus ausinc qui n'ont cure
> de leauté ne de droiture;
> et leur promet en ses ydees,
> des euvres qu'eus avront ouvrees,
> sauvement ou dampnacion:
> c'est la predestinacion,
> c'est la presciance divine,
> qui tout set et riens ne devine,
> qui seult au genz sa grace estandre
> quant el les voit a vien antandre,
> ne n'a pas por ce souplanté
> poair de franche volanté.
> Tuit home euvrent par franc vouloir
> soit por joïr ou por douloir.
> C'est sa presante vision,
> car qui la diffinicion
> de pardurableté dellie,
> ce est possession de vie
> qui par fin ne peut estre prise,
> tretoute ansamble, san devise.
> (Vv. 17441–68)

This mirror is the same one from which we took our beginning. In this beautiful, polished mirror, which he keeps and has always kept with him, in which he sees all that will happen and will keep it always present, he sees where the souls will go who will serve him loyally; he sees also the place of those who have no concern for loyalty or justice, and in his ideas he promises them salvation or damnation for the deeds that they will have done. It is predestination, it is divine prescience, which knows all and divines nothing, which is accustomed to extend its grace to men when it sees them directed toward good, and which has not, for all that, supplanted the power of free will. All men work by free will, either for joy or sorrow. It is his present vision, for if one invokes the definition of eternity, it is the possession of life which cannot be grasped by an end, a life that is a complete whole, without any division. (292)

When one examines it closely, the "beautiful, polished mirror" shows itself to be far more than the "expression" of a "fundamental Christian doctrine," as Paré claims.[60] It is certainly true that the mirror, resolving the debate, constitutes the occasion for the text's conclusive citation of the canonical Boethian definition of *aeternitas: interminabilis vitae tota simul et perfecta possessio*,[61] which is rendered here as *possession de vie / qui par fin ne peut estre prise / tretoute ansamble, san devise* (vv. 17466–68). But, as an instrument without which divine intellection would not be itself, the mirror introduces a lack into the divine presence precisely by filling it; it undermines the perfection of God's knowledge to the very extent to which it renders it possible. For the mirror functions here as a decisive supplement, which demands, in turn, a further supplement: God must make use of his lens if he is to contemplate his own "ideas" (*ydees*), and his lens, in turn, must be intermittently "polished" (v. 17439) if its reflective surface is to be intelligible. Despite its qualification as "everlasting" (*pardurables*), the mirror is in this sense curiously corruptible, simultaneously subject to the two determinations that Nature elsewhere presents as antithetical: "God never made anything *everlasting*, but everything I make is *corruptible*" (*Onques ne fis riens pardurable; / quan que je faz est corrumpable*, vv. 19031–32). As such, the beautiful, polished mirror is not only in itself irreducible to both contingency and necessity, human temporality and divine vision, which it reconciles; at the same time, being both divine and subject to decay, it collapses—or, alternately, displaces—the fundamental metaphysical opposition between *ens increatum* and *ens creatum*. The *mirouer* allows for the precise definition of the relation of *presciance* and *predestinacion* (vv. 17453–54; cf. 17072–73) to *volanté* (v. 17460; cf. 17075) insofar as it itself thus exceeds both the divine and the human; it furnishes the resolution to the *question* by introducing an entirely novel term into the discussion.

How is one, then, to read the figure of the *mirouer?* The question must first of all be posed in philological terms that concern the literary and philosophical tradition so often invoked and transformed by the *Roman de la Rose.* In a rich article Patricia Eberle has suggested that the "ultimate source" of the image is a passage in the Book of Wisdom (7:27) in which the wisdom of divine providence is described as a *speculum sine macula,* a "mirror without a flaw."[62] Such a gloss is valuable; but interpretations that situate the figure in the context of the philosophical tradition are perhaps more pertinent in this context, which is more Scholastic than scriptural. As a figure that functions to articulate the simultaneous identity and difference of freedom and foreknowledge, contingency and necessity, the *mirouers pardurables* can be read as a figural presentation of a classical philosophical metaphor for the relation between divine eternity and human temporality: a circle whose center, God, is equally present in each point of its circumference, time. This image is already to be found in the fourth book of *De Consolatione Philosophiae,* in which Lady Philosophy explains that, "as reasoning is to understanding, as that which becomes is to that which is, as time is to eternity, as the circle is to its center, so is the moving course of fate to the unmoving simplicity of providence" (*uti est ad intellectum ratiocinatio, ad id quod est id quod gignitur, ad aeternitatem tempus, ad punctum medium circulus, ita est fati series mobilis ad providentiae stabilem simplicitatem*).[63] Developing the analogy at length in the first book of his *Summa contra gentiles,* Thomas invokes the same figure to define the relation of *aeternitas* to *tempus:*

> cum aeterni esse nunquam deficiat, cuilibet tempori vel instanti temporis praesentialiter adest aeternitas. cuius exemplum utcumque in circulo est videre: punctum enim in circumferentia signatum, etsi indivisibile sit, non tamen cuilibet puncto alii secundum situm coexistit simul, ordo enim situs continuitatem circumferentiae facit; centrum vero, quod est extra circumferentiam, ad quodlibet punctum in circumferentia signatum directe oppositionem habet. quicquid igitur in quacumque parte temporis est, coexistit aeterno quasi praesens eidem: etsi respectu alterius partis temporis sit praeteritum vel futurum. aeterno autem non potest aliquid praesentialiter coexistere nisi toti: quia successionis durationem non habet. quicquid igitur per totum decursum temporis agitur, divinus intellectus in tota sua aeternitate intuetur quasi praesens.[64]

> Since the being of what is eternal never decays, eternity is present in all its presence to any time or instant of time. The circle illustrates the point. A determined point on the circumference of a circle is indivisible, yet it does not coexist simultaneously with any other point as to position; for it is the

order of position that produces the continuity of the circumference. Now, the center of the circle, which lies outside the circumference, is directly opposed to any given determinate point on the circumference. In the same way, whatever is found in any part of time coexists with what is eternal as being present to it, although with respect to some other time it may be past or future. A thing can be present to what is eternal only by being present to the whole of it, since the eternal does not have the duration of succession. The divine intellect, therefore, sees in the whole of its eternity, as being present to it, everything that takes place through the whole course of time.

The *mirouer* of which Nature speaks can be read as a figural transposition of precisely this *exemplum*. The circle of the philosophers, in which eternity and time coincide while remaining distinct, thus becomes the spherical looking-glass in which divine knowledge and human *perception* are reconciled and yet maintained in their independence. By virtue of a singular *translatio* of philosophical conceptuality into poetic figuration, the *circulus* in which eternity is present to time now shines in the surface of the *biau mirouer poli*.

The term *mirouer* itself may also be of importance in this context. As the Old French equivalent of the Latin word *speculum*, it can be read as a lexical transposition of a formulation often employed by medieval philosophers to designate the nature of divine knowledge. A passage from De Consolatione Philosophiae, as is so often the case, is decisive here. Defining the nature of providence, Lady Philosophy employs the word *specula*, "watch-tower," "lookout," and, by extension, "height, summit, eminence," calling God "he who has looked out from the lofty watch-tower of his providence," *qui cum ex alta providentiae specula respexit*.[65] The persistence of this phrase in the history of medieval theological reflection can be measured by the fact that, when Thomas discusses the problem of predestination and providence in his commentaries on the *Sententiae*, he makes use of the very same expression, arguing that God views the whole of time "as if from a watch-tower of eternity," *quasi ab aeternitatis specula*.[66] *Specula*, a term etymologically and semantically related to *speculum*, thus occupies a prominent place in medieval definitions of the notion of eternity; and, as such, it allows us to interpret the *mirouers pardurables* of the *Roman de la Rose* in a new light. A complex lexical and semantic *translatio* from Latin to Old French and from the field of philosophy to that of poetry may, once again, be at play here: the canonical definition of eternity as vision *ab specula* can be understood to give rise, by means of the Latin *speculum*, to the text's *mirouer*, in which—in a striking revision of theological doctrine—divine vision is figured not as *ab specula*, "from a watch-tower," but, instead, as *per speculum,* "through a looking-glass," the product of the reciprocal mirroring of contingency and necessity.

Such interpretations of the *mirouer pardurable* acquire their true sense only when they are integrated into a properly critical reading of the figure. The text of the work alone, at this level of analysis, can be of assistance. As a mirror, the instrument of divine intellection demands to be situated in the context of the treatise on optics that soon follows the discussion of the *question* in the poem (v. 18001ff.); its singular activity, which both reconciles and preserves the difference between freedom and foreknowledge, contingency and necessity, cannot but be classed among the many "wondrous powers" (*merveilleus pouers,* v. 18016) ascribed to lenses later in the poem.[67] But this much, in any case, is certain: the "everlasting mirror" with which the discussion of freedom and foreknowledge ends cannot count as merely one among the many mirrors of the two-part romance, from the *miroër* with which Oiseuse welcomes the narrator into the orchard at the start of the poem (v. 556), to the *miroërs perilleus* (v. 1569) of Narcissus and its subsequent appearances and reflections in the poem (cf. vv. 19870, 20380, and 20848),[68] the *miroër* in which Bel Acueill contemplates himself (v. 12704),[69] and the many "figures of mirrors" (*figures / des mirouers,* vv. 18218–19) discussed in Nature's discussion of optics. For, as the crucial instrument that allows for the simultaneous identity and difference of contingency and necessity, the "eternal mirror" is the perfect figure for the work that incessantly maintains itself in its capacity to be otherwise but which, once produced, must nevertheless be as it is, determined by the implacable, irrevocable "retrospective necessity" (*necessitez en regart*) of its actual form. As the medium in which actuality and possibility are incessantly reflected, the *mirouers pardurables* is the image of the very mirror that the *Roman de la Rose* calls itself: the "Mirror of Lovers," *li Miroërs aus Amoreus* (v. 10621).[70]

A reflection of reflection, the *mirouers pardurables,* therefore, is the supreme emblem of the work itself: a mirror that, in a vertiginous and perpetual *mise en abîme,* mirrors its own mirroring, exposing the possibility and actuality of its own taking place. It is, in the words of the text, *li mirouers . . . de cui conmancement preïsmes* (vv. 17441–42): the point at which "we began," the *fons* of not only creaturely but also poetic life, the origin from which the romance itself draws its *matere . . . bone et neuve* (v. 39). As such, the mirror makes it possible to read the entire discussion of necessity and contingency in the romance in a new light. Considered from the point of its specular resolution, the *question* broached by Nature no longer appears as a more or less unmotivated "chapter" in the romance; it ceases to have the form of a "digression" unrelated to the drama of the work as a whole. The text's discussion of the modal categories reveals itself, instead, as a crucial moment in the development of the poem, in which the work, in the most explicit and programmatic fashion, explores the structure of its own taking place—its own contingency and necessity—with the aid of the complex conceptual vocabulary of thirteenth-century thought. As such, the discussion of free will and divine omniscience marks perhaps the final point of the text's *translatio* from the discourse of philosophy into the language of poetry; it may well constitute the poem's ultimate departure from the theological tradition, illustrating the transformation that philosophical conceptuality undergoes in being incorporated, transcribed, and "described" in the poetic text. Decomposed and recomposed by the arguments of the romance, the *quaestio de futuribus contingentibus* shows itself, in the end, to concern a fact of literary composition alone: the point at which necessity and contingency, actuality and possibility, coincide, while remaining distinct in a work that could always have been otherwise but which, from the moment of its production, must have the form it does. What is reflected in the everlasting mirror, in this sense, is the simultaneous fortuitousness and irrevocability of the poetic work; the image sheltered in the perfect, "present vision" (*presante vision*) of which we now read is of nothing other than the *Roman de la Rose*. Here, on the "beautiful, polished" surface of its looking-glass of contingency, the poem thus shows itself for what it is: a work dedicated, through its language, its form, its rhetoric, and its organization, to an exploration of the many forms of its own possibility and actuality.

Conclusion
Diverse Verses

Close to the center of the *Roman de la Rose* a new figure emerges on the scene of the medieval psychomachia: "False Seeming" (*Faussemblant,* v. 10429), son of "trickery" (*Barat*) and "hypocrisy" (*Hypocrisie*), clothed in the "habit of religion" (v. 10444) and accompanied by his constant companion, "Constrained Abstinence" (*Contreinte Atenence*). Once described, however, False Seeming retreats into the background of the work, stepping forward again, in one of the most extended discourses of the romance, almost a thousand lines later. Here the figure presents himself in his own words, enjoining his interlocutors, with the greatest sincerity, never to take him at his word:

> Sanz faille traïstres sui gié
> et por larron m'a Diex juigié.
> Parjurs sui; mes ce que j'afin,
> set l'en enviz devant la fin;
> car pluseur par moi mort reçurent
> qui onc mon barat n'aperçurent,
> et reçoivent et recevront
> qui ja mes ne l'apercevront.
> (Vv. 11139–46)

Without doubt, I am a traitor, and God has judged me a thief. I am a perjurer, but one hardly knows before the end what I am bringing to an end, for several who never perceived my trickery have received their deaths through me, and many are receiving them and will receive them without ever perceiving it. (196)

Conclusion

The figure of false semblance introduces himself, in these verses, in terms that are not what they seem. What begins in these lines as an act of self-identification and consequent self-denunciation (*sainz failles traïtres sui gié, / et por larron m'a Diex jugié,* "Without doubt, I am a traitor, and God has judged me a thief") can barely be separated from an utterance that calls into question the very possibility of his identification and, as a result, his condemnation. For with the words *parjurs sui,* "I am a perjurer," False Seeming offers an exemplary formulation of one of the greatest and most ancient of logical paradoxes, which was elaborated and debated widely in classical and late antiquity before being transmitted to the Middle Ages, during which it was confronted anew among the *insolubilia* taught and analyzed in the university faculties of the twelfth and thirteenth centuries.[1] Here the figure must therefore be said at once to identify himself and to strip himself of every possible condition of identification: with a circular and destructive movement of self-reference which recalls that of the propositions debated in the *scholae, ego dico falsum* or *propositio scripto in illo folio est falsum,*[2] the force of the utterance *parjurs sui* turns immediately upon itself, refuting, by necessity, the very claim it proposes and simultaneously rendering its contradiction equally untenable. No matter how they are interpreted, the words lead to paradox. If the phrase *parjurs sui* is understood to be true, then it, too, is the utterance of a "perjurer," and it is then itself an act of "perjury"; the proposition, in other words, is false if it is held to be true. If the phrase *parjurs sui,* by contrast, is understood to be false, then it is not the utterance of a perjurer, and it is not then an act of perjury; the proposition, in other words, is true if it is taken to be false. The statement, like all those of its logical form, contradicts itself in whatever form it is interpreted; as a proposition that is itself true if it is false and false if it is true, it is barely a proposition at all, and it defines its speaker in rendering him strictly indefinite.

The terms by which False Seeming describes himself a little later in the text constitute an amplification of the simultaneous determination and indetermination that follow from his initial utterance. "I know very well how to change my clothes," he tells us,

> Trop sé bien mes habiz changier,
> prendre l'un et l'autre estrangier.
> Or sui chevaliers, or sui moines,
> or sui prelaz, or sui chanoines
> or sui clers, autre heure sui prestres,
> or sui deciples, or sui mestres,

> or chateleins, or forestiers:
> briefment je sui de touz mestiers.
> Or resui princes, or sui pages,
> et sai par queur restouz langages;
> autre heure sui vieuz et chenuz,
> or resui jennes devenuz;
> or sui Roberz, or sui Robins,
> or cordeliers, or jacobins;
> si pregn por sivre ma compaigne,
> qui me solace et m'acompaigne
> (c'est dame Attenance Contrainte),
> autre desguiseüre mainte,
> si com il li vient a plesir,
> por acomplir li son desir.
> Autre eure vest robe de fame,
> or sui damoisele, or sui dame;
> autre eure sui religieuse,
> or sui rendue, or sui prieuse,
> or sui nonnain, or abbeesse,
> or sui novice, or sui professe,
> et vois par toutes regions
> çarchant toutes religions;
> mes de religion sanz faille
> j'en lés le grain et pregn la paille.
> Por genz enbacler i habit,
> je n'en quier sanz plus que l'abit.
> Que vos diroie? En tele guise
> con il me plest je me desguise.
> Mout est en moi muez li vers,
> mout sunt li fet au diz divers.
>   (Vv.11157–92)

I know very well how to change my clothes, to take one and then another foreign to it. Now I am a knight, now a monk; at one time I am a prelate, another a canon; at one hour a clerk, at another a priest; now disciple, now master, now lord of the manor, now forester. In short, I am of all trades. At times I am a prince, at times a page, and I know all languages by heart. At one hour I am old and white, and then I have become young again. Now I am Robert, now Robin, now Cordelier, now Jacobin. And in order to follow my companion, Lady Constrained Abstinence, who comforts me and goes along with me, I take on many another disguise, just as it strikes her pleasure, to fulfill her desire. At one time I wear a woman's robe; now I am a girl, now a lad. At another time I become a religious lady: now I am a devotee, now a prioress, nun, or abbess; now a novice, now a pressed nun. I go through every locality seeking all religions. But, without fail, I leave the kernel of religion and take the husk. I dwell in religion in order to trick people; I seek only its habit, no more. What should I tell you? I disguise myself in the way that pleases me. The tune is very much changed in me; my deeds are very different from my words. (196–97)

Like Proteus, "who used to change into everything whenever he wanted" (*se soloit / muer en tout quan qu'il vouloit,* vv. 11151–52), the figure who speaks in these lines is not one. The very unit of the work, the verse, here bears the marks of the movement of antithesis and alteration which characterizes False Seeming. At its caesura, the line, falling into two symmetrical halves, articulates the passage between the identities of the speaker, whether they be those of occupation, class, name, or gender: in the metrical space between the *now* of "now I am a knight" and that of *now* of "now I am a clerk," of "now I am a lad" and "now I am a girl," the voice of duplicity has narrated, within a single octosyllable, the passage between his multiple forms. Exploiting the possibilities of segmentation of the verse of the romance, the figure thus reveals his every "guise," according to one of the telling rhyme pairs of which he makes use, to be but a "disguise" (vv. 11189–90).

Regularly irregular, multiform by his very form, False Seeming has lent himself to numerous and varied interpretations, which have in turn assigned him diverse and often incompatible functions in the economy of the romance. Lewis long ago dismissed False Seeming as one of Jean's regrettable "digressions";[3] many of the most prominent successive readers of the work, from Charles Muscatine to Carolyn Van Dyke, concurred with his judgment.[4] But the critical estimation of the figure has grown in recent criticism, to the point where, by means of a metamorphosis worthy of the personification himself, False Seeming has cast off the position William Ryding once assigned him as an "unfortunate presence" in the poem and acquired a title of notable prestige in the work as a whole:[5] for Susan Stakel the figure thus marks the point at which the fundamental "conceptual field of deceit" in the text "attains far and away its greatest density";[6] for Lee Patterson he illustrates a series of traits that characterize the organization of the romance;[7] for Sylvia Huot, who has considered the figure on a number of occasions, he constitutes Love's own "parodic double"[8] as well as "the embodiment of fiction";[9] and for Kevin Brownlee, who has dedicated a rich study to the polymorphous figure, he plays the roles at once of reader and writer, functioning in the romance as "a kind of emblem of multivoicedness."[10]

The reading of the *Roman de la Rose* proposed in the chapters of this book make it possible to build on these analyses, offering a further interpretation of the figure. Simultaneously himself and another and, more precisely, himself *as* another, False Seeming is a figure of the two-part romance itself as this book has presented it, doubled through its unitary bipartition, multiplied by its single "I," fractured by the temporal and hermeneutic structures of its allegory, set in movement by its figures of instability and impermanence. Like the named and nameless narrator ("now Guillaume," one is tempted to suggest, "now Jean," and "now neither"), like the phoenix, like Fortune, like all the creaturely life reflected on the surface of the simultaneously divine and corruptible looking-glass, False Seeming remains himself and other than himself in the incessant self-differentiation imposed upon him by the irreducible contingency of his form. The disguises that cloak his persona are the guises of the poem itself. It is perhaps in this sense that we are to read the words by which False Seeming characterizes himself, which are, after all, borrowed from the technical terminology of versification:

> Que vos diroie? En tele guise
> con il me plest je me desguise.
> Mout est en moi muez li vers,
> mout sunt li fet au diz divers.
> (Vv. 11189–92)

What should I tell you? I disguise myself in the way that pleases me. The tune is very much changed in me; my deeds are very different from my words. (196–97)

False Seeming here makes use of an expression that ties the structure of his form to that of the literary work itself. The text of the published English translation cited earlier, "The tune is very much changed in me," is doubtless correct, but it fails to capture the specific force of the term invoked at this point in the romance to designate the object of the perpetual "change" staged by False Seeming, which is not so much *tune* or *music* as it is exactly the unit of poetry, *vers* (*Mout est en moi muez li* vers). The word, to be sure, contains a figurative sense in its thirteenth-century usage: dictionaries of Old French list "state, state of affairs, condition" as attested meanings of *vers*,[11] and the line of False Seeming's discourse can therefore certainly be translated, "With me, things are very much changed," as Strubel suggests in his modern French rendition.[12] But throughout the Middle Ages, the primary sense of the term remains the one that derives from the Latin *vertere*, to "turn around," *versus*,

Conclusion

"line" or "furrow," and which is therefore semantically linked to the entire agricultural lexicon at the origin of the modern metrical terminology; and it is therefore possible to hear a decidedly metapoetic resonance in the figure's words, which furnishes undeniable textual evidence for the interpretation of False Seeming as a figure of the poem itself. "With me," False Seeming quite literally says, "the *verse* is very much changed." Uttered by a figure who can be interpreted as an emblem of the joint work of Guillaume and Jean, the claim holds for the two-part work as a whole: with the *Roman de la Rose* the elements of poetry—"verse" (*li vers*, v. 11191)—are "changed," "altered," and set into a movement of metamorphosis in which, as announced by the rhyme pair of the text, they become, within themselves, "diverse" (*divers*, vv. 11192).

It is these "diverse verses" that this book has taken as its objects of study, defining them as the elements of a single poetic exploration of the linguistic, rhetorical, figural, and theological dimensions of contingency. At each of the levels of its construction, within each of its "verses," the *Roman de la Rose* confronts the diverse dimensions of its own possibility to be and to have been otherwise than it is: in its poetic subject, who is himself in being capable of being someone other than himself; in the figures of its rhetoric, which are exposed to the very instability and metamorphosis they would depict; and in its discussion of the concept of possibility, in which a *quaestio* of thirteenth-century philosophy, displaced from the terrain of theology and epistemology to that of poetics, functions to pose the question of the logical and metaphysical status of the romance itself. The work, in each of its literary structures, thus reflects upon the force of contingency and is itself moved by it, unfolding *per accidens* throughout its exploration of accidentality and occurring, like the "fortune" of the medieval philosophers, "not as itself, but as something else," *non in quantum ipsum sed in quantum alterum*. It presents itself as the very contingency of which it speaks: as a "possible thing" (*chose possible*, v. 17175) which could always have been otherwise than it is but which, from the moment of its production, is irrevocability determined, by the implacable force of "retrospective necessity" (*necessitez en regart*, v. 17198), to assume its actual form.

Calling attention to the contingency at play within its own language, its figures, and its organization, the *Roman de la Rose* brings to light, in its own way, the single event that the lyric poets of Provence bequeathed to the literatures of Europe as the fundamental matter of writing: the finding (*trobar*) of poetry, the taking place (*contingere*) of language in the literary text. The many ruptures and discontinuities within the romance of Guillaume de Lorris and Jean de Meun mark this event throughout the registers of the text; they reveal the irreducible capacity of the poem to occur and not to occur and, in this way, expose the mode in which the two-part romance takes place. Defining the techniques of this exposition and situating them in the context of thirteenth-century philosophy, this study, therefore, has necessarily considered a restricted set of the formal, rhetorical, and topical structures by which the text of the *Roman de la Rose* unfolds. But at the same time, in its consideration of a poetic work that is in many senses exemplary in the history of medieval and modern European literature, this book has sought to investigate a far more general matter. It is the most fundamental of all questions of poetics, to which every work, in its own way, is devoted: how language, in literature, takes place. Or, more simply: what it means for a poem to be.

Notes

Introduction

1. The annotation is to be found in BN fr 12786, edited recently by Armand Strubel in his *Le Roman de la Rose,* Lettres Gothiques (Paris: Le Livre de Poché, 1992), 244. The copyist's addition is not unique among the manuscripts of the romance. In the fourteenth-century BN 1569, for example, we also read, between the two parts of the romance, that Jean de Meun "parfinit" the romance of the "aucteur dit Guient" (28 b).

2. On the influence and reception of the romance in medieval France, see the invaluable studies of Pierre-Yves Badel, *Le Roman de la Rose au XIVe siècle: Étude de la réception de l'œuvre* (Geneva: Droz, 1980); Sylvia Huot, *The Romance of the Rose and Its Medieval Readers: Interpretation, Reception, Manuscript Transmission* (Cambridge: Cambridge University Press, 1993); as well as her essays "Authors, Scribes, Remanieurs: A Note on the Textual History of the *Roman de la Rose,*" in *Rethinking the* Romance of the Rose*: Text, Image, Reception,* ed. Kevin Brownlee and Sylvia Huot (Philadelphia: University of Pennsylvania Press, 1992), 203–33; and "Medieval Readers of the *Roman de la Rose:* The Evidence of Marginal Notations," *Romance Philology* 43 (1990): 400–420. On the *querelle de la Rose,* see in addition Eric Hicks, ed., *Christine de Pizan, Jean Gerson, Jean de Montreuil, Gontier and Pierre Col: Le débat sur le Roman de la Rose,* Bibliotèque du XVe siècle, 43 (Paris: Champion, 1977); A. J. Minnis, "Theorizing the *Rose:* Crises of Textual Authority in the *Querelle de la Rose,*" in *Magister amoris: The* Roman de la Rose *and Vernacular Hermeneutics* (Oxford: Oxford University Press, 2001), 209–56; David F. Hult, "Words and Deeds: Jean de Meun's *Romance of the Rose* and the Hermeneutics of Censorship," *New Literary History* 28 (1997): 345–66; and John V. Fleming, "The Moral Reputation of the *Roman de la Rose* before 1400," *Romance Philology* 18 (1964–65): 430–35. On the partial Italian translation of the romance often attributed to Dante, see Luigi Vanossi, *Dante e il "Roman de la Rose": Saggi sul "Fiore,"* Biblioteca dell' 'Archivium Romanicum,' ser. 1, 144 (Florence: Olschki, 1979); Earl Jeffrey Richards, *Dante and the "Roman de la Rose": An Investigation into the Vernacular Context of Dante's "Commedia,"* Beihefte zur Zeitschrift der romanischen Philologie, 184 (Tübingen: Niemeyer, 1981); Gianfranco Contini, "Un nodo della cultura medievale: la serie Roman de la Rose-Fiore-Divina Commedia," in *Un'idea di Dante* (Turin: Einaudi, 1970), 245–83; and, more recently, *The*

Fiore in Context: Dante, France, Tuscany, ed. Zygmunt Baransky and Patrick Boyde, William and Katherine Devers series in Dante studies, 2 (South Bend: University of Notre Dame Press, 1996). For the English *romaunt,* see Ronald Sutherland, ed., *The Romaunt of the Rose and Le Roman de la Rose* (Berkeley: University of California Press, 1969). On the Dutch reception of the poem, see Dieuwke van der Poel, *De Vlaamse "Rose" en "Die Rose" van Heinric: Onderzoekingen over Twee Middelnederlandse Bewerkingen van de "Roman de la Rose" (avec un résumé en français),* Middeleeuwse Studies en Bronnen, 13 (Hilversum, Neth.: Verloren, 1989); and "A Romance of a Rose and Florentine: The Flemish Adaptation of the *Romance of the Rose,*" in Brownlee and Huot, *Rethinking the* Romance of the Rose, 304–15. On the posterity of the romance in Italian and European literature, see John V. Fleming's study, "Augustinus and Franciscus," in *Reason and the Lover* (Princeton, N.J.: Princeton University Press, 1984), 136–83. The romance even had an afterlife in Byzantium: see Henry Kahane and Renée Kahane, "The Hidden Narcissus in the Byzantine Romance of *Belthandros and Chrysantza,*" *Jahrbuch der österreichischen Byzantinistik* 33 (1983): 199–219.

3. Paulin Paris, "Fin du treizième siècle. Trouvères: Le *Roman de la Rose,*" *Histoire Littéraire de la France* 23 (1856): 15.

4. Gaston Paris, *La littérature française au moyen âge,* 5th ed. (1888; rpt., Paris: 1913), 183. In his 1926 essay, "'Le Roman de la Rose' et la pensée du XIIIe siècle," Edmond Faral appears to refer implicitly to this judgment in writing that "le fait est . . . qu'aux quelque quatre mille vers de Guillaume, à ce corps d'œuvre artistiquement mesuré, il [sc., Jean de Meun] a appliqué, sous prétexte de l'achever, une queue monstrueuse de dix-huit mille vers." See *Revue des Deux Mondes,* 7th ser., 35 (1926): 435.

5. Ernest Langlois, *Le Roman de la Rose,* Société des Anciens Textes Français (SATF) (Paris: Firmin-Didot, 1914–24), 1:25.

6. Alfred Jeanroy, *Histoire des lettres,* vol. 1: *Des origines à Ronsard,* ed. Alfred Jeanroy, Joseph Bédier, and F. Picavet (Paris: Plon, 1921) (= Vol. 12 of *Histoire de la nation française,* ed. G. Hanotaux), 411.

7. Edmond Faral, "La littérature allégorique et le Roman de la Rose," in *Histoire de la littérature française illustrée,* ed. Joseph Bédier and Paul Hazard (Paris: Larousse, 1923), 69.

8. C. S. Lewis, *The Allegory of Love: A Study in Mediaeval Tradition* (Oxford: Oxford University Press, 1938), 137, 140. As a rule, C. S. Lewis comments, "it is rash to differ" from Ernest Langlois (136).

9. Paulin Paris, "Fin du treizième siècle. Trouvères: Le *Roman de la Rose,*" 15.

10. Gaston Paris, *La littérature française au moyen âge,* 184.

11. Ernest Langlois, *Origines et sources du Roman de la Rose* (Paris: Ernest Thorin, 1890), 93.

12. Alfred Jeanroy, "Introduction," *Le Roman de la Rose: Principaux episodes traduits,* trans. B.A. Jeanroy (Paris: E. de Boccard,1928), xv; "Le Roman de la Rose," 411.

13. Ibid. Jeanroy's pointed figure, which calls into question the very status of Jean's poem as a *textum* in the literal sense, is echoed in C. S. Lewis's characterization of the second *Rose* as a "huge, disheveled, violent poem of eighteen thousand lines" (*Allegory of Love*, 137), as well as in George Lyman Kittridge's statement that Jean de Meun "chose to string his observations on a thread of allegory" (*Chaucer and His Poetry* [Cambridge: Harvard University Press, 1915], 25).

14. Faral, "La littérature allégorique et le *Roman de la Rose*," 72.

15. Louis Thuasne, *Le Roman de la Rose* (Paris: Société Française d'Éditions Littéraires et Techniques, 1929), 76.

16. Jean-Claude Milner is the author of this felicitous definition of the *excursus*. See *L'Oeuvre claire: Lacan, la science, la philosophie* (Paris: Seuil, 1995), 25.

17. Lewis, *Allegory of Love*, 137, 141.

18. Ibid., 141. Cf. Ezra Pound's not dissimilar remarks on the two-part poem in *The Spirit of Romance* (1952; rpt., New York: New Directions, 1968), 84–86.

19. Langlois, *Le Roman de la Rose*, 1:3. On the reception of the romance in nineteenth- and twentieth-century criticism, see the helpful summary given in chapters 2 and 3 of Karl August Ott's *Der Rosenroman* (Darmstadt, Germ.: Wissenschaftliche Buchgesellschaft, 1980), 46–123.

20. Langlois, *Les origines et les sources du Roman de la Rose*, 94.

21. Alan M. F. Gunn, *The Mirror of Love: A Reinterpretation of "The Roman de la Rose"* (Lubbock: Texas Tech Press, 1952), 23.

22. Ibid., 28. Despite this thesis, Gunn adds the following statement within parentheses, which appears to constitute a significant disavowal: "We are concerned at this point with the poet's theme in its most general meaning, and not with his special interpretation of love. It does not matter in this connection that his views on love were somewhat different from those of Guillaume de Lorris."

23. John V. Fleming, *The Roman de la Rose: A Study in Allegory and Iconography* (Princeton, N.J.: Princeton University Press, 1969), 104, 50. See also Fleming's later reformulation of his position in his *Reason and the Lover*.

24. Roger Dragonetti, "Pygmalion ou les pièges de la fiction dans le *Roman de la Rose*," in *Orbis Mediaevalis: Mélanges d'études de langue et de littérature médiévales offerts à R. R. Bezzola*, ed. Georges Güntert, Marc-René Jung, and Kurt Ringger (Bern: Francke, 1978), rpt. in Dragonetti, *La musique et les lettres: Études de littérature médiévale* (Geneva: Droz, 1986), 346.

25. Roger Dragonetti, "Le 'Singe de Nature' dans le *Roman de la Rose*," now in *La musique et les lettres*, 371.

26. Ibid., 345.

27. Ibid. Dragonetti further develops this thesis in *Le mirage des sources: L'art du faux dans le roman médiéval* (Paris: Seuil, 1987), 200–225.

28. These are only the most significant contributions to the question of the organization of Jean de Meun's text and its relation to the whole of the *Roman de la Rose*. For a more detailed summary of critical perspectives, see Ott, *Der Rosenro-*

man; and Heather M. Arden, *The Roman de la rose: An Annotated Bibliography*, Garland Medieval Bibliographies, 8 (New York: Garland, 1993).

29. For a summary of recent criticism of the manuscript tradition of the romance, see Huot, *Romance of the Rose and Its Medieval Readers*, 1–15. See also David Hult, *Self-Fulfilling Prophecies: Readership and Authority in the First Roman de la Rose* (Cambridge: Cambridge University Press, 1986), 10–55.

30. Fleming, *Reason and the Lover*. It is important to recall that Fleming's earlier book on the romance distinguished itself from almost all of the critical literature on the poem precisely in its insistence on the need to read the two parts of the work as a unity.

31. Hult, *Self-Fulfilling Prophecies*. Cf. Hult's two later articles, "Language and Dismemberment: Abelard, Origen and the *Romance of the Rose*," in *Rethinking the Romance of the Rose*, 101–30; and "Words and Deeds."

32. Susan Stakel, *False Roses: Structures of Duality and Deceit in Jean de Meun's Roman de la Rose*, Stanford French and Italian Studies 49 (Stanford: Anima Libri, 1991).

33. Sylvia Huot, *The* Romance of the Rose *and Its Medieval Readers*. Huot has also made a number of other important contributions to the study of the romance: see her articles "Bodily Peril: Sexuality and the Subversion of Order in Jean de Meun's *Roman de la Rose*," *Modern Language Review* 95 (2000): 41–61; "Confronting Misogyny: Christine de Pizan and the *Roman de la Rose*," in *Translatio studii: Essays by his students in honor of Karl D. Uitti for his sixty-fifth birthday*, ed. Renate Blumenfeld-Kosinski, Kevin Brownlee, Mary B. Speer, and Lori Walters (Amsterdam: Rodopi, 2000), 169–87; "The Scribe as Editor: Rubrication as Critical Apparatus in Two Manuscripts of the *Roman de la Rose*," *L'Esprit Créateur* 27 (1987): 67–78; "Seduction and Sublimation: Christine de Pizan, Jean de Meun, and Dante," *Romance Notes* 25 (1985): 361–73.

34. Douglas Kelly, *Internal Difference and Meanings in the* Roman de la Rose (Madison: University of Wisconsin Press, 1995).

35. Minnis, *Magister Amoris*.

36. Heather Arden, *The Romance of the Rose*, Twayne's World Author Series (Boston: Twayne Publishers, 1987); Sarah Kay, *The Romance of the Rose*, Critical Introductions to French Literature 110 (London: Grant and Cutler, 1995). Cf. Kay's three additional articles on the romance: "The Birth of Venus in the *Roman de la Rose*," *Exemplaria* 1 (1997): 7–37; "Women's Body of Knowledge in the *Romance of the Rose*," in *Framing Medieval Bodies*, ed. Sarah Kay and Miri Rubin (New York: Manchester University Press, 1994), 210–35; and "Sexual Knowledge: The Once and Future Texts of the *Romance of the Rose*," in *Textuality and Sexuality: Reading Theories and Practices*, ed. Judith Still and Michael Worton (New York: Manchester University Press, 1993), 69–83, 4.

37. The two early manuscripts that present Guillaume's text without its continuation by Jean de Meun are the late-thirteenth- or early-fourteenth-century BN

Notes to Pages 6–7

fr 12786 and the late-thirteenth-century BN fr 1573. See Pierre-Yves Badel, *Le Roman de la Rose au XIVe siècle*, 55. Cf. the findings summarized by Ernest Langlois in his *Les manuscrits du Roman de la Rose: Description et classement* (Paris: Champion, 1910); see also the diagram offered by Hult in *Self-Fulfilling Prophecies*, 89.

38. Badel, *Le Roman de la Rose au XIVe siècle*, 55.

39. Paul Zumthor, *Essai de poétique médiévale* (Paris: Seuil, 1972), 375. Cf. Zumthor's important essay on the two parts of the romance: "De Guillaume de Lorris à Jean de Meung," in *Études de langue et de littérature du Moyen Âge offerts à Félix Lecoy* (Paris: Champion, 1973), 609–20.

40. The material form of the medieval work, the manuscript, is in this sense exemplary: it is the product of scribal additions, glosses, and interpolations that constitute a work without necessarily giving rise to the fixed text of any author in the modern sense. On the emergence of the concept of authorship, see Foucault's seminal essay "Qu'est-ce qu'un auteur?" *Bulletin de la Société Française de Philosophie* 64 (1969): 77–95 (reprinted in *Dits et écrits*, vol. 1: *1954–1969* [Paris: Gallimard, 1994], 789–821); on the classical and medieval juridical prehistory of the notion of authorship, see Kantorowicz, "The Sovereignty of the Artist: A Note on Legal Notions and Renaissance Theories of Art," in Ernst H. Kantorowicz, *Selected Studies* (Locust Valley, N.Y.: J. J. Augustin, 1965), 352–65. See also Hult's helpful discussion of the "medieval author" in "The Spectral Author," the first chapter of *Self-Fulfilling Prophecies* (10–104); see also A. J. Minnis, *Medieval Theory of Authorship: Scholastic Literary Attitudes in the Later Middle Ages* (London: Scolar Press, 1984). On the manuscript as the paradigm of the medieval text, see Bernard Cerquiglini's remarks on medieval works in his *Éloge de la variante: Histoire critique de la philologie* (Paris: Seuil, 1989), 58–59; on the importance of the manuscript as a model for the medieval literary text, see Stephen G. Nichols, "Why Material Philology? Some Thoughts," in *Philologie als Textwissenschaft: Alte und neue Horizonte*, ed. Helmut Tervooren and Horst Wenzel, *Zeitschrift für deutsche Philologie*, special issue, 116 (1997): 10–30; and, on the scribal presence in the medieval text, see Elspeth Kennedy, "The Scribe as Editor," in *Mélanges de langue et de littérature du Moyen Âge et de la Renaissance offerts à Jean Frappier* (Geneva: Droz, 1970), 523–31; Roy Rosenstein, "*Mouvance* and the Editor as Scribe: *Trascrittore Traditore?*" *Romanic Review* 80 (1989): 157–71; and, with particular reference to the *Roman de la Rose*, Sylvia Huot, "The Scribe as Editor: Rubrication as Critical Apparatus in Two *Roman de la Rose* Manuscripts," *L'Esprit Créateur* 27 (1987): 67–78.

41. Hult, *Self-Fulfilling Prophecies*, 6.

42. Hult notes as much when he writes that Jean's *Rose* and the scribal continuation that separates it from Guillaume's *Rose* "incorporate R1 [that is, the poem attributed to Guillaume de Lorris] into its their own redefined textualities" (ibid., 92).

43. *Allegory of Love*, 141 and 142.

44. See Roger Dragonetti, *La vie de la lettre au Moyen Âge (Le Conte du Graal)* (Paris: Seuil, 1980), 9.

45. Cf. *Allegory of Love*, 136.

46. On the *dispositio* of the romance, see Daniel Poirion, *Le Roman de la Rose* (Paris: Hatier, 1973), esp. "L'amplification de l'allégorie," 98–144; cf. Kay, *The Romance of the Rose*, 160–65; see Kelly's treatment of the *modus digressivus* in *Internal Differences and Meanings in the Roman de la Rose*, 122–27; and Lee Patterson, "'For the Wyves love of Bathe': Feminine Rhetoric and Poetic Resolution in the *Roman de la Rose* and the *Canterbury Tales*," *Speculum* 58 (1983): 656–95, which subsequently appeared in revised form as chap. 6 ("The Wife of Bath and the Triumph of the Subject") in Patterson's *Chaucer and the Subject of History* (Madison: University of Wisconsin Press, 1991), 280–321; and still later as "Feminine Rhetoric and the Politics of Subjectivity: La Vieille and the Wife of Bath," in Brownlee and Huot, *Rethinking the Romance of the Rose*, 316–58.

One: Inventio Linguae

1. *De interpretatione*, 16 a 4 ff, *Aristotle in Twenty-Three Volumes*, vol. 1: *The Categories, On Interpretation, Prior Analytics*, trans. Harold. Cooke and Hugh Tredennick (Cambridge: Harvard University Press, 1983), 114. All translations from the Greek, unless otherwise noted, are my own. The Latin text quoted is that of Boethius' translation, as printed in *Aristoteles Latinus*, II, 1–2: *De interpretatione vel Periermeneias*, ed. Lorenzo Minio-Paluello (Leiden: Brill, 1965).

2. On the intepretation of this difficult passage, see, among many others: Jean Pépin, "Σύμβολα, Σγμεῖα, Ὁμοιώματα: À propos de *De Interpretatione* 1, 16 a 3–8 et *Politique* VIII 5, 1340 a 6–39," in *Aristoteles Werk und Wirkung: Paul Moraux gewidmet*, Vol. 1: *Aristoteles und seine Schule*, ed. Jürgen Weisner (Berlin: De Gruyter, 1985), 22–44; Curzio Chiesa, "Symbole etsigne dans le *De Interpretatione*," in *Philosophie du langage et grammaire dans l'antiquité* (Bruxelles: Ousia, 1986), 203–18; and John Magee, *Boethius on Signification and Mind* Philosophia antiqua Vol. 52 (Leiden: Brill, 1989), esp. ch.1, 7–48.

3. Ibid., 16 a 12–14: "For the true and the false exist with respect to synthesis and division" (περὶ γὰρ σύνθεσιν καὶ διαίρεσίν ἐστι τὸ ψεῦδος καὶ τὸ ἀληθές, *circa compositionem enim et divisionem est falsitas veritasque*). Aristotle insists upon the com-positional form of truth in several texts: cf. *De anima*, 430 b 3 ff, in *Aristotle in Twenty-Three Volumes*, vol. 8: *On the Soul, Parva Naturalia, On Breath*, trans. W. S. Hett, 170: "in truth and falsity, there is a certain composition" (ἐν οἷς δὲ καὶ τὸ ψεῦδος καὶ τὸ ἀληθές, σύνθεσίς τις); cf. also *Metaphysica* 1027 b 19 ff, in which Aristotle writes that "the true and the false are with respect to composition and division" (περὶ σύνθεσιν . . . καὶ διαίρεσιν).

4. Ibid., 17 a 25: κατάφασις δέ ἔστιν ἀποφανσίς τινος κατά τινος, *Adfirmatio vero est enuntiatio alicuis de aliquo*. It goes without saying that the negative statement, which speaks "one thing away from another thing," τινος ἀπό τινος, *alicuius ab aliquo*, is merely the inversion of the affirmative, which, for Aristotle, constitutes the model of correct speech in general.

5. On truth as *adequatio rei et intellectus*, see *De interpretatione*, chap. 9 and the final chapter of *De praedicamentis*. On the presence of truth in the judgment, and not the concept, see *De interpretatione*, chap. 1; *Metaphysica*, bk. 4, chap. 29; bk. 5, chap. 4; bk. 8, chap. 10; and *De anima*, 3: chap. 6.

6. 18 a 29–30.

7. 18 a 32.

8. 19 a 29.

9. 18 b 6.

10. 19 a 18.

11. Jan Lukasiewicz was the first to identify this principle as such, in a series of extremely influential essays on Aristotle's logical works and the possibility of a many-valued propositional logic. Lukasiewicz was careful to distinguish the theorem of bivalence, according to which every proposition is either true or false, from the law of the excluded middle, which he reserved for the principle that two contradictory propositions cannot be false simultaneously. Lukasiewicz, who gives a brief history of this principle from Aristotle to the Stoics, notes that it is already formulated by Aristotle himself in *De interpretatione* (17 a 2), where he defines propositions as those utterances that contain truth or falsity (ἀποφαντικὸς δε οὐ πας [λόγοι] ἀλλ' ἐω ᾧ τὸ ἀληθεύειν ἢ ψεύδεσθαι ὑπάρχει). In modern logic the law of bivalence appears in exemplary terms in Frege, who writes: "I understand a statement's truth value to be the fact that it is true or false. There are no other truth conditions" (Gottlob Frege, "Über Sinn und Bedeutung," in *Funktion, Begriff, Bedeutung*, ed. Günter Patzig [Göttingen: Vandenhoeck and Ruprecht, 1994], 48). On logical systems that are not restricted by the law of bivalence, see Lukasiewicz's groundbreaking "Philosophical Remarks on Many-Valued Systems of Propositional Logic," in *Polish Logic: 1920–1939*, ed. Storrs McCall (Oxford: Clarendon Press, 1967), 40–65; on the problem of contingency and possibility, see also Lukasiewicz, "On the Notion of Possibility," "On Three-Valued Logic," and "On Determinism," in *Polish Logic*, 15–16, 16–18, 19–39, respectively. Cf. Lukasiewicz's later treatment of Aristotelian logic in his important study, *Aristotle's Syllogistic from the Standpoint of Modern Formal Logic*, 2d ed. (Oxford: Oxford University Press, 1951). On Aristotle and the restriction of the law of bivalence, see also Jules Vuillemin, *Nécessité et contingence: L'aporie de Diodore et les systèmes philosophiques* (Paris: Minuit, 1984), esp. 161–66.

12. 19 a.

13. On the theological dimension of the problem of contingency, see chap. 4, "Through the Looking-Glass: The Knowledge of Contingency."

14. 17 a 6–8.

15. J. Isaac, *Le Peri Hermeneias en Occident, de Boèce à Saint Thomas: Histoire littéraire d'un traité d'Aristote*, Bibliothèque Thomiste, vol. 29 (Paris: Vrin, 1953).

16. Ibid., 16. Isaac refers here to the editors of *Aristoteles latinus* (45), who are insistent on this point: "Nullam deteximus *Periermeneias* versionem novam. Qui in codicibus extant sine commentariis textus, omnes sunt Boethii."

17. Boethius, *De institutione arithmetica libri duo,* ed. G. Friedlein (Leipzig: Teubner, 1867), 3 (also in *Patrologia Latina* 63, col. 1079); cited in Isaac, 17 n. 2.

18. See Pierre Courcelle, *Les lettres grecques en Occident de Macrobe à Cassiodore,* rev. ed. (Paris: Bibliothèque des Écoles Françaises d'Athènes et de Rome, 1948), 285–94. See also Isaac, 23.

19. *Apulei Peri hermeneias,* in *Apuleius,* vol. 3: *De philosophia libri,* ed. Thomas (Leipzig: Teubner, 1908).

20. Martiani Capellae, *De nuptiis Philologiae et Mercurii,* ed. A. Dick (Leipzig: Teubner, 1925). See Isaac, 26–27, which relies on the account of the two authors provided by Thomas in his edition of Apuleius.

21. Isaac, *Le Peri Hermeneias en Occident,* 34.

22. Ibid., 26.

23. Ibid., 38.

24. See Isaac, *Le Peri Hermeneias en Occident,* 44–47; and Pier Damiani, *De divina omnipotentia e altri opusculi,* ed. Brezzi and Bruno Nardi (Florence: Ed. Nazion. D. Class. D. Pens. Ital., 1943; also in *Patrologia Latina* 145).

25. Aristotle's distinction between the two types of necesssity can be found, *in nuce,* at *De interpretatione,* 19 a 24–19 b 5. For Anselm's treatment of the problem, see in particular *De concordia, Quaestio* 1; *Cur deus homo,* 2; *De casu diaboli,* 21; see also Léon Baudry, "La prescience divine chez S. Anselme," *Archives d'Histoire Doctrinale et Littéraire du Moyen Âge,* 13 (1940–42): 223–37.

26. See Isaac, *Le Peri Hermeneias en Occident,* 61–74.

27. See the table of readings, for the instruction of the *trivium* at Chartres and Paris, comp. Isaac (ibid., 64).

28. Ibid., 96.

29. On the *Kategorica* and the formation of the term *substantia,* see Jean-François Courtine, "Note complémentaire pour l'histoire du vocabulaire de l'être (Les Traductions latines d' ΟΥΣΙΑ et la compréhension romano-stoïcienne de l'être)," in *Concepts et catégories dans la pensée antique,* ed. Pierre Aubenque (Paris: Vrin, 1980), 33–87.

30. Here it is not necessary to enter into the much debated question of the identity or difference between the two terms. It is enough to note Bonitz's plausible solution to the question, which he proposes in his edition of the *Metaphysics:* "Potentiae notionem quum duobus vocabulis Aristoteles significet, τὸ δυνατόν et τὸ ἐνδεχόμενον, haec ubi accuratius usurpat, ita videtur distinguere, ut τὸ δυνατόν propria ac sua vi ad principium agendi vel patiendi re insitum pertineat, τὸ ἐνδεχόμvον autem eam signficet possibilitatem, per quam, si quid ponamus esse quod ἐνδέχεσθαι diximus, non verendum sit, ne nobis contradicamus ipsi" (*Metaphysik* 2 [1849]: 386–87; cited by Albrecht Becker-Freysing, *Die Vorgeschichte des philosophischen Terminus "contingens": Die Bedeutungen von 'contingens' bei Boethius und ihr Verhältnis zu den Aristotelischen Möglichkeitsbegriffen* (Heidelberg: F. Bilabel, 1938), 14 n.).

31. 22 b 21.

32. 32 b 5–15.

33. Aristotle's phrase reads literally as follows: "for all potentiality is impotentiality of the same and with respect to the same" (τοῦ αὐτοῦ καὶ κατὰ τὸ αὐτὸ πᾶσα δύναμις ἀδυνανία, *Metaphysics* 1046 a 32); see also 1050 b 10, in which Aristotle defines the possible as "possible both to be and not to be" (τὸ δυνατόν εἶναι καὶ εἶναι καὶ μὴ εἶναι).

34. See Becker-Freysing, *Die Vorgeschichte des philosophischen Terminus "contingens,"* 14–20.

35. At 18 b 16ff., for example, Boethius makes use of the form *contingit* to render the Greek ἐδέχεται, translating ἀλλὰ μὴν οὐδ' ὡς οὐδέτερόν γε ἀληθὲς ἐδέχεται λέγειν as "at vero nec quoniam neutrum verum est contingit dicere"; yet at 18 b 20 Boethius uses *contingere* as an equivalent of συμβαίνειν, proposing the Latin phrase *contingit affirmationem esse non veram* for the Greek τὴν κατάφασιν συμβαίνειν μὴ ἀληθὲς εἶναι. See Becker-Freysing, *Die Vorgeschichte des philosophischen Terminus "contingens,"* 16–17. Becker-Freysing notes, however, that Boethius consistently translates the perfective forms συμβεβηκός and συμβέηκεν by *accidens* and *accidit* (17 n. 29).

36. Ibid., 20.

37. Becker-Freysing refers, in particular, to Cassiodorus' statement in the *Institutiones* (ed. R. A. B. Mynors [Oxford: Clarendon Press, 1937], 128) that "Perihermeneias supra memoratus Victorinus transtulit in Latinum; cuius commentum sex libris patricius Boethius minutissima disputatione tractavit."

38. Whereas the Greek text reads συμβεβηκός ἐστιν, δ' ἐνδέχεται τῷ αὐτῷ ὑπαρχειν καὶ μὴ ὑπάρχειν, Victorinus' Latin rendition has "Accidens est, quod contingit alicui et esse et non esse." See Becker-Freysing, *Die Vorgeschichte des philosophischen Terminus "contingens,"* 21.

39. The force of Boethius' rendition can still be registered in William of Moerbeke's thirteenth-century translation of Aristotle's text. Although it is in many respects more literal than Boethius' version and although it avoids Boethius' translation of συμβαίνειν by *contingere* (opting instead for *accidere*), William of Moerbeke's *De interpretatione* does not call into question the translation of ἐνδεχόμενον by *contingens*.

40. See *Metaphysics* Θ, chaps. 1–3.

41. Ancii Manlii Severini Boethi, *Commentarii in librum Aristotelis Peri hermeneias*, ed. Karl Meiser (Leipzig: Teubner, 1877–80), 2:228.

42. On fire, see, for example, Ibid., 2:187.29; on snow, 2:236.5; on man, 187.27–29. Here I am indebted to Norman Kretzmann's essay "Nos Ipsi Principia Sumus: Boethius and the Basis of Contingency," in *Divine Omniscience and Omnipotence in Medieval Philosophy: Islamic, Jewish and Christian Perspectives*, ed. Tamar Rudavsky (Dordrecht: D. Reidel, 1985), 23–50, esp. 27–28.

43. A list of the passages in which Boethius gives examples of such necessitation can be found in Kretzmann, "Nos Ipsi Principa Sumus," 28.

44. *Commentarii in librum Aristotelis Peri hermeneias*, II, 190.1–6.

45. Ibid., II, 415.24–25.

46. Ibid., I, 105.29–106.1.

47. Becker-Freysing notes this ambiguity of Boethius' use of the predicate *contingens*, which he judges to be an "eigentümliche Bezeichung" and does not consider as such (*Die Vorgeschichte des philosophischen Terminus "contingens,"* 31). No doubt this is a case of a philological and linguistic trait that, once again, is of great philosophical importance. It is not difficult to imagine that Boethius' use constitutes a radicalization of Aristotle's treatment of contingency, which, in the wake of the Stoic notion of λόγος ἐνδιάθετος, insists on the unity of things and their expression. On λόγος ἐνδιάθετος and φαντασία λογική, see Claude Imbert, "Théorie de la représentation et doctrine logique dans le stoïcisme ancien," in *Les Stoïciens et leur logique, actes du colloque de Chantilly, 18–22 Septembre, 1976*, ed. Jacques Brunschwig (Paris: Vrin, 1978), 223–49.

48. See, for example, *Commentarii in librum Aristotelis Peri hermeneias*, 2:206; 1:105; 1:111. This principle is also stated in a number of other forms, as for example, at 2:216, in which we read that "propositonum veritas ex rerum substantia pendet."

49. Ibid., 2:208. In an influential essay Konstanty Michalski argued that this passage already expresses the idea of a "third truth value," which Lukasiewicz formulates in his works on multi-valued logic and which a number of fourteenth-century philosophers, according to Michalski, understand to be the specific truth value of future contingents. See Konstanty Michalsky, "Le problème de la volonté au XIVe siècle," in *Studia Philosophica, Commentarii Societatis Philosophiae Polonorum* (Leopoli, Poland: Ksazka, 1937), 2:286ff. Michalsky's claims have been called into question, most notably by Philotheus Boehner. See the essay that accompanies Boehner's edition of *The Tractatus de Praedesitatione et de praescientia dei et de futuris contingentibus of William Ockam* (New York: Franciscan Institute, 1945).

50. Ibid., 2:199.

51. Ibid., 2:193.

52. Ibid., 1:126.

53. Ibid., 1:108, 123.

54. Ibid., 2:240.

55. Ibid., 2:213.

56. Ibid., 1:126.

57. Ibid., 2:246, 247–48.

58. See *De concordia praescentia et praedestinationis et gratiae Dei cum libero arbitrio*, Vol. 1, chaps. 2 and 3, in *L'Oeuvre de S. Anselme de Cantorbéry*, ed. Michel Corbin (Paris: Éditions du Cerf, 1998), 5:247–252.

59. See the helpful comments on the subject by Léon Baudry, ed. *La querelle des futurs contingents (Louvain 1465–1475)* (Paris: Vrin, 1950), 10–11, who refers here to Anselm's *De veritate*, chap. 10; *Cur deus homo*, II, chaps. 17 and 18; and *Monologion*, chap. 18.

60. Petrus Abaelardus, *Dialectica: First Complete Edition of the Parisian Man-*

uscripts, ed. L. M. de Rijk (Assen: Van Gorcum and Com, 1956), bk. 2: *De Categoricis: De spiecierum differentiis categoricarum,* 210-13. All translations from the Latin are my own.

61. Ibid., 211.

62. Abelard's *Editio super Aristotelem de Interpretatione* is to be found in Mario Dal Pra, ed., *Pietro Abelardo: Scritti di logica* (Firenze: La Nuova Italia, 1969), in which Abelard's commentary on chap. 9 of Περὶ ἑρμηνείας appears on 99-113. Abelard's *glossae* on the same chapter in the *Logica Ingredientibus* are to be found in *Peter Abaelards Philosophische Schriften,* ed. Bernhard Geyer, Beiträge zur Geschichte der Philosophie des Mittelalters, vols. 1-3 (Münster: Aschendorffsche Verlagsbuchhandlung, 1919), 417-47. All translations from Abelard are my own.

63. This term, which might well merit a philological and philosophical study of its own, appears to have been formed by Boethius in his translation of Aristotle's text as a rendition of the Greek ὁπότερος, before becoming a technical term in medieval accounts of contingency. Thus, at 18 b 5, Boethius translates οὐδεν ἄρα οὔτε ἔστιν γίγνεται οὔτε ἀπὸ τύχης οὔ' ὁπότερ' ἔτυχεν as *nihil igitur neque est neque fit nec a casu nec utrumlibet.* Indicating "whichever," "either of the two," and, literally, "whichever you like" (*uter + libet*), it is a perfect expression of contingency: the necessary alternative between a term and its negation.

64. *Peter Abaelards Philosophische Schriften,* 435.23-25. This definition should be read together with the definition offered of *utrumlibet* in the *Editio super Aristotelem:* "Utrumlibet enim nihil magis habet se in propinquo futuro ad hoc ut dicatur sic est, quam ad hoc ut dicatur non sic est; vel non magis habet se ad hoc ut dicatur non sic est, quam ad hoc ut dicatur sic est, aut habebit in longunquo futuro" (*Pietro Abelardo: Scritti di logica,* 103).

65. I. M. Bochenski, *Formale Logik* (Munich: Karl Alber, 1956), 98.

66. *Peter Abaelards Philosophische Schriften,* 440.38-40.

67. 19 a 29-33. The Greek text reads as follows: λέγω δὲ οἷον ἀνάγκη μὲν ἔσεσθαι ναυμαχίαν αὔριον ἢ μὴ ἔσεσθαι, οὐ μέντοι ἔσεσθαι γε αὔριον ναυμαχίαν ἀναγκαῖον οὐδὲ μὴ γενέσθαι. γενέσθαι μέντοι ἢ μὴ γενέσθαι ἀναγκαῖον.

68. *Pietro Abelardo: Scritti di logica,* 112.

69. Ibid.

70. Ibid.

71. *Peter Abaelards Philosophische Schriften,* 443.16-19.

72. See, for example, *Commentarii in librum Aristotelis Peri hermeneias,* 2:206; 1:105; 1:111. This principle is also stated in a number of other forms, as for example, at 2:216, in which we read that "propositonum veritas ex rerum substanta pendet."

73. See Werner Hamacher, "Ou, séance, touche de Nancy, ici," in *Paragraph* 16:2 (1994): 219. Cf. Daniel Heller-Roazen, "Language, or No Language," *Diacritics* 29:3 (1999): 22-39.

74. Here I rely on the historical information provided by Isaac (*Le Peri*

Hermeneias en Occident, 87–97), who relates that Thomas attended Albert's lectures in Paris from 1248 to 1252. Albert's commentary can be found in *Alberti Magni Opera omnia,* ed. Auguste and Émile Borgnet, vol. 1, *Liber I Perihermeneias,* Tract. V: *De Passione partium enuntiantionis quae est oppositio* (Paris: Ludovic Vivès 1890–99), 411–23. Thomas's text has been recently republished in I. Leonis XIII, ed. *Sancti Thomae de Aquino, Opera omnia,* vol. 1: *Expositio libri peryermeneia (editio altera retractata)* (Rome: Commissio Leonina and Vrin, 1989).

75. *Alberti Magna Opera omnia,* 1:422.

76. Ibid.

77. Ibid., 423.

78. Cf. *Commentarii in librum Aristotelis Peri hermeneias,* 2:240.

79. I have elsewhere offered such a reading of Guilhem's *vers de dreit nien.* See Daniel Heller-Roazen, "The Matter of Language: Guilhem de Peitieus and the Platonic Tradition," *MLN* 113 (1998): 851–80.

80. Dante, *Convivio,* I, XII, 5–6, in *Opere minori,* II, vol. 1: *Convivio,* ed. Cesare Vasoli and Domenico De Robertis (1988; rpt., Milan-Naples: Ricciardi, 1995), 80–81: "E così il volgare è più prossimo quanto è più unito, che uno e solo è prima ne la mente che alcuno altro, e che non solamente per sé è unito, ma per accidente, in quanto è congiunto con le più prossime persone, sì come con li parenti e con li propri cittadini e con la propria gente. E questo è lo volgare proprio; lo quale è non prossimo, ma massimamente prossimo a ciascuno."

81. See Dante Alighieri, *Opere minori,* III, vol. 1: *De vulgari Eloquentia* and *Monarchia,* ed. Pier Vincenzo Mengaldo and Bruno Nardi (1979; rpt., Milan: Riccardo Ricciardi, 1996). Dante defines the vernacular as "prima locutio," in opposition to Latin, which he calls "locutio secundaria nobis, quam Romani grammaticam vocant," in bk. 1, I–II, 26–39. On Dante's distinction between the vernacular and Latin and its significance for medieval vernacular love poetry, see Giorgio Agamben, "The Dream of Language," in *The End of the Poem: Studies in Poetics,* trans. Daniel Heller-Roazen (Stanford: Stanford University Press, 1999), 53–56. On Dante and the grammarians, see André Pézard, *Dante sous la pluie de feu (Enfer, chant XV)* (Paris: Vrin, 1950), 133–222.

Two: The Nameless Lover

1. Spitzer's essay, which first appeared in *Traditio* 4, 414–22, can be found in Leo Spitzer, *Romanische Literaturstudien: 1936–1956* (Tübingen: Niemeyer, 1959), 100–113. On Spitzer's essay, see Paul Zumthor's observations in "From the Universal to the Particular in Medieval Poetry," *MLN* 85 (1970): 815–23.

2. See Charles S. Singleton, *Dante Studies I: Commedia, Elements of Structure* (Cambridge: Harvard University Press, 1954); as well as its continuation, *Journey to Beatrice* (Baltimore: Johns Hopkins University Press, 1958). On Singleton's reading of Dante, see Contini, "Un libro americano su Dante," in *Un'idea di Dante,* 217–24.

3. Roger Dragonetti, "Trois motifs de la lyrique courtoise confrontés avec les *Arts d'aimer* (Contribution à l'étude de la thématologie courtoise)," in *Romanica Gandensia VII: Études de philologie romane* (Ghent: Romanica Gandensia, 1959), 33.

4. Paul Zumthor, *Langue, texte, énigme* (Paris: Seuil, 1975), 163. The phrase is taken from the introduction to Zumthor's study of "Le 'je' du poète" (163–216).

5. Michel Zink, *La subjectivité littéraire* (Paris: Presses Universitaires de France, 1985), 16–17. Zink's formulation is Hegelian in inspiration, as Zink himself is the first to indicate; it draws on Hegel's own characterization of the Middle Ages, in his *Lectures on Aesthetics,* as the first period of the Romantic—that is, subjective—art form. For Hegel's discussion of Romantic art, see Georg Wilhelm Friedrich Hegel, *Werke in zwanzig Bänden,* 14: *Vorlesungen über die Ästhetik,* ed. Eva Moldenhauer and Karl Markus Michel (Frankfurt: Suhrkamp, 1994), 2:127–242.

6. See Spitzer, "Note on the Poetic and the Empirical 'I' in Medieval Authors," esp. 104, in which we read: "All the modern misunderstandings on the parts of commentators of the 'biographical approach' school are due to their confusion of the 'poetic I' with the empirical or pragmatical 'I' of the poet—who, in the very first lines of his poem, has taken care to present his 'poetic I' as representative of humanity: 'Nel mezzo del cammin di *nostra vita / Mi ritrovai* per una selva oscura.'" Spitzer argues, moreover, that the "I" of the Comedy is also double in its designation of "Dante the protagonist" and "Dante the narrator," two figures that, Spitzer notes, are "quite distinct" (ibid., 104 n. 1).

7. Zumthor, *Langue, énigme, texte,* 163.

8. Dragonetti, *Le mirage des sources: L'art du faux dans le roman medieval,* 218.

9. Sarah Kay, *Subjectivity in Troubadour Poetry* (Cambridge: Cambridge University Press, 1990), 1.

10. On the sense of *subjectum* as a translation of ὑποκείμενον and as the *subjectum metaphysicae* of medieval philosophy, see Jean-François Courtine, *Suarez et le système de la métaphysique* (Paris: Presses Universitaires de France, 1990), chap. 1, "Qu'est-ce que la métaphysique? L'horizon de la problématique scolastique," 9–30. On the term *mawḍuʿ,* see A.-M. Goichon, *Lexique de la langue philosophique d'Ibn Sina* (Paris: Brouwer, 1938), 438–39; and see A.-M. Goichon, *Introduction à Avicenne: Son épître des définitions* (Paris: Brouwer, 1933), 79–80.

11. This project is already apparent in the first of the Cartesian *Regulae ad directionem ingenii,* which clearly states that the ground of human knowledge (*humana sapientia, quae semper est*) is to be found not in a diversity of domains, as the Scholastics maintained, but, rather, in a single, constant realm—namely, that of the representative activity of the "I." Hence the second *regula:* "Circa illa tantum objecta oportet versari, ad quorum certam et indubitatam cognitionem nostra ingenia videntur sufficere." See René Descartes, *Oeuvres,* ed. Charles Adam and Paul Tannery (Paris: Vrin, 1996), 10:359–62.

12. See Émile Benveniste, "La nature des pronoms," "Structures de relations de personne dans le verbe," and "De la subjectivité dans le langage," in *Problèmes de linguistique générale* (Paris: Gallimard, 1966); and Roman Jakobson, "Shifters, Ver-

bal Catgeories and the Russian Verb," in *Selected Writings* (The Hague: Mouton, 1971), 2:130–47. It would doubtless be foolish to argue that Abelard "anticipated" Benveniste and Jakobson; the intellectual, institutional, and cultural differences between works of twelfth-century logic and twentieth-century structural linguistics are too great to be hastily assimilated.

13. On shifters, see Roman Jakobson, "Shifters, Verbal Categories, and the Russian Verb."

14. Geyer, *Peter Abaelards Philosophische Schriften*, 39.17–18.

15. Ibid., 39.18–26.

16. Ibid., 397.8–9.

17. See, for example, Apollonius Dyskolos, *Pron.* 26, 14: αἱ δε ἀντωνομίαι οὐδενοι τούτων παραστιτκαί, μόνον δὲ ουσίαι. Priscian continues this tradition when he defines *pronomina* as signifying "substantiam sine aliqua certa qualitate."

18. See Abelard, *Glosulae super Porphyriam*, in *Peter Abaelards Philosophische Schriften*, 527.7–9.

19. See Abelard's glosses on the *Categories*, in ibid., 221.4–6.

20. Louis Holtz, *Donat et la tradition de l'enseignement grammatical: Étude sur l'Ars Donati et sa diffusion (IVe–IXe siècle) et édition critique* (Paris: Centre National de la Recherche Scientifique, 1981), 588.2–3. The same definition is given in the *Ars maior* (ibid., 629.2–3).

21. This substitution is clearly expressed in a definition of the pronoun often found after the fifth century: "Pronomen est quasi pro nomine, eo quod fungitur officio nominis," Expl. 498, 35; "ideo pronomen dicitur, quia uicem fungitur nominis," Ps. Aug., *reg.*, 507, 7; "Pronomen dictum est quoniam fungitur officio nominis," Pom, 199, 20. See Holtz, *Donat et la tradition de l'enseignement grammatical*, 125, n. 1.

22. Dyonisius Thrax, in *Grammatici Graeci*, vol. 2, pt. 1, 1, 63: Ἀντωομία ἐστὶ λέξις ἀντι ὀνόματος παραλαμβανουένη ὁρισμένον δηλωτική, "the pronoun is a word that is placed in the position of a noun and that shows determinate *personae*." Apollonius Dyskolos, in *Grammatici Graeci*, vol. 2/1, 1, 9, 11: λέξιν ἀντ' ὀνόματος προσώπων ὡρισμένων παραστατικήν, "a word used in place of nouns for determinate *personae*." Priscian's definition of the pronoun (2, 577, 3) is a restatement of Donatus': "Pronomen est pars oriationis quae pro nomie proprio unius cuisque acciptur personasque finitas recipit." See Holtz, *Donat et la tradition de l'enseignement grammatical*, 126 n. 11.

23. See C. T. Lewis and C. Short, *A Latin Dictionary* (Oxford: Clarendon Press, 1879), 1355. On προσώπον and προσώπειον in Greek antiquity, see Françoise Frontisi-Ducroux, *Du masque au visage: Aspects de l'identité en Grèce ancienne* (Paris: Flammarion, 1995); on *persona*, see Philippe Cormier, *Généalogie de personne*, with a preface by Jean-Luc Marion (Paris: Criterion, 1994).

24. Priscian, for example, thus defines the *personae* of the pronouns as follows:

"prima est cum ipsa quae loquitur de se pronuntiat; secunda, cum de ea ad quam directo sermone loquitur; terita, cum de ea quae nec loquitur nec ad se directum accipt sermonem" (Keil, Heinrich, ed. *Grammatici Latini* [Leipzig: Teubner, 1855–80]), 2:584, 11.

25. See *Contra Eutychen* III, in Boethius, *The Theological Tractates and The Consolation of Philosophy,* trans. E. K. Rand, H. F. Stewart, and S. J. Tester (Cambridge: Harvard University Press, 1973), 86, in which we read: "Nomen enim personae videtur aliunde traductum, ex his scilicet personis quae in comoediis tragoediisque eos quorum interest homines repraesentabant. Persona vero dicta est a personando, circumflexa paenultima. Quod si acuatur antepaenultima, apertissime a sono dicta videbitur; idcirco autem a sono, quia concavitate ipsa maior necesse est volvatur sonus." In *Dictionnaire étymologique de la langue latine: Histoire des mots,* 4th ed. (Paris: Klincksieck, 1959, 500), A. Ernout and A. Meillet also refer to the Etruscan Φ*ersu,* "mask," as a possible origin of the term.

26. On Chrétien's prologues, see Tony Hunt, "The Rhetorical Background to the Arthurian Prologue: Tradition and the Old French Vernacular Prologues," *Forum for Modern Language Studies* 6 (1970): 1–23; on the medieval rhetorical treatments of beginnings, see Edmond Faral, *Les arts poétiques du XIIe et du XIIIe siècle: Recherches et documents sur la technique littéraire du Moyen Age* (Paris: Champion, 1962), 55–60.

27. Faral, *Les arts poétiques du XIIe et du XIIIe siècle,* 113, sec. 16. On Guillaume's use of the *sententia* as an opening device, see Karl D. Uitti, "Understanding Guillaume de Lorris: The Truth of the Couple in Guillaume's *Romance of the Rose,*" *Contemporary Readings of Medieval Literature* 8 (1989): 51–70, esp. 53.

28. See Badel, *Le Roman de la Rose au XIVe siècle,* 337. Hult makes a similar observation in characterizing the dream as a "paradigm for the human imperative to tell stories" (*Self-Fulfilling Prophecies,* 117). Scholars have often noted the general function of dreams in medieval literature as figures for literary works. See, for example, Steven F. Kruger, *Dreaming in the Middle Ages* (Cambridge: Cambridge University Press, 1992), 134: "The dream fiction, by representing in the dream an imaginative entity like fiction itself, often becomes self-reflexive. Dream fiction is especially liable to become metafiction, thematizing issues of representation and interpretation." On the poetic function of the dream, see also Jacqueline Cerquiglini-Toulet's remarks in the introduction to her edition and translation of Guillaume de Machaut, *La Fontaine amoureuse* (Paris: Stock, 1993), 16–19. On the historical background to Guillaume's invocation of the figure, see Ernest Langlois, *Origines et sources du Roman de la Rose* (Paris: Ernest Thorin, 1891).

29. The association of *songe* and *mensonge,* which is at once lexical and semantic, precedes, to be sure, the *Roman de la Rose,* and it extends far beyond it, to the point that, as a rhyme, it has justly been said to continue to "haunt" the literary production of the fourteenth century. See Jacqueline Cerquiglini[-Toulet], *"Un Engin si soutil": Guillaume de Machaut et l'écriture poétique au XIVe siècle,* Biblio-

thèque du XVe siècle, vol. 47 (Paris: Champion, 1985), 172. See also Renate Blumenfeld[-Kosinski], "Remarques sur *Songe/Mensonge*," *Romania* 101 (1980): 385–90; as well as Yakov Malkiel, "Ancient Hispanic *vera(s)* and *mentira(s)*: A Study in Lexical Polarization," *Romance Philology* 6 (1952–53): 121–72. Jean de Meun often invokes the association of the two terms in rhyming his octosyllables, as in the prologue, by the assonance of *songe* and *mençonge*. See, for example, vv. 9853–54, vv. 18464–65.

30. For a study of the problems of deceit, lying, and falsehood in the "second" *Roman de la Rose*, see Stakel, *False Roses*. On the problem of falsification in the Middle Ages more generally, see the rich study by Giles Constable, "Forgery and Plagiarism in the Middle Ages," *Archiv für Diplomatik* 29 (1983): 1–41.

31. Kruger, *Dreaming in the Middle Ages*, 135.

32. *Ad Herennium*, I, viii, 13. See *Cicero in Twenty Eight Volumes*, vol. 1: *Ad. C. Herennium, De Ratione Dicendi (Rhetorica ad Herennium)*, trans. Harry Caplan (Cambridge: Harvard University Press, 1989), 22.

33. *De inventione*, I, xix, 27. See *Cicero in Twenty Eight Volumes*, vol. 2: *De inventione, De Optimo Genere Oratorum, Topica*, trans. H. M. Hubbell (Cambridge: Harvard University Press, 1949), 54. The question of the truth value of dreams in the work of the *auctor* to whom Guillaume refers, Macrobius' *Commentarii in Somnium Scipionis*, remains an open one; but it is worth noting that the claim that dreams "may encourage the reader to good works (*in bonam frugem*)" by no means implies their veracity. See Macrobius, *Commentarii in Somnium Scipionis*, ed. Iacobus Willlis (Leipzig: Teubner, 1963), I, ii, 7. On theories of the *fabula* in the Middle Ages, see also Peter Dronke, *Fabula: Explorations into the Uses of Myth in Medieval Platonism* (Leiden: Brill, 1974). On Guillaume and Macrobius, see Jean Dornbush, "'Songes est senefiance': Macrobius and Guillaume de Lorris' *Roman de la Rose*," in Blumenfeld-Kosinski, Brownlee, Speer, and Walters, *Translatio studii*, 105–16; and, on Macrobius and the romance more generally, see Charles Dahlberg, "Macrobius and the Unity of the *Roman de la Rose*," *Studies in Philology* 58 (1961): 573–82; cf. Dahlberg's later essay "Love and the *Roman de la Rose*," *Speculum* 4 (1969): 568–84.

34. *De interpretatione*, 17 a 6–8.

35. *De lingua latina*, VI, 55.

36. Isidore of Seville, *Etymologiarum sive originum*, I, De gram., chap. 121. Cited in Edgar De Bruyne, *Études d'esthétique médiévale*, with a preface by Maurice de Gandillac (1946; rpt., Paris: Albin Michel, 1998), 1:97.

37. *Diff*, c. 221. Cited in De Bruyne, *Études d'esthétique médiévale*, 1:99.

38. Cited in De Bruyne, *Études d'esthétique médiévale*, 2:308 (in 1998 ed., 1:678).

39. On the loci classici for the formulation of this concept, see chapter 1 and, in particular, n. 4.

40. On the terms *overt* and *covert*, see Renate Blumenfeld-Kosinski, "*Overt*

and *Covert:* Amorous and Interpretative Strategies in the *Roman de la Rose,*" *Romania* 111 (1990): 443–44.

41. Jean de Meun refers to these notions at vv. 7135–38, in which Reason mentions *les integumanz aus poetes* (v. 7138). On the term *involucrum,* see M.-D. Chenu, "Involucrum: Le mythe selon les théologiens médiévaux," *Archives d'Histoire Doctrinale et Littéraire du Moyen Âge* 22 (1956): 75–79. Concerning "integumentum" (in particular in William of Conches), see Édouard Jeauneau, "L'usage de la notion d'*integumentum* à travers les gloses de Guillaume de Conches," in *Archives d'Histoire Doctrinale et Littéraire du Moyen Âge* 24 (1957): 35–100. On the general relation of myth to theoretical discourse in the twelfth century, see Brian Stock, *Myth and Science in the Twelfth Century: A Study of Bernard Sylvester* (Princeton, N.J.: Princeton University Press, 1972), 31–62; Dronke, *Fabula: Explorations into the Uses of Myth in Medieval Platonism;* and, on the so-called school of Chartres in particular, Winthrop Wetherbee, *Platonism and Poetry in the Twelfth Century: The Literary Influence of the School of Chartres* (Princeton, N.J.: Princeton University Press, 1972).

42. Erich Auerbach, "Figura," in *Scenes from the Drama of European Literature,* foreword by Paolo Valesio (Minneapolis: University of Minnesota Press, 1984), 11–76. On the affinities of Guillaume's *somnium* to Scripture as it was interpreted by the exegetical tradition, see also Rupert T. Pickens, "*Somnium* and Interpretation in Guillaume de Lorris," *Symposium* 28 (1974): 175–86, esp. 175–76.

43. See Auerbach, *Scenes from the Drama of European Literature,* 49–51. For Paul's use of the term τύπος see, for example, I Cor. 10:6, in which the Jews are called "figures of ourselves," τύποι ἡμῶν. See also I Cor. 11. For Paul's use of "allegory," see Gal. 4:21–31. In their conception of *figura,* the Church Fathers no doubt also develop a number of notions (such as those of τύπος and σκιά) already present in the exegetical theory of Philo Judaeus. On Philo and the Church Fathers, see Harry Austryn Wolfson, *The Philosophy of the Church Fathers* (Cambridge: Harvard University Press, 1970), esp. "Allegorical Method," 24–73.

44. Tertullian, *Adversus Marcionem* (3, 16), cited in Auerbach, *Scenes from the Drama of European Literature,* 28.

45. See *De doctrina christiana,* I, II: "Ex quo intellegitur quid appellem signa, res eas videlicet quae ad significandum aliquid adhibentur" (*L'istruzione christiana,* ed. Manlio Simonetti [Milan: Mondadori, 1994], 20.11–12).

46. On *glose* and *gloser,* see also vv. 18432–33 and 21543–44. Cf. Badel's incisive remarks on the terms *gloss* and *allegory* in *Le Roman de la Rose au XIVe siècle,* 13–20; Nancy Freeman Regalado, "'Des Contraires Choses: La Fonction poétique de la citation et des *exempla* dans le 'Roman de la Rose,'" *Littérature* 41 (1981): 62–81; and, in a different context, John Fleming's important chapter "Text and *Glose,*" in *The Roman de la Rose: A Study in Allegory and Iconography* (Princeton, N.J.: Princeton University Press, 1969), 3–53.

47. Marie de France, *Lais,* ed. Karl Warnke and trans. Laurence Harf-Lancner,

Livres de Poche: Lettres Gothiques 4523 (Paris: Le Livre de Poche, 1990, "Prologue," vv. 9–16: "Costume fu ans anciëns, / ces testimoine Priciëns, / es livres que jadis faiseient / assez oscurement diseient / pur cels ki a venir esteient / e ki aprendre le deveient, / que peüssent gloser la letre / e de lur sen le surplus metre." On Marie's prologue and the expression *gloser la letre,* see Leo Spitzer's classic essay, "The Prologue to the *Lais* of Marie de France and Medieval Poetics," *Romanische Literaturstudien,* 3–14.

48. On the concept of *allegoria* and its pertinence to the *Roman de la Rose,* see Badel's important discussion in *Le Roman de la Rose au XIVe siècle,* 13–14. Badel observes that, although the term *allegory* is often invoked by modern critics of the *Roman de la Rose* as a stylistic and rhetorical term, it was not used by the authors of the thirteenth and fourteenth centuries with reference to vernacular literature; in the Middle Ages *allegoria* appears to have been tied to the exegesis of Scripture alone. On allegory as a fundamental and in every sense essential structure of the literary work, see Martin Heidegger, "Der Ursprung des Kunstwerkes," in *Holzwege* (Frankfurt am Main: Klosterman, 1957), 7–68, esp. 9; for an English translation, see Martin Heidegger, *Poetry, Language, Thought,* trans. Alfred Hofstadter (New York: Harper and Row, 1971), 17–81, esp. 19–20. See also Walter Benjamin, *Ursprung des deutschen Trauerspiels,* in *Gesammelte Schriften,* ed. Rolf Tiedemann and Hermann Schweppenhäuser, vol. 1, pt. 1: 203–430, esp. "Allegorie und Trauerspiel," 336–409; Walter Benjamin, *The Origin of the German Tragic Drama,* trans. John Osborne (London: Verso, 1977), esp. 159–235.

49. Isidore of Seville, *Etymologiarum sive originum,* I, 37, 22.

50. *Le Roman de la Rose au XIVe siècle,* 340.

51. Evelyn Birge Vitz, "The 'I' of the *Roman de la Rose,*" *Genre* 6 (1973): 49.

52. See Émile Benveniste, "Les relations de temps dans le verbe français," in *Problèmes de linguistique générale,* 237–50.

53. *La subjectivité littéraire,* 161.

54. Ibid., 128.

55. A number of critics have judged the *Roman de la Rose* to be an autobiography. In Vitz's terms, for example, the *Rose* constitutes nothing less than "the first autobiographical novel—or romance—in French literature" ("'I' of the *Roman de la Rose,*" 50). On the *Rose* and autobiography, see also Kay, *Subjectivity in Troubadour Poetry,* 171ff.; Sarah Kay, *The Romance of the Rose,* Critical Introductions to French Literature, 100, 34–44; Hult's discussion in "Autobiographical Prophecy: Gates of Horn or Gates of Ivory?" (in *Self-Fulfilling Prophecies,* 137–69); and Claire Nouvet's incisive remarks in her essay "A Reversing Mirror: Guillaume de Lorris' *Romance of the Rose,*" in Blumenfeld-Kosinski, Brownlee, Speer, and Walters, *Translatio studii,* 189–205. On the applicability of the category of autobiography to medieval literature, see Zumthor, "Autobiographie au Moyen Âge?" in *Langue, texte, énigme,* 165–80; and Zink, *La subjectivité littéraire,* 171ff. On certain theoretical and historical problems implicit in the concept of the autobiographical

genre, see Paul de Man's remarks in "Autobiography as De-facement," in *The Rhetoric of Romanticism* (New York: Columbia University Press, 1984), 67–82. On the rhetorical structure of the poetic "I" of the romance more generally, see Stephen G. Nichols, "The Rhetoric of Sincerity in the *Roman de la Rose*," in *Romance Studies in Memory of Edward Billings Ham,* ed. Urban T. Holmes, California State College Publications, 2 (Hayward: California State College, 1967), 115–29.

56. See Emmanuelle Baumgartner, "The Play of Temporalities; or, The Reported Dream of Guillaume de Lorris," in Brownlee and Huot, *Rethinking the Romance of the Rose,* 22–38.

57. Claire Nouvet, "A Reversing Mirror: Guillaume de Lorris' *Romance of the Rose,*" 190.

58. Juan Ruiz, *Libro de buen amor,* ed. G. B. Gybbon-Monypenny (Madrid: Editorial Castalia, 1988), vv. 20–21.

59. Philippe Lejeune, *Le pacte autobiographique* (Paris: Seuil, 1975), 14. Lejeune's entire definition reads as follows: "Récit rétrospectif en prose qu'une personne réelle fait de sa propre existence, lorsqu'elle met l'accent sur sa vie intellectuelle, en particulier sur l'histoire de sa personnalité." On Lejeune's notion of autobiography, which is in many cases paradigmatic among literary critics, see De Man's comments in *Rhetoric of Romanticism,* 72–73.

60. To cite only five examples, from a corpus of almost three hundred manuscripts: BN fr 1559, a late-thirteenth-century manuscript, thus marks the rupture in the romance by means of a one-line comment printed in red, "Ci conmance maistre Jehan de Meun" (fol. 34 v); BN fr 25926, a fourteenth-century text, follows the same practice, briefly indicating the *incipit* of Jean's poem (fol. 30 r: "Ci conmence mestre Jehan de Meun"). BN fr 1567, another fourteenth-century text, indicates the start of Jean's text through the capitalization of the *E* with which the continuation begins (fol. 31 v): "Et si l'ai je perdu . . ."); BN fr 1569, also from the fourteenth century, contains a seven-line addition on the death of Guillaume and the "love" that "generously" motivated Jean to complete the romance (fol. 28 v). The practice of the earlier manuscripts of the *Rose* is still followed two centuries later, as shown by BN fr 19153, a fifteenth-century manuscript that indicates the beginning of the continuation both by a textual addition and an image of the second poet (fol. 31 v). For a summary of the textual and iconographic demarcations in a larger corpus of manuscripts of the romance, see Lori Walters, "Author Portraits and Textual Demarcation in Manuscripts of the *Romance of the Rose,*" in Brownlee and Huot, *Rethinking the Romance of the Rose,* 359–73; see also Sylvia Huot's essays, "'Ci parle l'aucteur': Rubrication of Voice and Authorship in the *Roman de la Rose* Manuscripts," *SubStance* 17 (1988): 42–48; "Scribe as Editor," 67–78; and, on the manuscript segmentation and reception of the work more generally, see Huot's fundamental study, *The Romance of the Rose and Its Medieval Readers.* See also David F. Hult's remarks on rubrication in his essay "Closed Quo-

tations: The Speaking Voice in the *Roman de la Rose*," *Yale French Studies* 67 (1984): 248–69, esp. 260–61.

61. Guillaume de Lorris and Jean de Meun, *Le Roman de la Rose*, ed. Armand Strubel, Lettres gothiques (Paris: Le Livre de Poche, 1992), 245n. In his translation Strubel has recourse to parentheses to introduce the term that is in fact lacking from the text of the original: "Et pourtant, je l'ai peut-être perdue (votre bienveillance): il ne manque pas grand-chose pour que j'en tombe dans le désespoir."

62. Cf. Paul Zumthor's penetrating remarks on the "welding" achieved by these verses in his essay "De Guillaume de Lorris à Jean de Meung," in *Études de langue et de littérature du Moyen Âge offerts à Félix Lecoy* (Paris: Champion, 1973), 609–20, esp. 661; cf. Hult, "Closed Quotations," 261–62.

63. The original prosodic and material forms of the *Roman de la Rose* may well also have called into question the identity of the object that may be "lost" at the opening of Jean's continuation. In the recitation of the verse with which the second part of the poem begins, *Et si l'ai je perdue, espoir,* the terminal *e* that marks *fiance* or *bienveillance* as the object of loss might have been effaced: before a word beginning with a vowel, a post-tonic *e* is often elided in Old French versification. The object of "loss," in this way, might become indeterminate; the discourse of the poem would then threaten to contain no mark of the grammatical identity of what has been lost. The loss, *a limine,* would itself be lost. On elision in Old French poetry, see Georges Lote, *Histoire du vers français*, pt. 1: *Le Moyen Âge,* vol. 3: *La poétique, le vers et la musique* (Paris: Hatier, 1955), "L'élision et l'hiatus," 73–93 and, on the feminine post-tonic *e* before a word beginning with a vowel, 79–84. Such an *e*, Lote writes, "is elided, as a general rule, starting with the oldest French texts, which clearly means that it was effaced in ordinary pronunciation" (79). On the elision of the feminine *e* at the end of polysyllables that precede words beginning with vowels, see Adolf Tobler, *Le vers français ancien et moderne,* trans. Karl Breul and Léopold Sudre (Paris: F. Viewer, 1885), 69; and A. Piaget, "Le 'Chemin de Vaillance' de Jean de Courcy, et l'hiatus de l'*e* final des Polysyllabes au XIVe et XVe siècles," *Romania* 27 (1898): 591. It would be well worth continuing the line of inquiry begun by Lori Walters in her important article "Author Portraits and Textual Demarcation in Manuscripts of the *Romance of the Rose,*" through a comparative examination of the exact textual forms of these crucial lines in the manuscript tradition.

64. On the figure of "martyrdom" in the *trouvères,* see Roger Dragonetti, *La technique poétique dans la chanson courtoise: Contribution à l'étude de la rhétorique médiévale* (Brugge: De Tempel, 1960), 114–15. Dragonetti cites, among others, *Drouart la Vache,* in which love appears as more of a *martire* "Que nus hom ne vous porroit dire" (*Drouart la Vache: Li Livres d'Amours,* ed. Robert Bossuat [Paris: Champion, 1926], vv. 176, 6). The *tópos* of "martyrdom" is Provençal in origin; on its function in Bernard de Ventadour, see Pierre Bec, "La douleur et son univers

poétique chez Bernard de Ventadour," in *Écrits sur les troubadours et la lyrique médiévale (1961–1991)* (Paris: Paradigme, 1992), 177–78.

65. It is worth recalling that, according to the medieval literary tradition, Jean de Meun is also the author of a *Testament,* which appears to make him the inventor of the "testamentary" genre in general. See Silvia Buzzetti Gallarati, *Le Testament Maistre Jehan de Meun: Un caso letterario* (Turin: Dell'Orso, 1989); on the literary structure and posterity of the the *Testament* attributed to Jean, see the enlightening study by Nancy Freeman Regalado, "Villon's Legacy from *Le Testament of Jean de Meun:* Misquotation, Memory, and the Wisdom of Fools," in *Villon at Oxford: The Drama of the Text, Proceedings of the conference held at St. Hilda's College Oxford, March 1996,* ed. Michael Freeman and Jane H. M. Taylor (Amsterdam: Rodopi, 1999), 282–311.

66. It is worth noting that the scene at issue is in fact located approximately 250 lines before the actual "midpoint" of the poem (in Lecoy's edition, for example, in which the poem ends at v. 21750, v. 10875 constitutes the numerical midpoint of the work). It is doubtful, in any case, that one could ever determine the exact "midpoint" of an octosyllabic poem, such as the *Roman de la Rose,* whose line numbering often differs significantly from manuscript to manuscript. The decisive scene has justly attracted the attention of the critics: see Karl D. Uitti, "From *Clerc* to *Poète:* The Relevance of the *Romance of the Rose* to Machaut's World," in *Machaut's World: Science and Art in the Fourteenth Century,* Annals of the New York Academy of Sciences, 314 (New York: New York Academy of Sciences, 1978), esp. 112–14; Kevin Brownlee, "Jean de Meun and the Limits of Romance: Genius as Rewriter of Guillaume de Lorris," in *Romance: Generic Transformations from Chrétien de Troyes to Cervantes,* ed. Kevin Brownlee and Marina Scordilis Brownlee (Hanover: Dartmouth College–University Press of New England, 1985), 114–34; Kevin Brownlee, "The Problem of Faux Semblant: Language, History, and Truth in the *Roman de la Rose,*" in *The New Medievalism,* ed. Marina S. Brownlee, Kevin Brownlee, and Stephen G. Nichols (Baltimore: Johns Hopkins University Press, 1991), 253–71, esp. 256–57; Nouvet, "A Reversing Mirror: Guillaume de Lorris' *Romance of the Rose*"; Sylvia Huot, *From Song to Book: The Poetics of Writing in Old French Lyric and Narrative Poetry* (Ithaca: Cornell University Press, 1987), 90–94; David F. Hult, "Language and Dismemberment: Abelard, Origen and the *Romance of the Rose,*" in Brownlee and Huot, *Rethinking the Rose;* Kay, *Romance of the Rose,* 39–41; Simon Gaunt, *Retelling the Tale: An Introduction to French Medieval Literature* (London: Duckworth Academic, 2001), chap. 5.

67. Dragonetti, *Le mirage des sources,* 204. Dragonetti, to be sure, considers there to be a second surprise implicit in this passage, which consists in the fact that the reader did not notice that "un conteur autre que Guillaume, déjà décédé . . . avrait pris la plume." It is difficult to see, however, how the medieval reader could experience such surprise, for he was informed of the end of Guillaume's text by the manuscript itself through rubrics and, often, anonymous scribal interventions

concerning the two authors (such as one finds, for example, in the version edited by Poirion and Strubel [see *Le Roman de la Rose,* 240–45]). On this instance of "textual autocitation," see also Brownlee, "Jean de Meun and the Limits of Romance," 130–31.

68. Love's commemoration of the love poets of Roman antiquity at vv. 10492–95 demands to be read together with the Ovidian text, of which it constitutes at once a "modernization" and a radicalization. Here Ovid himself is inscribed among the *sacri uates* (*Amores,* III, 9, v. 17) he once mourned; for, alongside "Tibullus" (v. 10478), "Gallus," and "Catillus," the romance now mentions "Ovides," the author of the original elegy in their honor. What is more, the first author of the romance itself is also classed among the dead poets, as Ovid's deictic indication of the fallen Tibullus, *Ecce puer veneris* (v. 7), is now translated and referred to Guillaume himself, who risks his life for love: *Vez ci Guillaume de Lorris* (v. 10496). See P. Ovidi Nasonis, *Amores, Medicamenta faciei femineae, Ars amatoria, Remedia amoris,* ed. E. J. Kenney (Oxford: Clarendon Press, 1961). As David Wallace has observed, the four poets mentioned by Amors appear to constitute the model for the society of the poetic *bella scuola* which greets Dante at the threshold of the Inferno. See David Wallace, "Chaucer and Boccaccio's Early Writings," in *Chaucer and the Italian Trecento,* ed. Piero Boitani (Cambridge: Cambridge University Press, 1983), 151. On Jean de Meun and Ovid more generally, see Minnis, *Magister amoris,* 35–118; John V. Flemimg, "Jean de Meun and the Ancient Poets," in Brownlee and Huot, *Rethinking the* Romance of the Rose, 81–100; Sylvia Huot, "The Medusa Interpolation in the *Romance of the Rose:* Mythographic Program and Ovidian Intertext," *Speculum* 62 (1987): 865–77; Kevin Brownlee, "Orpheus' Song Re-Sung: Jean de Meun's Reworking of *Metamorphoses,* X," *Romance Philology* 36 (1982): 201–9; Dragonetti, "Pygmalion ou les pièges de la fiction dans le *Roman de la Rose,*" in *Orbis Mediaevalis: Mélanges d'études de langue et de littérature médiévales offerts à R. R. Bezzola,* ed. Georges Güntert, Marc-René Jung, and Kurt Ringger (Bern: Francke, 1978), 89–111, rpt. in *La musique et les lettres,* 345–67; Thérèse Bouché, "Ovide et Jean de Meun," *Le Moyen Âge* 83 (1977): 71–87; Daniel Poirion, "Narcisse et Pygmalion dans le Roman de la Rose," in *Essays in Honor of Louis Francis Solano* (Chapel Hill: University of North Carolina Press, 1970), 153–65.

69. On Dante's naming and its affinities to the attribution of the name "Marcel" to the "I" of the *Recherche,* see Gianfranco Contini's observations in "Leggere Dante," in *Postremi esercizî ed elzeviri* (Turin: Einaudi, 1998), 5–12, esp. 8.

70. This essay appears in Contini's important volume, *Un'idea di Dante,* 245–83.

71. Ibid., 261.

72. *Inferno,* XXXIV, 25.

73. This figure appears, of course, well before the French and Italian poets, in their Provençal precursors. In a poem of Bernard de Ventadour, for example, we

thus read: "Deus! Devinar degra oimai / qu'eu MOR s'amor! Et a que?" (*Bernard de Ventadour, Troubadour du XIIe siècle: Chansons d'amour,* ed. by Moshe Lazar [Paris: Klincksieck, 1966], XL, vv. 35–36).

74. In Old French the quality of the vowel in *amour/amor* and in *mort* is not identical: see Mildred Katherine Pope, *From Latin to Modern French, with Especial Consideration of Anglo-Norman: Phonology and Morphology,* 2d rev. ed. (1882; rpt., New York: Barnes and Noble, 1973), 248–49; and Langlois comments on the language of the *Rose* in the first volume of his edition, 214–16. I am grateful to Simon Gaunt for having alerted me to this important phonetic distinction.

75. *Iambi et Elegi Graeci Ante Alexandrum Cantati,* vol. 1: *Archilochus, Hipponax, Theognidea,* ed. M. L. West (Oxford: Oxford University Press, 1971), Archilochos, fr. 191.

76. *Pindari carmina cum Fragmenta,* ed. B. Snell and H. Maehler (Leipzig: Teubner, 1975–80), fr. 123.

77. *Poetae melici Graeci,* ed. Denys Page (Oxford: Oxford University Press, 1962), Alkman 3.

78. *Poetarum Lesbiorum fragmenta,* ed. E. Loebel and D. Page (Oxford: Oxford University Press, 1955), fr. 31. 15–16.

79. *Catullus, Tibullus, and Pervigilium Veneris,* trans. F. W. Cornish, J. Postgate, and J. W. Mackail, 2d ed., revised by G. Goold (Cambridge: Harvard University Press, 1988), L, 58–61.

80. Guilhem de Peitieus, "Farai un vers de dreit nien" (183, 7), vv. 1–2; v. 19, in Nicolò Pasero, ed. *Guglielmo IX: Poesie* (Modena: S. T. E. M.-Mucchi, 1963), 92–93.

81. Raimbaut d'Aurenga, "Escotatz, mas no say que s'es" (389, 28), vv. 1–2, in *The Life and Works of the Troubadour Raimbaut d'Orange,* ed. Walter T. Pattison (Minneapolis: University of Minnesota Press, 1952), 152–53.

82. Ponç d'Ortafà, "Si ai perdut mon saber" (379, 2), vv. 1–8, in Martín de Riquer, *Los trovadores: Historia literaria y textos* (Barcelona: Planeta, 1975), 3:1313.

83. Moshe Lazar, *Bernard de Ventadour, Troubadour du XIIe siècle,* XLI, v. 7.

84. Giraut de Borneil, *The* Cansos *and* Sirventes *of Giraut de Borneil: A Critical Edition,* ed. Ruth Verity Sharman (Cambridge: Cambridge University Press, 1989), 62 (242, 3).

85. Moshe Lazar, *Bernard de Ventadour, Troubadour du XIIe siècle,* XLIII, v. 28.

86. Bonifaci Calvo, "Ora non moiro, nen uiuo, nen sei" (Tavani, 23, 2), in *The Poems of Bonifacio Calvo: A Critical Edition,* ed. William D. Horan (The Hague: Mouton and Co., 1966), 90–91, vv. 1–2.

87. "Trois motifs de la lyrique courtoise confrontés avec les *Arts d'aimer* (Contribution à l'étude de la thématologie courtoise)," 10. On the characterization of the trouvère as a suffering lover, see also Gioia Zaganelli, *Aimer, sofrir, joïr: I paradigmi della soggettività nella lirica francese dei secoli XII e XIII* (Florence: La Nuova Italia, 1982).

88. Holger Petersen Dyggve, *Gace Brulé, Trouvère champenois: Edition des chansons et étude historique* (Helsinki: Sociéte de Littérature Finnoise, 1951), R. 1414 v. 48; *The Lyrics and Melodies of Gace Brulé,* ed. and trans. Samuel N. Rosenberg and Samuel Danon, Garland Library of Medieval Literature, vol. 39 (New York: Garland, 1985), 24, vv. 48, 84–85. The Old French and English texts cited here, unless otherwise indicated, are those of Rosenberg and Danon's edition.

89. Dyggve, *Gace Brulé,* R. 686, v. 29; Rosenberg and Danon, *Lyrics and Melodies of Gace Brulé,* 52, v. 29, 176–77.

90. Dyggve, *Gace Brulé,* R. 828, vv. 37–40; Rosenberg and Danon, *Lyrics and Melodies of Gace Brulé,* 77, vv. 37–40, 260–61.

91. "Trois motifs de la lyrique courtoise confrontés avec les *Arts d'aimer* (Contribution à l'étude de la thématologie courtoise)," 29.

92. Cited by Langlois, *Le Roman de la Rose,* 2:334.

93. Guido Cavalcanti, *Rime, con le rime di Iacopo Cavalcanti,* ed. Domenico de Robertis (Turin: Einaudi, 1986), poem 8, "Tu m'hai sì piena di dolor la mente," vv. 9–14, p. 29.

94. Ezra Pound, *Translations,* intro. Hugh Kenner (New York: New Directions Press, 1963), 37.

95. *Purgatorio,* XXIV, 52–54: "E io a lui: 'I' mi son un che, quando, / Amor mi spira, noto, e al quel modo / ch'e' ditta dentro vo significando." On this passage and Dante's encounter with Bonagiunta, see Guglielmo Gorni, "Il nodo della lingua," in *Il nodo della lingua e il verbo d'amore: Studi su Dante e altro duecentisti,* Saggi di "Lettere italiane," vol. 29 (Florence: Leo Olschki, 1981), 13–21.

96. On this motif, see Pierre Bec, *Écrits sur les troubadours et la lyrique médiévale (1961–1991),* 186; see also Simon Gaunt, "A Martyr to Love: Sacrificial Desire in the Poetry of Bernart de Ventadorn," *Journal of Medieval and Early Modern Studies* 31 (2001): 477–506.

97. On Pygmalion, see Dragonetti, "Pygmalion ou les pièges de la fiction dans le Roman de la Rose," 89–111, rpt. in *La musique et les letters,* 345–67; cf. Poirion, "Narcisse et Pygmalion dans le Roman de la Rose"; and Douglas Kelly, *Internal Differences and Meanings in the* Roman de la rose (Madison: University of Wisconsin Press, 1995), 76–78.

98. *Langue, text, énigme,* 170; Huot, *From Song to Book,* 1ff.

99. Langlois has noted that Jean's singular discussion of the phoenix cannot be reduced to any of the accounts of the mythical bird in the *auctores* (such as Ovid, *Met.* XV, 392ff; Statius, *Silue* II, IV, 37; Martial, Epig., VI, VII, 1). See Langlois, *Origines et sources du Roman de la Rose,* 165–66. On the phoenix in Nature's account of genus and species, see Pierre-Yves Badel's essay "Jean de Meun, le phénix et les logiciens," *Romania* 110 (1989): 167–80; see also Faith Lyons, "Some Notes on the *Roman de la Rose*—the Golden Chain and Other Topics in Jean de Meun," in *Studies in Medieval Literature and Languages in Memory of Frederick Whitehead,* ed. W. Rothwell, W. R. J. Barron, David Blamires, and Lewis Thorpe (New York: Manchester University Press, 1973), 201–8, esp. 206–8.

100. In the Ovidian elegy evoked earlier by the romance, the love poet appears to "burn" in his death: we read that Tibullus *ardet in extructo corpus inane rogo* (*Amores*, III, 9, 6).

101. See Frédéric Godefroy, *Dictionnaire de l'ancienne langue française et de tous ses dialectes: Du IXe au XVe siècle* (1884; rpt., New York: Kraus Reprint Corp., 1961), 3:567–68, in which this passage in the *Rose* is cited as an example of the sense of *essart* as "destruction." In their *Altfranzösisches Wörterbuch* (Wiesbaden: Franz Steiner, 1954), 3:1291–92, Adolf Tobler and Erhard Lommatzsch follow Godefroy's definition of the word, also citing its appearance in the *Rose's* discussion of the phoenix. Strubel translates Jean's phrase as follows: "Voilà comment il achève la destruction de son corps" (*Le Roman de la Rose,* 839).

102. See Alain Rey, *Dictionnaire historique de la langue française* (Paris: Le Robert, 1992), 1:729.

103. See S. F. Niemeyer, *Mediae Latinitatis Lexicon minus* (Leiden: Brill, 1976), 386.

104. See, for example, A. J. Greimas, *Dictionnaire de l'ancien français* (Paris: Larousse Bordas, 1997), 221.

Three: Fortune

1. The relative wealth of secondary literature concerning Fortune in the *Roman de la Rose* bears witness to the importance of this figure in the poem as a whole. See Stanley Leman Galpin, "Fortune's Wheel in the *Roman de la Rose*," *PMLA* 24 (1909): 332–42; André Pézard, "Lune et Fortune chez Jean de Meung et chez Dante," in *Studi in onore di Italo Siciliano* (Florence: Olschki, 1966), 2:985–95; Armand Strubel, "La personnification allégorique, Avatar du mythe: Fortune, Raison, Nature et Mort chez Jean de Meun," in *Pour une mythologie du Moyen Âge,* ed. Laurence Harf-Lancner and Dominique Boutet (Paris: École Normale Supérieure, 1988), 61–72; Valérie Gallent-Fasseur, "Des deux arcs d'Amour à la maison de Fortune: Graces et disgraces selon le *Roman de la Rose*," in *Le Beau et le laid au Moyen Âge: Actes du 24e colloque, Aix-en-Provence, février 1999 du Centre universitaire d'études et de recherches médiévales d'Aix* (Aix-en-Provence: CUERMA, Université de Provence, 2000), 105–21; Barbara Thompson, "The Paradoxes of Fortune in the *Roman de la Rose*," *Chimères* (Fall 1972): 13–47. The figure of Reason has been the subject of one of the most extensive debates among scholars of the romance, who have disagreed on the authority with which she speaks in the poem. For the position that she constitutes a privileged representative of the author of the work, see D. W. Robertson, *A Preface to Chaucer: Studies in Medieval Perspectives* (Princeton, N.J.: Princeton University Press, 1962), esp. 91–104, 196, and 361; Fleming, *Romance of the Rose;* as well as *Reason and the Lover;* against such a thesis, see Winthrop Wetherbee, "The Literal and the Allegorical: Jean de Meun and the *de Planctu Naturae,*" *Mediaeval Studies* 33 (1971): 264–91; Thomas D. Hill, "Narcissus, Pygmalion, and the Castration of Saturn: Two Mythological Themes

in the *Roman de la Rose*," *Studies in Philology* 71 (1974): 404–26; Michael D. Cherniss, "Jean de Meun's *Reson* and Boethius," *Romance Notes* 6 (1975): 678–85; Donald W. Rowe, "Reson in Jean's *Roman de la Rose:* Modes of Characterization and Dimensions of Meaning," *Mediaevalia* 10 (1988): 97–126. See also, in a different context, Pierre-Yves Badel, "Raison 'fille de Dieu' et le rationalisme de Jean de Meun," in *Mélanges de langue et de littérature du moyen âge et de la renaissance offerts à Jean Frappier* (Geneva: Droz, 1970), 1:41–52; and see Lionel J. Freedman, "Jean de Meun and Ethelred of Rievaulx," *L'Esprit Créateur* 2 (1962): 135–41.

2. Roger Dragonetti has commented on this anagram in "Pygmalion ou les pièges de la fiction dans le *Roman de la Rose*," 99.

3. On Jean's use of the *auctores* in his discussion of Fortune, see later discussion, in particular, sec. 2 and 4; for other discussions of the subject, see Galpin, "Fortune's Wheel in the *Roman de la Rose*"; Langlois, *Origines et sources du Roman de la Rose* (Paris: Ernest Thorin, 1891), 95–97 and 148–50; Patch, *Fortuna in Old French Literature, Smith College Studies in Modern Languages* 4:4 (July 1923): 6–11; Lecoy, *Le Roman de la Rose,* 1:280–89.

4. Langlois, *Origines et sources du Roman de la Rose,* 94. On the severe judgments passed on Jean de Meun by so many of the first Romance philologists, see "Introduction."

5. De Lorris and de Meun, *Le Roman de la Rose,* 283n, in which Strubel remarks: "Plutôt qu'Amour, c'est Fortune qui se pose désormais en principal adversaire de Raison: le point de départ est oublié, et le discours cède à son propre mouvement, tendant vers l'exhaustivité."

6. See W. Walde Fowler, "Fortuna (Roman)," in *The Encyclopaedia of Religion and Ethics,* ed. James Hastings (1926–76; rpt., Edinburgh: T. and T. Clark, 1994), 6:98.

7. For an example of the expression *Fors Fortuna,* see Petron. 120, v. 78ff. On the synonymy of the two terms, see the entry under "Fortuna," in *Paulys Real-Encyclopädie der Classischen Altertumswissenschaft,* ed. Georg Wissowa and Wilhelm Kroll (Stuttgart: J. B. Metzlersche Buchhandlung, 1912), 7:12–42.

8. On the etymology of *Fortuna,* see Jacqueline Champeaux, *Fortuna: Le culte de la fortune à Rome et dans le monde romain,* vol. 1: *Fortuna dans la religion archaïque* (Rome: École Française de Rome, 1982), 428–37. On the root **bher-* and its Latin representative, *fero,* see the observations in Émile Benveniste, *Le vocabulaire des institutions indo-européennes* (Paris: Minuit, 1969), 1:11.

9. Georges Dumézil, *La religion romaine archaïque, avec un appendice sur la religion des Étrusques,* 2d ed. (1966; rpt., Paris: Payot, 1974), 424.

10. On the distinction between *di indigetes* and *di novensides,* see the classic work by Jesse Bendict Carter, *The Religion of Numa and Other Essays in the Religion of Ancient Rome* (London: Macmillan, 1906), 9.

11. See Jerold C. Frakes, *The Fate of Fortune in the Early Middle Ages: The Boethian Tradition,* Studien und Texte zur Geistesgeschichte des Mittelalters, vol. 23 (Leiden: Brill, 1988), 11.

12. See Jacqueline Champeaux, *Fortuna: Le culte de la fortune à Rome et dans le monde romain*, vol. 1: *Fortuna dans la religion archaïque*.

13. See *Paulys Real-Encyclopädie der Classischen Altertumswissenschaft* (12), which refers to Ennius in Cic., *off.* 38: *quidve ferat fors.*

14. On τύχη, see St. George Stock, "Fortune (Greek)," in Hastings, *Encyclopaedia of Religion and Ethics*, 6:93–96.

15. On Fortuna in Roman letters, see Howard Rollin Patch, *The Tradition of the Goddess Fortuna in Roman Literature and the Transitional Period*, Smith College Studies in Modern Languages 3:3 (1922).

16. Fowler, "Fortuna (Roman)," 99.

17. Cic. *Div.*, 2, 15.

18. *Ex Ponto*, IV, *E* III, 31.

19. *Tristia*, V, *Eleg.* VIII, 15.

20. *Historia naturalia*, II, 22.

21. Cic., *De divinatione*, II, 7.

22. Jacqueline Champeaux, *Fortuna: Le culte de la fortune à Rome et dans le monde romain*, vol. 1: *Fortuna dans la religion archaïque*, 428.

23. Augustine, *De civ. Dei*, 4, 11.

24. Ibid., 18, 5, 9.

25. Isidore of Seville, *Etymologiarum sive originum*, VIII, xi, 94.

26. Cic., *De divinatione*, II, 7.

27. Boethius, *Theological Tractates* and *The Consolation of Philosophy*, trans. E. K. Rand, H. F. Stewart and S. J. Tester (Cambridge: Harvard University Press, 1973), 174. 6; 175. Unless otherwise indicated, the English text quoted is that of this edition. The first number cited is that of the Latin text, which is followed by the line number; the second page number is that of the English translation.

28. Ibid., 224.5–18; 225.

29. On *fortuna bona* and *fortuna mala*, see Gottfried Kirchner, *Fortuna in der Dichtung und Emblematik des Barock: Tradition und Bedeutungswandel eines Motivs* (Stuttgart: Metzler, 1970), 6.

30. Jean's translation has been most recently published and edited by V. L. Dedeck-Héry, "Boethius' *De Consolatione* by Jean de Meun," *Mediaeval Studies* 14 (1952): 165–275. On Jean de Meun's translation of Boethius, see Glynnis M. Cropp, "Le Livre de Boece de Consolacion: From Translation to the Glossed Text," in *The Medieval Boethius: Studies of the Vernacular Translations of De Consolatione Philosophiae*, ed. A. J. Minnis (Cambridge: D. S. Brewer, 1987), 63–88; Howard Rollin Patch, *The Tradition of Boethius: A Study of His Importance in Medieval Culture* (New York: Oxford University Press, 1935), 63–65. On the medieval French translations of *De Consolatione* more generally, see Gynnis M. Cropp, "The Medieval Tradition," in *Boethius in the Middle Ages: Latin and Vernacular Tradition of the Consolatio Philosophiae*, ed. Maarten J. F. M. Hoenen and Lodi Nauta (Leiden: Brill, 1997), 243–66. On Jean de Meun and Boethius, see Karl August Ott, "Jean de Meun und Boethius: Über Aufbau und Quellen des Rosenro-

mans," in *Philologische Studien: Gedenkschrift für Richard Kienast,* ed. Ute Schwab and Elfriede Stutz, Germanische Bibliothek, ser. 3: Untersuchungen und Einzeldarstellungen (Heidelberg: C. Winter, 1978), 193–227.

31. V. L. Dedeck-Hery, "Boethius' *De Consolatione* by Jean de Meun," 204, bk. 2, prose 8, ll. 11–12.

32. Boethius, *Theological Tractates* and *The Consolation of Philosophy,* 224.5–11.

33. V. L. Dedeck-Hery, "Boethius' *De Consolatione* by Jean de Meun," 203–4, ll. 6–12.

34. Boethius, *Theological Tractates* and *The Consolation of Philosophy,* 225.

35. It has often been noted by historical linguists that the Gallo-Roman language does not fully preserve the complex system of the Latin demonstrative pronouns, which function to denote three distinct spatial fields—the near, the distant, and the medial, represented respectively by *hic, ille,* and *iste.* Instead of three positions defined with reference to the speaker, there are thus only two in Old French, expressed by the words *cist* (derived from *iste*) and *cil* (derived from *ille*). It is these two forms that Jean might have used in his translation of *De Consolatione Philosophiae,* had he not chosen the form we discussed earlier. On the morphology of demonstrative pronouns in Old French, see Gaston Zink, *Morphologie du français médiéval* (Paris: Presses Universitaires de France, 1989), 73–78. On their syntactic function, see Philippe Ménard, *Syntaxe de l'ancien français,* 4th ed. (Bordeaux: Éditions Bière, 1994), 30–34. See also the summary remarks in Gérard Moignet, *Grammaire de l'ancien français: Morphologie-Syntaxe,* 2d ed. (Paris: Klincksieck, 1979), 42–44.

36. V. L. Dedeck-Hery, "Boethius' *De Consolatione* by Jean de Meun," bk. 2, prose 8, 204; Boethius, *Theological Tractates* and *The Consolation of Philosophy,* 224. 7–8.

37. See Langlois, *Origines et sources du Roman de la Rose,* 136.

38. See note to v. 4813 in Lecoy, *Le Roman de la Rose,* 1:281.

39. See v. 3958: *Ele* [Fortune] *a une roe qui torne.* . . . On the figure of the wheel of Fortune and its history, see Alfred Doren, "Fortuna im Mittelalter und in der Renaissance," in *Vorträge der Bibliothek Warburg,* ed. Fritz Saxl, vol. 2: *Vorträge 1922–1923,* pt. 1 (Leipzig: B. G. Teubner, 1924), 71–144; Pierre Courcelle, *La Consolation de philosophie dans la tradition littéraire: Antécédents et postérité de Boèce* (Paris: Études Augustiniennes, 1967), 101–58; Galpin, "Fortune's Wheel in the *Roman de la Rose.*" On Fortune and her wheel in medieval poetry, see Jean Frappier, *Étude sur la Mort le Roi Artu: Roman du XIIIe siècle* (Geneva: Droz-Minard, 1961), chap. 3, "La roue de Fortune," 258–88; and see Jacqueline Cerquiglini[-Toulet], *"Un Engin si soutil": Guillaume de Machaut et l'écriture poétique au XIVe siècle* Bibliothèque du XVe siècle, vol. 47 (Paris: Champion, 1985), 56–76.

40. See *De Consolatione* II, prose 1, in which Philosophy says: "Tu vero volventis rotae impetum retinere conaris? At, omnium mortalium stolidissime, si manere incipit, fors esse desistit" (Boethius, *Theological Tractates* and *The Conso-*

lation of Philosophy, 178. 59–62). Jean refers to this passage at vv. 6380–82, in which Reason says: "Veuz tu sa roe retenir, / qui ne peut estre retenue / ne par grant gent ne par menue?" The text of Jean's translation of passage in *De Consolatione,* which is very close to that of the *Rose,* makes this clear: "Te efforces tu a retenir le cours isnel de sa roe tournant? O tu li tres fols de touz les mortiex hommes, se elle commence a estre estable, elle delaisse a estre Fortune" (V. L. Dedeck-Hery, "Boethius' *De Consolatione* by Jean de Meun," 188.59–61).

41. *Peter Abaelards Philosophische Schriften,* ed. Bernhard Geyer, Beiträge zur Geschichte der Philosophie des Mittelalters, vols. 1–3 (Münster: Aschendorffsche Verlagsbuchhandlung, 1919), 440.38–40.

42. Cf. vv. 7995–7998, in which Ami calls into question the possibility of speaking of Fortune's "taking" any of her goods: "Toli? Par foi, non pas, je ment, / ainz prist ses choses proprement, / car por voir sai que se mien fussent, / ja por lui lessié ne m'eüssent."

43. Boethius, *Theological Tractates* and *The Consolation of Philosophy,* 176.31.

44. Gérard Paré, *Les idées et les lettres au XIIIe siècle: Le Roman de la Rose,* Bibliothèque de philosophie, vol. 1 (Montreal: Université de Montréal, 1947). Franz Walter Müller's *Der Rosenroman und der lateinische Averroismus des 13. Jahrhunderts* (Frankfurt am Main: Vittorio Klostermann, 1947) constitutes a further work on the relation of the *Rose* to thirteenth-century thought; yet it is unfortunately of little use, on account of the lack of precision with which it treats both "Latin Averroism" and the *Rose,* as Badel has indicated (see *Le Roman de la Rose au XIVe siècle,* 34 n. 80).

45. Poirion, *Le Roman de la Rose,* 128.

46. Gisela Hilder, *Der scholastische Wortschatz bei Jean de Meun: Die Artes Liberales,* Beihefte zur Zeitschrift für Romanische Philologie, vol. 129 (Tübingen: Max Niemeyer, 1972). On Jean de Meun and Scholasticism more generally, see also Mario Mancini "Parigi 1270: Filosofia e racconto nel 'Roman de la Rose' di Jean de Meun," *Rivista di Estetica* 34-35 (1994-95): 3-27; and Mary Katherine Tilman, "Scholastic and Averroistic Influences on the *Roman de la Rose,*" *Annuale Mediaevale* 11 (1970): 89-106.

47. Ibid., xi. See also Hilder's "Zusammenfassende Bemerkungen," 170-84. Hilder's important research thus led her to disprove Curtius' claim that "Jean de Meun ist Literat, . . . nicht Universitätsphilosoph" (Ernst Robert Curtius, *Europäische Literatur und lateinisches Mittelalter* [Bern: Francke, 1965], 478) as well as Zumthor's similar contention that Jean de Meun remains "untouched" by Scholasticism.

48. The editors of the *Aristoteles latinus* believe the *translatio vetus* of the *Physics,* which is attributed to Jacob of Venice, to have been completed before the middle of the twelfth century. See *Aristoteles Latinus,* ed. Gérard Verbeke, 7:1-2: *Physica: Translatio vetus,* ed. Fernard Bossier and Jozef Brams (Leiden: Brill, 1990), pt. 1, xxii. All Latin citations from Aristotle's *Physics* in this chapter, unless other-

wise indicated, refer to the text of this edition. On the *Physics* more generally in the Middle Ages, see Helen S. Lang, *Aristotle's Physics and Its Medieval Varieties* (Albany: State University of New York Press, 1992), which unfortunately does not consider the problem of fortune and chance.

49. For Siger's texts on fortune, see *Siger de Brabant: Écrits de logique, de morale et de physique,* ed. Bernardo Bazán (Louvain: Publications Universitaires, 1974), 162–71.

50. *Physics,* 197 a 5 ff. The Greek text cited throughout the chapter, unless otherwise indicated, is that printed in *Aristotle in Twenty-Three Volumes,* vol. 4: *The Physics, Books I–IV,* trans. Philip H. Wicksteed and Francis M. Cornford, rev. ed. (Cambridge: Harvard University Press, 1957).

51. See 197 a 36 ff.

52. Pierre Aubenque, *Le problème de l'être chez Aristote: Essai sur la problématique aristotélicienne* (Paris: Presses Universitaires de France, 1962), 141–44.

53. See, for example, *Metaphysics,* E 1026 a 33–b 2, in which "Being by accident" appears as one of the ways in which Being is said.

54. Rémi Brague, *Aristote et le problème du monde: Essai sur le contexte cosmologique et anthropologique de l'ontologie* (Paris: Presses Universitaires de France, 1988), 359.

55. See *Physics,* 197 a 5 ff.

56. *Physics,* 196 b 25–30.

57. This formulation is to be found at *An. Pr.* 32 b 10.

58. *Metaphysics,* 1026 b 21.

59. 1064 b 30.

60. 1065 a 4.

61. 1027 a 20.

62. Aet. I. 29. 7: Ἀναξαγόρας καὶ Δημόκριτος καὶ οἱ Στωικοὶ ἄδηγον αἰτίαν ἀνθρωπίνῳ λογισμῷ. Aristotle himself seems to refer to this doctrine when he writes that to some, fortune seems "inscrutable to the human mind" (*causa inmanifesta humano intellectui,* ἄδηλος δὲ ἀνθρωπίνῃ διανοίᾳ, 196 b 5). Cf. also 197 a 10, in which Aristotle uses a similar phrase, describing fortune as ἄδηλος ἀνθρώπῳ.

63. 197 a 18–22. The Greek text reads as follows: καὶ τὸ φάναι εἶναί τι παράλογον τὴν τύχην ὀρθῶς. ὁ γὰρ λόγος ἢ τῶν ἀεὶ ὄντων ἢ τῶν ὡς ἐπὶ τὸ πολύ, ἡ δὲ τύχη ἐν τοῖς γιγνομένοις παρὰ ταῦτα. ὥστ' ἐπειδὴ ἀόριστα τὰ οὕτως αἴτια, καὶ ἡ τύχη ἀόριστον.

64. *Sancti Thomae Aquinitatis, doctoris angelici, Opera omnia, iussu impensaque Leonis XIII. M. Edita, Tomus secunda: Commentarius in octo libros physicorum Aristoteles* (Rome: Ex Typographia Polyglotta, 1884), 80: "Ponit autem differentiam inter causam per se et causam per accidens: quia causa per se est finita et determinata; causa autem per accidens est infinita et indeterminata, eo quod infinita uni possunt accidere."

65. Ibid., 82.

66. Ibid., 80. The same example is to be found again on 84.

67. Boethius, *Theological Tractates* and *The Consolation of Philosophy*, V, prose 1, 386–88, ll. 40–42.

68. 1025 a 15–1025 a 30; the text cited is that printed in *Aristoteles Latinus*, ed. Gérard Verbeke, vol. 25, pt. 3. 2: *Metaphysica, Lib. I–XIV, recensio et translatio Guillelmi de Moerbeka,* ed. Gudrun Vuillemin-Diem (Leiden: Brill, 1995). According to the most recent editors of this text, it constitutes one of William's first translations, probably dating from between 1260 and 1270 (ibid., pt. 3. 1, 2).

69. *Alberti Magni Ordinis Fratrum Praedicatorum, Opera Omnia*, vol. 16, pt. 1: *Metaphysica, Librus quinque priores,* ed. Bernhard Geyer (Westphalia: Aschendorff, 1960), 299.

70. Both the translation of W. D. Ross and Hugh Tredennick render the relative pronoun ᾗ in the phrase οὐχ ᾗ ἀλλα' ᾗ ἕτερον by "in virtue of," thereby falsifying the sense of the Aristotelian original. For D. W. Ross's version, see *Aristotle's Metaphysics* (Oxford: Clarendon Press, 1924, rpt. in *The Complete Works of Aristotle: The Revised Oxford Translation,* ed. Jonathan Barnes [Princeton, N.J.: Princeton University Press, 1984]): "The accident has happened or exists,—not in virtue of itself, however, but of something else." Cf. *Aristotle in Twenty-Three Volumes: The Metaphysics, Books I–IX,* trans. Hugh Tredennick (Cambridge: Harvard University Press, 1933): "The accident happens or exists, but in virtue not of itself but of something else."

71. Helene Weiss was perhaps the first to call attention to the importance of the Aristotelian formula οὐχ ᾗ αὐτὸ ἀλλα' ᾗ ἕτερον. See Helene Weiss, *Der Zufall in der Philosophie des Aristoteles* (London: Wyndham Printers, 1935), 187–92. See also Brague's analysis of the phrase in *Aristote et le problème du monde,* 360–62.

72. As such, Fortune thus appears as a case of the figure that, in the words of one eminent historian of medieval poetics, "the Middle Ages overused to the point of abuse." See Faral, *Les arts poétiques du XIIe et du XIIIe siècle,* 73. On personification in thirteenth-century literature, see also Armand Strubel, *La Rose, Renart et le graal: La littérature allégorique en France au XIIIe siècle* (Geneva: Slatkine, 1989), 69–76. Many scholarly works have been dedicated to medieval literary works of allegorical personification. See, among others, R. Glaser, "Abstractum agens und Allegorie im älteren Französisch," *Zeitschrift für romanische Philologie* 59 (1953): 43–122; Siegfried Heinimann, *Das Abstraktum in der französischen Literatursprache des Mittelalters,* Romanica Helvetica, vol. 73 (Bern: Francke, 1963); Charles Muscatine, "The Emergence of Psychological Allegory in the Old French *Roman*," *PMLA* 68 (1953): 1160–82; Marc-René Jung, *Études sur le poème allégorique en France au Moyen Âge,* Romanica Helvetica, vol. 82 (Bern: Francke, 1971); R. W. Franck, "The Art of Reading Medieval Personification Allegory," *English Literary History* 20 (1953): 237–50; B. H. Bronson, "Personification Reconsidered," *English Literary History* 14 (1947): 163–77; C. S. Lewis, *The Allegory of Love: A Study in*

Notes to Pages 86–87

Mediaeval Tradition (Oxford: Oxford University Press, 1938); and, with attention to the *Rose,* Paul Zumthor, "Narrative and Anti-Narrative: *Le Roman de la Rose,*" *Yale French Studies* 51 (1974): 181–204.

73. *Ad Herennium* IV, 52, 65, in *Cicero in Twenty-Eight Volumes,* vol. 1: *[Cicero] Ad C. Herennium, De Rationi Dicendi (Rhetorica ad Herennium),* 394.

74. Quintilian IX, 2, 31: *Ac sunt quidam, qui has demum* προσωποποιΐας *dicant, in quibus et corpora et verba fingimus.*

75. Cic., *De oratore,* III, 20.

76. *Ad Herennium* IV, 53, 66, as printed in *[Cicero] Ad C. Herennium, De Rationi Dicendi (Rhetorica ad Herennium),* 66. This passage appears to be the source for the definition of *conformatio* one finds in Isidore's *Etymologiae* (II, 13, 1): "conformatio est, cum aliqua, quae non adest, persona configitur quasi adsit, aut rest muta aut informis fit eloquens."

77. *Ex Ponto,* IV, *E* III, 31.

78. Boethius, *Theological Tractates* and *The Consolation of Philosophy,* II, prose 1, 176, l. 31.

79. Ibid., bk. 1, metre 1, 132, ll. 19–20: "Nunc quia fallacem mutavit nubila vultum, / Protrahit ingratas impia vita moras" ("Now that her clouded, cheating face is changed / My cursed life drags on its long, unwanting days" [133]).

80. Ibid., bk. 2, prose I, ll. 33–34.

81. Pierre Courcelle, *La Consolation de Philosophie dans la tradition littéraire,* 135–39. In particular, Courcelle notes a passage in Henry of Settimello's Boethian *De diuersitate Fortunae et Philosophiae* (1:4), in which we read (*Patrologia Latina,* 204:844a): "Numinis ambiguos uultus deprendo. Nouercam / sentio Fortunam, quae modo mater erat." Courcelle refers the lines to the passage from the *Consolatio* we have cited above (bk. 2, prose 1, ll. 33–34).

82. Alain de Lille, *Anticlaudianus: Texte critique avec une introduction et des tables,* ed. R. Bossuat (Paris: Vrin, 1955), VIII, v. 31, 173; VIII, vv. 36–37, 174.

83. See illustrations 82, 66, 78, and 88 in Pierre Courcelle, *La Consolation de philosophie dans la tradition littéraire.* On the iconography of Fortune in the *Roman de la Rose,* see Fleming, *The* Roman de la Rose, 124–26.

84. On this convention, see Italo Siciliano, *François Villon et les thèmes poétiques du Moyen Âge* (Paris: Armand Colin, 1934), 293–94. Cf. vv. 3956–57: *em poi d'eure son semblant mue / une eure rit, autre eure est morne.*

85. See Arthur Langfors, ed., Gervais de Bus, *Le Roman de Fauvel,* Sociéte des anciens textes français, 75 (Paris: Firmin-Dodot, 1914–19), vv. 1908–12: "L'une face ot oscure et brune / et a regarder trop hideuse, / Et l'autre bele et graciëuse, / Tendre, blance, clere et rouvente." Cited in Sicilano, *François Villon et les thèmes poétiques du Moyen Âge,* 294n.

86. Pierre Michault, *Oeuvres poétiques,* ed. Barbara Folkart, Série "Bibliothèque médiévale" (Paris: Union Générale, 1980), *La dance aux aveugles,* prose 8, 97–98. Cited in Sicilano, *François Villon et les thèmes poétiques du Moyen Âge,* 294n.

87. Guillaume de Machaut, *Le Livre du Voir Dit (Le Dit véridique)*, ed. and trans. by Paul Imbs, rev. and coord. by Jacqueline Cerquiglini-Toulet, Lettres Gothiques (Paris: Le Livre de Poche, 1999), vv. 8620–23.

88. Cf. also vv. 6067–68, in which the term *desguise* appears again with regard to Fortune: *n'onc si desguisee meson / ne vit, ce cuit, onques mes hon.*

89. Without noting the ambiguity that the term implies, A. J. Greimas thus tells us that *desguisier* signifies both "sortir de sa guise, de sa manière d'être" and "se travestir." See *Dictionnaire de l'ancien français,* 166.

90. The medieval rhetoricians often use the term *deformatio,* in addition to *conformatio* and *fictio personae,* to render the Greek προσωποποιΐα. See Faral, *Les Arts poétiques,* 72. See also *Rutili Lupi Schemata lexeos,* 2, 6, in which *deformare* is used in a technical sense: " προσωποποιΐα: hoc fit, cum personas in rebus constituimus, que sine persona sunt, aut eorum hominum qui fuerent tamquam vivorum et praesentium actionem sermonemque deformamus."

91. The clear source of Jean's account is Alain de Lille's *Anticlaudianus,* VII, v. 405 to VIII, v. 14 (ed. Bossuat), as has been often noted: see Langlois, *Origines et sources du Roman de la Rose,* 149; Lecoy, *Le Roman de la Rose,* 1:284; and, more recently, Maxwell Luria, *A Reader's Guide to the Roman de la Rose* (Hamden, Conn.: Archon Books, 1982), 160–63. On Jean de Meun and Alain de Lille more generally, see Daniel Poirion, "Alain de Lille et Jean de Meun," in *Alain de Lille, Gauthier de Châtillon, Jackemart Giélée et leur temps,* ed. H. Roussel and F. Suard (Lille: Presses Universitaires de Lille, 1980), 134–51.

92. Paré, *Les idées et les lettres au XIIe siècle: Le Roman de la Rose,* 120.

93. *Anticlaudianus: Texte critique avec une introduction et des tables,* VII, v. 427.

94. On the *topos* of the "inverted world," which the classical and medieval rhetoricians treat under the heading of ἀδύνατα, or *impossibilia,* see Curtius, *Europäische Literatur und lateinisches Mittelalter,* "Verkehrte Welt," 104–8. Curtius does not mention the description of Fortune's island in the *Rose,* although he cites Alain de Lille's corresponding discussion in the *Anticlaudianus.*

95. Chrétien de Troyes, *Cligès,* ed. and trans. Charles Méla and Olivier Collet, Lettres Gothiques (Paris: Livre de Poche, 1994), v. 3806.

96. Curtius defines the *impossibile* as a "Reihung unmöglicher Dinge" (*Europäische Literatur und lateinisches Mittelalter,* 105).

97. Lanctantius, *De iustitia divina,* III, chap. 29: "Fortuna ergo per se nihil est . . . siquidem fortuna est accidentium subitus atque inopinatus adventus."

98. This principle is clearly stated by the figure of Philosophy in the fourth book of *De Consolatione Philosophiae,* in which we read: "Est enim quod ordinem retinet servatque naturam; quod vero ab hac deficit, esse etiam, quod in sua natura situm est, derelinquit"; "For that *is,* which keeps its order and preserves its nature; and whatever falls from this also abandons its being, which is dependent on its nature" (Boethius, *Theological Tractates* and *The Consolation of Philosophy,* 326, ll. 110–12; 327).

99. Langlois (*Origines et sources du Roman de la Rose,* 137) and Lecoy (*Le Roman de la Rose,* 1:285–86) have noted that the immediate source of Jean's discussion is the Boethian *Consolatio,* III, prose 12; and IV, prose 2.

100. In this sense the *Roman de la Rose* can be read as the source of those literary works that, in the subsequent course of French letters, bind the figure of Fortune ever more closely to that of Love, such as the *Dit de la Panthère* and, above all, the *Voir Dit.* See Cerquiglini[-Toulet], *"Un Engin si soutil": Guillaume de Machaut et l'écriture poétique au XIVe siècle,* 64–69, who also discusses the "proximité contextuelle des deux termes: Désir et Fortune" (68).

101. *Metamorphoses,* III, v. 434. It is worth recalling, in this context, that in Ovid's text, Narcissus's love is defined above all by the fact that it is directed not toward an existing being but, rather, toward a mere shadow. We read (*Metamorphoses,* bk. 3, v. 417): *corpus putat esse, quod umbra est.*

102. For the classical association of Fortune and her wheel, see, for example, Tacitus, *Dial. De orationibus,* 23; Cicero, *In Pisonem,* 10, 22; Horace, *Carmina,* III, 10, v. 9ff.; Tibullus, *Elegiae,* I, 5, v. 69ff. For other passages, see Doren, "Fortuna im Mittelalter und in der Renaissance," 80–82.

103. An example of this tradition can be found in the miniatures of certain manuscripts of the *Rose* itself, such as BN fr 25926 (fol. xlviii v), in which Fortune appears (ca. v. 6139), blindfolded, inside her own wheel. On the representation of Fortune in thirteenth-century art, see Émile Mâle, *L'art religieux du XIIIe siècle en France,* Livre de Poche (1898; rpt., Paris: Colin, 1958), 1:183–88.

104. Reason's identification of the ends of language, for which she invokes the authority of Plato (*Ceste sentence ci rimee / touveras escrite en Thimee / de Platon, qui ne fut pas nices*) (vv. 7073–75), can be read as a restatement of Augustine's definition of *teaching* (*docere*) and *remembering* (*commemorare*) as the goals of speech in *De Magistro,* 1.1.

Four: Through the Looking-Glass

1. On the function of Genius in Jean de Meun, see Brownlee, "Jean de Meun and the Limits of Romance: Genius as Rewriter of Guillaume de Lorris," 114–34; Minnis, *Magister amoris,* 108–13 and 166–71; on the relation of Genius to Nature, see Fleming, *Roman de la Rose,* 214–18; and Kay, "Sexual Knowledge," 69–83, esp. 72–76; and see Huot's reflections on Genius in her article, "Bodily Peril," 41–61. For a general study of the figure of Nature, see George D. Economou, *The Goddess Natura in Medieval Literature* (Cambridge: Harvard University Press, 1972).

2. Jean's *chaene doree* appears to owe much to the Neo-Platonic notion of *aurea catena.* In his notes to this passage Lecoy identifies two passages as possible sources for Jean's expression: Alain de Lille, *De planctu naturae,* col. 453; and Bernardus Sylvestris, *De universitate mundi,* ed. Barach and Wrobel, 31.76–80, noting that, although both texts contain references to a *catena,* neither qualifies it

as *aurea* (*Roman de la Rose,* 3:163–64). On the notion of *aurea catena,* see Pierre Levêque, *Aurea catena Homeri* (Paris: Les Belles Lettres, 1959). Cf. Faith Lyons, "Some Notes on the *Roman de la Rose*—the Golden Chain and Other Topics in Jean de Meun," in *Studies in Medieval Literature and Languages in Memory of Frederick Whitehead,* ed. W. Rothwell, W. R. J. Barron, David Blamires, and Lewis Thorpe (New York: Manchester University Press, 1973), 201–8, esp. 201–4.

3. As Langlois observes in the notes to his edition of the romance, the expression *laiz genz* appears no less than five times in Jean's continuation, four of which are to be found in Nature's confession: vv. 5009, 17186, 17165, 17364, 18247 (line numbers refer here to Lecoy's ed.). See Langlois, *Le Roman de la Rose,* 4:308n.

4. On Jean de Meun's philosophical vocabulary, see Paré, *Les idées et les lettres au XIIIe siècle,* 15–52; as well as Hilder, *Der scholastische Wortschatz bei Jean de Meun.*

5. It is worth noting that the first modern French equivalent Godefroy lists for *descrire* is simply *écrire* (citing Richel. 901 Bible, fol. 56: "*Descris* en ton cuer tot çou que tu donneras et tot ce que tu prendras"). See Godefroy, *Dictionnaire de l'ancienne langue française et de tous ses dialects,* vol. 2: *Casteilon-Dyvis,* 571. The primary meaning of the classical Latin *descrivere* is likewise "copy out, transcribe"; only in a secondary sense can it be said to signify, like the modern English form, "sketching off, describing in painting." See Charleton T. Lewis and Charles Short, *A Latin Dictionary, Founded on Arden's Edition of Freud's Latin Dictionary, Revised, Enlarged, and in Great Part Rewritten* (Oxford: Oxford University Press, 1975), 555.

6. See Arden, *Roman de la rose.* For Paré's discussion, see *Les Idées et les lettres au XIIIe siècle,* 231–51.

7. Faith Lyons, "Some Notes on the *Roman de la Rose*—the Golden Chain and Other Topics in Jean de Meun," esp. 204–5. See also Mary Katherine Tilman's reformulation of part of the discussion in terms of a Scholastic topic in her article "Scholastic and Averroistic Influences on the *Roman de la Rose,*" *Annuale Mediaevale* 11 (1970), 93–94.

8. Hilder, *Der scholastische Wortschatz bei Jean de Meun.* Paré's brief discussion of Jean de Meun's vocabulary is all the more significant in this context. See *Les idées et les lettres au XIIIe siècle,* 15–52.

9. Langlois, *Origines et sources du Roman de la Rose,* 137–38.

10. Langlois, *Le Roman de la Rose,* 4:307n.

11. Lecoy, *Le Roman de la Rose,* 3:168.

12. Ibid.

13. Daniel Poirion, *Le Roman de la Rose* (Paris: Hatier, 1973), 178.

14. Strubel, *Le Roman de la Rose,* 893n.

15. Lecoy, *Le Roman de la Rose,* III, 170.

16. Ibid., 901n.

17. Paré, *Les idées et les lettres au XIIIe siècle,* 42.

18. *De interpretatione,* 17 a 25.

19. Boethius, *Commentarii in librum Aristotelis Peri hermeneias,* 1:105, 111;

2:206. On this principle and its importance for medieval philosophy of language, see chap. 1.

20. On the noun *convertibilité* and the adjective *convertible* in Jean de Meun and their relation to thirteenth-century thought, see Paré, *Les idées et les lettres au XIIIe siècle,* 39–40; and Hilder, *Der scholastische Wortschatz bei Jean de Meun,* 51–54.

21. Boethius, *Commentarii in librum Aristotelis Peri hermeneias,* 2:199.

22. Joachim Roland Söder, *Kontingenz und Wissen: Die Lehre von den* futura contingentia *bei Johannes Duns Scotus,* Beiträge zur Geschichte der Philosophie und Theologie des Mitelaters, Neue Folge, 49 (Münster: Aschendorff, 1999), 19.

23. For Augustine's formulation of the question, see *De libero arbitrio,* III, 3–4 and *De civitate dei,* V, 9. The title "the first philosopher of the Will" is due to Hannah Arendt, who argues that the Augustinian *liberum arbitrium* constitutes a faculty that, in its irreducibility to judging and thinking alike, is fundamentally distinct from its classical philosophical precursors, in particular the Aristotelian notion of προαίρεσις ("the Greeks," she wrote, "had no notion of the faculty of the Will," in *The Life of the Mind: One-Volume Edition* [New York: Harcourt Brace Jovanovich, 1978], vol. 2: *Willing,* 18, but, more generally, see 9–110). On the Aristotelian concept of will, see, among others, Michael Wittmann's two works: *Aristoteles und die Willensfreiheit: Eine historisch-kritische Untersuchung* (Fulda: Fuldaer Actiendruckerei, 1921); and *Die Ethik des Aristoteles in ihrer systematischen Einheit und in ihrer geschichtlichen Stellung untersucht* (Regensburg: G. J. Manz, 1920). On the Christian origin of the concept of *liberum arbitrium,* see also the rich chapter on free will and divine foreknowledge in Étienne Gilson's *L'esprit de la philosophie médiévale,* 2d ed. (Paris: Vrin, 1948), 284–303.

24. Boethius, *Theological Tractates* and *The Consolation of Philosophy,* 394–95.

25. Ibid.

26. Ibid.

27. Anselm of Canterbury, *De casu diaboli,* chap. 21, in *Opera omnia,* vol. 1, ed. F. S. Schmitt (Edinburgh: Thomas Nelson and Sons, 1946), 267.26.

28. On the *De Concordia* and its relations to Anselm's other works, see Léon Baudry, "La prescience divine chez S. Anselme," *Archives d'Histoire Doctrinale et Littéraire au Moyen Âge* 13 (1940–42): 223–37.

29. Anselm of Canterbury, *De Concordia praescientia et praedestinationis et gratiae dei cum libero arbitrio,* chap. 1, in *Opera omnia,* vol. 2, ed. F. S. Schmitt (Edinburgh: Thomas Nelson and Sons, 1946), 245.9–246.1.

30. Marica Colish, *Peter Lombard* (Leiden: Brill, 1994), 1:25.

31. Peter Lombard, *Sententiae in IV libris distinctae,* 3d rev. ed., ed. Ignatius C. Brady (Grottaferrata, Italy: Collegii S. Bonaventurae ad Claras Aquas, 1971–81), I, d. 35: "De scientia, praescientia, providentia, etc." (254). The *Sententiae* will be hereafter cited in their usual form: volume, distinction (abbreviated as "d."), chapter (abbreviated as "cap."), and page number.

32. Ibid., I. d. 35, cap. 7, 255.

33. Ibid., I, d. 37, cap. 1, 275.

34. Ibid., I, d. 39, cap. 1, 280.

35. Alain de Libera, *La philosophie médiévale,* Collection Premier Cycle (Paris: Presses Universitaires de France, 1993), 339.

36. See Calvin Normore, "Future Contingents," in *The Cambridge History of Late Medieval Philosophy: From the Rediscovery of Aristotle to the Disintegration of Scholasticism, 1110–1600,* ed. Norman Kretzmann, Anthony Kenny, and Jan Pinborg (Eleanor Stump, assoc. ed.) (Cambridge: Cambridge University Press, 1982), 359–81. Normore states that the relevant distinctions of the Lombard's *Sentences* constitute "the most influential twelfth-century work on future contingents" (363).

37. Fernand van Steenberghen, *La philosophie au XIIIe siècle,* 2d ed. (Louvain: Peeters, 1991), 422. On the condemnations of 1277, see Luca Bianchi, *Il vescovo e i filosofi: La condanna parigina del 1277 e l'evoluzione dell'aristotelismo scolastico,* Quodlibet 6 (Bergamo: Pierluigi Lubrina, 1990); on the articulation and distribution of the condemned articles, see Roland Hissette, *Enquête sur les 219 articles condamnés à Paris le 7 mars, 1277,* Philosophes médiévaux, 22 (Louvain: Publications universitaires, 1977).

38. David Piché, ed. and trans, with the collaboration of Claude Lafleur, *La condamnation parisienne de 1277: Texte latin, traduction, introduction* (Paris: Vrin, 1999), article 42 (15), p. 92. Cf. the earlier edition of Henryk Anzulewicz, "Eine weitere Überlieferung der *Collectio errorum in Anglia et Parisius condemnatorum* im *Ms. lat. fol. 456* der Staatsbibliothek Preußischer Kulturbesitz zu Berlin," *Franziskanische Studien* 74 (1992): 375–99, 384. Capitulum Sextum, art. 14: "Quod prima causa non habet scientiam futurorum contingetium. "

39. Ibid.

40. bid., 391: Capitulum Nonum, art. 12: "Quod nullum agens est ad utrumlibet, immo determinatur." Cf. art. 14 (391): "Quod voluntas nostra subiacet potestati corporum supercaelestium."

41. This is also why there can be no question here of simply identifying Jean de Meun as belonging to one of the currents—whether "Averroistic," "Thomist," or any other—of thirteenth-century Parisian intellectual life, as Müller, for example, does in *Der Rosenroman und der lateinische Averroismus des 13. Jahrhunderts.* On Jean de Meun's supposed "Averroism," see Fleming's judicious remarks in *The Roman de la Rose,* 214–18.

42. See de Libera's acute remarks on the "dialecticization of knowledge" in thirteenth-century systematic theology in *La philosophie médiévale,* 339–42.

43. Strubel translates the passage as follows: "En effet, à bien y regarder, il s'agit là de nécessité conditionnelle et non de nécessité absolue" (*Le Roman de la Rose,* 901); Dahlberg writes, rendering the passage more literally, "If one examines the case well, it is conditional necessity, not simple necessity" (289). In leveling the language of the text, both translators thereby also ignore the play on *regarder* in the lines *car s'il est qui bien i regart, / c'est necessitez en regart* (vv. 17197–98).

44. For Aristotle's distinction between the two types of necessity, see *De interpretatione,* 19 a 24–19 b 5.

45. As Courcelle has noted, Boethius' typology of necessity in the *De Consolatione Philosophiae* (bk. 3, prose 6) is largely borrowed from his treatment of the matter in his *Commentarii in librum Aristotelis Peri hermeneias,* which, in turn, owes much to Ammonius' commentary on the Aristotelian treatise. See Courcelle, *La Consolation de philosophie dans la tradition littéraire,* 218–21. In his translation of this passage Jean de Meun retains the Boethian expressions, writing that "deus manieres sont de neccessité: l'une est simple neccessité, si comme il couvient par neccessité que tuit homme soit mortel; l'autre est neccessité condicionnelle, si comme se tu sccs que un homme aille, il couvient par necessité que il aille." See Dedeck-Héry, "Boethius' *De Consolatione* by Jean de Meun," 273, 103–6.

46. *Cur deus homo,* 2, chaps. 17 and 18; *De Concordantia praesc. Dei cum lib. art.* q. 1, chaps. 2 and 3.

47. See, for instance, Albert's use of the term in his commentary on Peter Lombard's discussion of divine foreknowledge, in which he refers to Boethius and Anselm on the same matter, in *Opera omnia,* ed. Borgnet, vol. 26: *Commentarii in I Sententarum (Dist. XXVI–XCVIII)* (Paris: Ludovic Vivès, 1893), 289.

48. See, among other passages, Bonaventura, *Opera omnia,* ed. Collegium S. Bonaventurae (Ad Claras Aquas [Quarracchi]: Collegium S. Bonaventurae, 1882–1902), *Commentarium in Quatuor Libros Sententiarum Magistri Petri Lombardi,* vol. 1: *In Primum Librum Sententiarum,* 675.

49. These are the examples that Anselm gives for *necessitas antecedens* and *necessitas sequens* in *Cur deus homo,* 2, chap. 18.

50. *Sententiae in IV libris distinctae,* d. 38, c. 2.

51. Cf. the following sentence of *De Consolatione:* "Neque enima illam probo rationem qua se quidam credunt hunc quaestionis nodum posse dissolvere" (Boethius, *Theological Tractates* and *The Consolation of Philosophy,* 394.16–18).

52. Ibid., 396.46–51: "Iam vero quam praposterum est ut aeternae praescientiae temporalium rerum eventus causa esse dicatur! Quid est autem aluid arbitrari ideo deum futura quoniam sunt eventura providere, quam putare quae olim acciderunt causam summae illius esse providentiae?" (Translation on 397: "But now how preposterous it is that it should be said that the cause of eternal foreknowledge is the occurrence of temporal things! But what else is it, to think that God foresees future things because they are going to happen, than to think that those things, once they have happened, are the cause of his highest providence?").

53. Lecoy characterizes the passage as "quelque peu obscur dans les détails" (*Le Roman de la Rose,* 1:170).

54. Ibid., V, prose 6, 410. 75–77; 411. The principle, as the notes to the English edition of Boethius indicate, is already formulated by Ammonius in his commentary on Aristotle.

55. See André de Muralt's penetrating analysis of this tradition in *L'enjeu de la philosophie médiévale: Études thomistes, scotistes, occamiennes et grégoriennes* (Leiden: Brill, 1991), 290–92.

56. See in particular *De Trinitate*, 15:13, a passage cited by the Lombard (d. 39, c. 1) concerning the *immutabilitas* of divine knowledge.

57. On the concept of eternity, see Eleanore Stump and Norman Kretzmann, "Eternity," *Journal of Philosophy* 78 (August 1981): 429–58.

58. *Commentarii in I Sententarum*, 187: "Ad aliud dicendum, quod scitum a Deo omnino intemporale est, nec differentia temporis ponitur circa scitum, secundum quod est in scientia Dei, sed ponitur circa esse rei scitae: quia hoc habet se ut sequens scientiam, secundum quod causatum sequitur causam: et ideo respectu illius dicitur praescientia." As *De Consolatione Philosophiae* already indicates, it follows from such a definition of eternity that, with respect to God, it is less correct to speak of *praevidentia* than of *providentia*, since in the divine intellect there can be no temporal antecedence (no *prae* or *pre-*), but only an anticipatory "before" (*pro-*). See Boethius, *Theological Tractates* and *The Consolation of Philosophy*, 426.69–72; 427: "Unde non praevidentia sed providentia potius dicitur" ("and hence it is called providence rather than prevision" [trans. mod.]).

59. I Cor. 13:12: "Videmus nunc per speculum in aenigmate; tunc autem facie ad faciem" ("For now we see through a glass, darkly; but then, face to face"). Cf. II Cor. 3:18, in which the figure of the mirror appears again.

60. Paré, *Les idées et les letters au XIIIe siècle*, 243.

61. Boethius, *Theological Tractates* and *The Consolation of Philosophy*, 422.9–11; 423: "Eternity, then, is the whole, simultaneous and perfect possession of boundless life." In his translation of the *De Consolatione* Jean de Meun renders the passage in terms close to those of the *Roman de la Rose:* "Pardurableté donques est parfaite possession et toute ensemble de vie nommie terminable" (Dedeck-Héry, "Boethius' *De Consolatione* by Jean de Meun," 270.10–11).

62. Patricia J. Eberle, "The Lover's Glass: Nature's Discourse on Optics and the Optical Design of the *Roman de la Rose*," *University of Toronto Quarterly* 46 (1977): 252.

63. Boethius, *Theological Tractates* and *The Consolation of Philosophy*, 362.78–82; 363.

64. S. Thomae Aquinatis, *Opera omnia*, ed. Roverto Busa, vol. 2: *Summa contra gentiles* (Stuttgart: Fromann-Holzboog, 1980), c. 66 n. 8, 17.

65. Boethius, *Theological Tractates* and *The Consolation of Philosophy*, bk. 4, prose 6, 364. 121–22; 365.

66. S. Thomae Aquinatis, *Opera omnia*, ed. Roberto Busa, vol. 1: *In Quattuor Libros Sententiarum* (Stuttgart: Fromann-Holzboog, 1980), commentary on d. 38, art. 5: Utrum scientia dei sit contingentium, 102. The entire sentence reads as follows: "[Deus] non quasi futurum, sed omnia ut praesentia uno intuitu procul videt, quasi ab aeternitatis specula."

67. On Nature's discussion of mirrors later in the poem, see Eberle, "The Lover's Glass," 241–62. A large body of critical literature has been dedicated to the subject of mirrors in medieval French literature. On mirrors in the *Roman de la*

Rose, see Pascal Antonietti, "'*C'est li miroers perilleus*': Images et miroirs dans le *Roman de la Rose*," in *Le Moyen Âge dans la modernité: Mélanges offers à Roger Dragonetti*, ed. Jean R. Scheidegger, Sabine Girardet, and Eric Hicks (Geneva: Champion, 1996), 33–47. On mirrors in medieval French literature more generally, see, among other contributions, Jean Frappier's essay, "Variations sur le thème du miroir, de Bernard de Ventadour à Maurice Scève," *Cahiers de l'AIEF* 11 (1959): 134–58, rpt. in *Histoire, mythes et symboles, Études de littérature française* (Geneva: Droz, 1976), 149–68; and Frederick Goldin, *The Mirror of Narcissus in the Courtly Love Lyric* (Ithaca: Cornell University Press, 1967).

68. The figure of Narcissus in the romance has received a great deal of critical attention. See Hult, *Self-Fulfilling Prophecies*, 263–300; as well as his earlier article "The Allegorical Fountain: Narcissus in the *Roman de la Rose*," *Romanic Review* 72 (1981): 125–48; Nouvet, "A Reversing Mirror," 189–205; Jean-Charles Huchet, *Littérature médiévale et psychanalyse, Pour une clinique littéraire* (Paris: Presses Universitaires de France, 1990), 171–77; Martin Thut, "Narcisse *versus* Pygmalion: Une lecture du *Roman de la Rose*," *Vox romanica* 41 (1982): 104–32; Strubel, *La Rose, Renart et le Graal*, 208–9; Jean Dornbush, "'Songes est senefiance': Macrobius and Guillaume de Lorris' *Roman de la Rose*," in Blumenfeld-Kosinski, Brownlee, Speer, and Walters, *Translatio studii*, 105–16, esp. 109–11; Kay, *Romance of the Rose*, 110, 78–83; Thomas D. Hill, "Narcissus, Pygmalion, and the Castration of Saturn: Two Mythological Themes in the *Roman de la Rose*," *Studies in Philology* 71 (1974): 404–26; Daniel Poirion, "Narcisse et Pygmalion dans *Le Roman de la Rose*," in *Essays in Honor of Louis Francis Solano* (Chapel Hill: University of North Carolina Press, 1970), 153–65; Goldin, *Mirror of Narcissus in the Courtly Love Lyric*, 52–59; Jean Frappier, "Variations sur le thème du mirroir: De Bernard de Ventadour à Maurice Scève," *Cahiers de l'AIEF* 11 (1959): 134–58, rpt. in *Histoire, mythes et symboles: Études de littérature française* (Geneva: Droz, 1976), 149–68; Erich Köhler, "Narcisse, la fontaine d'Amour, et Guillaume de Lorris," in *L'Humanisme médiéval dans les littératures romanes du XIIe au XIVe siècle*, ed. Anthime Fourrier (Paris: Klincksieck, 1964), 147–66; Jean Rychner, "Le mythe de la fontaine de Narcisse dans le *Roman de la Rose* de Guillaume de Lorris," in *Le lieu et la formule: Hommage à Marc Eigeldinger*, ed. Yves Bonnefoy (Neuchâtel: Éditions de la Baconnière, 1978), 33–46; Douglas Kelly, "'Li chaistieus . . . Qu'Amors prist puis par ses esforz': The Conclusion of Guillaume de Lorris' *Rose*," in *A Medieval French Miscellany*, ed. Norris J. Lacy (Lawrence: University Press of Kansas, 1972), 61–78, esp. 65–66; Karl D. Uitti, "Understanding Guillaume de Lorris: The Truth of the Couple in Guillaume's *Romance of the Rose*," *Contemporary Readings of Medieval Literature* 8 (1989): 51–70, esp. 59–60; Karl D. Uitti, "'Cele [qui] doit estre Rose clamee (*Rose*, vv. 40–44): Guillaume's Intentionality," in Brownlee and Huot, *Rethinking the Romance of the Rose: Text, Image, Reception*, 39–64, 53–58; and Robert Gregory, "Reading as Narcissism: *Le Roman de la Rose*," *SubStance* 12 (1983): 37–48.

69. On Bel Acueil, see Simon Gaunt, "Bel Acueil and the Improper Allegory of the *Roman de la Rose*," *New Medieval Literatures* 2 (1988): 65–93.

70. On Jean de Meun's title for the work, see Alan M. F. Gunn, *The Mirror of Love*, 266–73; Eberle, "Lover's Glass"; Jean Batany, *Approches du Roman de la Rose: Ensemble de l'oeuvre et vers 8227 à 12456,* Études, 363 (Paris: Bordas, 1973), 53–54; Dragonetti, "Pygmalion ou les pièges de la fiction dans le *Roman de la Rose,*" rpt. in *La musique et les lettres,* 345–67; and Kevin Brownlee, "Reflections in the *Miroër aus Amoreus:* The Inscribed Reader in Jean de Meun's *Roman de la Rose,*" in Lyons and Nichols, *Mimesis,* 60–70; and "Jean de Meun and the Limits of Romance: Genius as Rewriter of Guillaume de Lorris." On the use of the term *speculum* as a title, see the lexicographic study by Sister Ritamary Bradley, "Backgrounds of the Title *Speculum* in Medieval Literature," *Speculum* 29 (1954): 100–115. It is significant, as Kevin Brownlee has noted (in "Jean de Meun and the Limits of Romance," 127–28) that, through the figure of Genius, Jean de Meun once refers to the work by the title given to it by Guillaume (v. 19852: *li jolis Romanz de la Rose*).

Conclusion

1. On the liar's paradox in the Middle Ages, see Paul Vincent Spade's excellent anthology, *The Medieval Liar: A Catalogue of the* Insolubilia-*Literature* (Toronto: Pontifical Institute of Mediaeval Studies, 1975).

2. See ibid. For the self-consciously textual formulation of the paradox, which displaces the locus of falsehood from an "I" who speaks to a "paper" on which something is "written," see John Buridan, *Sophismata,* chap. 2, cited in Spade, *Mediaeval Liar,* 58.

3. Lewis, *Allegory of Love,* 138–41.

4. In *False Roses* Stakel has offered an admirable summary of the critical positions on False Seeming (46–48; but see 46–82 for Stakel's entire reading of the figure); according to Charles Muscatine, Faussemblant numbers among the "grosser digressions" in the poem (*Chaucer and the French Tradition* [Berkeley: University of California Press, 1957], 73); for William Ryding, he is an "unfortunate presence" ("Faux Semblant: Hero or Hypocrite?" *Romanic Review* 60 [1969]: 163); Sister Faith McKean terms him an "interruption in the thought of the allegory" ("The Role of Faus Semblant and Astenance Contrainte in the *Roman de la Rose,*" in *Romance Studies in Memory of Edward Billings Ham,* ed. Urban T. Holmes, California State College Publications 2 [Hayward: California State College, 1967], 107); and Carolyn Van Dyke, in more nuanced terms, refers to his discourse as an "apparently digressive monologue" (*The Fiction of Truth: Structures of Meaning in Narrative and Dramatic Allegory* [Ithaca: Cornell University Press, 1985], 91). On Faussemblant, see also Fleming, *Roman de la Rose,* 161–71.

5. See n. 4.

6. Stakel, *False Roses,* 46.

7. Lee Patterson, "'For the Wyves love of Bathe': Feminine Rhetoric and Po-

etic Resolution in the *Roman de la Rose* and the *Canterbury Tales*," *Speculum* 58 (1983): 656–95, esp. 672.

8. Sylvia Huot, "Vignettes marginales comme glose marginale dans un manuscrit du *Roman de la Rose* au XIVe siècle," in *La présentation du livre,* ed. Emmanuelle Baumgartner and Nicole Boulestreau, Littérales: Cahiers du Département de Français, 2 (Paris: Centre de Recherche du Département de Français, 1987), 173–86.

9. Huot, *Romance of the Rose and Its Medieval Readers,* 324.

10. Brownlee, "Problem of Faux Semblant: Language, History, and Truth in the *Roman de la Rose*," 264.

11. Godefroy, *Dictionnaire de l'ancienne langue française et de tous ses dialects,* 8:203–4. The meaning of *vers* is first identified as that of "chanson, couplet, tirade verset," then, figuratively, as "gamme, ton," and finally, "état, situation." It is worth observing, however, that all three of the passages adduced for the third sense of the term are from the *Roman de la Rose.* Cf. Greimas, *Dictionnaire de l'ancien français,* 616.

12. De Lorris and de Meun, *Le Roman de la Rose,* 599: "Avec moi les choses sont bien changées."

Works Cited

I. Editions and Translations of the Roman de la Rose

Dahlberg, Charles. Trans. *The Romance of the Rose.* 1971. 3d ed. Princeton, N.J.: Princeton University Press, 1995.

Langlois, Ernest, ed. *Le Roman de la Rose.* 5 vols. Société des Anciens Textes Français. Paris: Firmin-Didot, 1914–24.

Lecoy, Félix, ed. *Le Roman de la Rose.* 3 vols. Classiques Français du Moyen Âge. Vols. 92, 95, and 98. Paris: Champion, 1965–70.

Strubel, Armand, ed. and trans. *Le Roman de la Rose.* Lettres Gothiques. Paris: Le Livre de Poche, 1992.

II. Editions and Translations of Classical and Medieval Works

Abelard, Peter. *Dialectica: First Complete Edition of the Parisian Manuscripts.* Ed. L. M. de Rijk. Assen: Van Gorcum and Co., 1956.

———. *Philosophische Schriften.* Beiträge zur Geschichte der Philosophie des Mittelalters. Vol. 1–3. Ed. Bernhard Geyer. Münster: Aschendorffsche Verlagsbuchhandlung, 1919.

———. *Scritti di logica.* Ed. Mario Dal Pra. Florence: La Nuova Italia, 1969.

Alain de Lille. *Anticlaudianus: Texte critique avec une introduction et des tables.* Ed. R. Bossuat. Paris: Vrin, 1955.

Albert the Great. *Opera omnia.* Ed. Auguste and Émile Borgnet. 38 vols. Paris: Ludovic Vivès, 1890–99.

Anselm of Canterbury. *Opera omnia.* Ed. F. S. Schmitt. Stuttgart-Bad Cannstaat: Fromann-Holzboog, 1938–61.

Anzulewicz, Henryk, ed. "Eine weitere Überlieferung der *Collectio errorum in Anglia et Parisius condemnatorum* im *Ms. lat. fol. 456* der Staatsbibliothek Preussischer Kulturbesitz zu Berlin." *Franziskanische Studien* 74 (1992): 375–99.

Aquinas, Thomas. *Opera omnia.* Vol. 1, pt. 1: *Expositio libri peryermeneia (editio altera retractata).* Ed. I. Leonis XIII. Rome: Commissio Leonina and Vrin, 1989.

———. *Opera omnia, iussu impensaque Leonis XIII. P. M. Edita, Tomus secunda: Commentarius in octo libros physicorum Aristoteles.* Rome: Ex typographia polyglotta, 1884.

Works Cited

———. *Opera omnia.* Vol. 1: *In Quattuor Libros Sententiarum.* Ed. Roberto Busa. Stuttgart: Fromann-Holzboog, 1980.

———. *Opera omnia.* Vol. 2: *Summa contra gentiles.* Ed. Roverto Busa. Stuttgart: Fromann-Holzboog, 1980.

Aristotle. *Aristoteles Latinus.* Ed. Gérard Verbeke. Vol. 2:1–2: *De interpretatione vel Periermeneias.* Ed. Lorenzo Minio-Paluello. Leiden: Brill, 1965.

———. *Aristoteles Latinus.* Ed. Gérard Verbeke. Vol. 7, pt. 1–2: *Physica: Translatio vetus.* Ed. Fernard Bossier and Jozef Brams. Leiden: Brill, 1990.

———. *Aristoteles Latinus.* Ed. Gérard Verbeke. Vol. 25, pt. 3. 2: *Metaphysica, Lib. I–XIV, recensio et translatio Guillelmi de Moerbeka.* Ed. Gudrun Vuillemin-Diem. Leiden: Brill, 1995.

———. *The Metaphysics, Books 1–10.* Trans. Hugh Tredennick. Cambridge: Harvard University Press, 1933.

———. *Metaphysics.* Trans. W. D. Ross. Rpt. in *The Complete Works of Aristotle: The Revised Oxford Translation.* Ed. Jonathan Barnes. Princeton, N.J.: Princeton University Press, 1984.

———. *The Physics, Books 1–5.* Trans. Philip H. Wicksteed and Francis M. Cornford. Rev. ed. Cambridge: Harvard University Press, 1957.

Augustine. *De doctrina christiana (L'istruzione christiana).* Ed. Manlio Simonetti. Milan: Mondadori, 1994.

Baudry, Léon, ed. *La querelle des futurs contingents (Louvain 1465–1475).* Paris: Vrin, 1950.

Bernard de Ventadour. *Chansons d'amour.* Ed. Moshe Lazar. Paris: Klincksieck, 1966.

Boethius. *Commentarii in librum Aristotelis Peri hermeneias.* Ed. C. Meiser. 2 vols. Leipzig: Teubner, 1877–80.

———. *De institutione arithmetica libri duo.* Ed. G. Friedlein. Leipzig: Teubner, 1867.

———. *The Theological Tractates* and *The Consolation of Philosophy.* Trans. E. K. Rand, H. F. Stewart, and S. J. Tester. Cambridge: Harvard University Press, 1973.

Bonaventura. *Opera omnia.* Ed. Collegium S. Bonaventurae. Ad Claras Aquas (Quarracchi): Collegium S. Bonaventurae, 1882–1902. *Commentarium in Quatuor Libros Sententiarum Magistri Petri Lombardi.* Vol. 1: *In Primum Librum Sententiarum.*

Bonifacio Calvo. *The Poems of Bonifacio Calvo: A Critical Edition.* Ed. William D. Horan. The Hague: Mouton, 1966.

Bossuat, Robert, ed. *Drouart la Vache: Li Livres d'Amours.* Paris: Champion, 1926.

Cassiodorus. *Institutiones.* Ed. R. A. B. Mynors. Oxford: Clarendon Press, 1937.

Catullus. *Catullus, Tibullus, and Pervigilium Veneris.* Trans. F. W. Cornish, J. P. Postgate, and J. W. Mackail. 2d ed, rev. G. P. Goold. Cambridge: Harvard University Press, 1988.

Cavalcanti, Guido. *Rime, con le rime di Iacopo Cavalcanti.* Ed. Domenico de Robertis. Turin: Einaudi, 1986.

Chrétien de Troyes. *Cligès.* Ed. and trans. Charles Méla and Olivier Collet. Lettres Gothiques. Paris: Livre de Poche, 1994.

Cicero. *Cicero in Twenty-Eight Volumes*. Vol. 1: *[Cicero] Ad C. Herennium, De Rationi Dicendi (Rhetorica ad Herennium)*. Trans. Harry Caplan. Cambridge: Harvard University Press, 1989.

———. *Cicero in Twenty-Eight Volumes*. Vol. 2: *De inventione, De Optimo Genere Oratorum, Topica*. Trans. H. M. Hubbell. Cambridge: Harvard University Press, 1949.

———. *Traité du destin*. Ed. Albert Yon. Paris: Les Belles Lettres, 1933.

Damian, Peter. *De divina omnipotentia e altri opusculi*. Ed. P. Brezzi and Bruno Nardi. Florence: Ed. Nazion. D. Class. D. Pens. Ital., 1943.

Dante Alighieri. *Opere minori*. Vol. 2: *Convivio*. Ed. Cesare Vasoli and Domenico De Robertis. 2 vols. 1988. Rpt. Milan-Naples: Ricciardi, 1995.

———. *Opere minori*. Vol. 3, pt. 1: *De vulgari Eloquentia* and *Monarchia*. Ed. Pier Vincenzo Mengaldo and Bruno Nardi. 1979. Rpt. Milan: Riccardo Ricciardi, 1996.

Faral, Edmond. *Les Arts poétiques du XIIe et du XIIIe siècle: Recherches et documents sur la technique littéraire du Moyen Âge*. Paris: Champion, 1962.

Gace Brulé. *Gace Brulé, Trouvère champenois: Edition des chansons et étude historique*. Ed. Holger Petersen Dyggve. Helsinki: Société de littérature finnoise, 1951.

———. *The Lyrics and Melodies of Gace Brulé*. Garland Library of Medieval Literature 39. Ed. Samuel N. Rosenberg and Samuel Danon. New York: Garland, 1985.

Gervais de Bus. *Le Roman de Fauvel*. Ed. Arthur Langfors. Sociéte des Anciens Textes Français 75. Paris: Firmin-Dodot, 1914–19.

Giraut de Borneil. *The Cansos and Sirventes of Giraut de Borneil: A Critical Edition*. Ed. Ruth Verity Sharman. Cambridge: Cambridge University Press, 1989.

Guillaume de Machaut. *La Fontaine amoureuse*. Ed. Jacqueline Cerquiligni-Toulet. Paris: Stock, 1993.

———. *Le Livre du voir dit (Le dit véridique)*. Ed. and trans. Paul Imbs. Revised and completed with an introduction by Jacqueline Cerquiglini-Toulet. Lettres Gothiques. Paris: Le Livre de Poche, 1999.

Hicks, Eric, ed. *Christine de Pizan, Jean Gerson, Jean de Montreuil, Gontier et Pierre Col: Le débat sur le Roman de la Rose*. Bibliotèque du XVe Siècle 43. Paris: Champion, 1977.

Jean de Meun. *Le Testament Maistre Jehan de Meun: Un caso letterario*. Ed. Silvia Buzzetti Gallarati. Turin: Dell'Orso, 1989.

———. "Boethius' *De Consolatione*." Ed. V. L. Dedeck-Héry. *Mediaeval Studies* 14 (1952): 165–275.

Juan Ruiz. *Libro de buen amor*. Ed. G. B. Gybbon-Monypenny. Madrid: Editorial Castalia, 1988.

Keil, Heinrich, ed. *Grammatici Latini*. Leipzig: Teubner, 1855–80.

Loebel, E., and D. Page, ed. *Poetarum Lesbiorum fragmenta*. Oxford: Oxford University Press, 1955.

Lombard, Peter. *Sententiae in IV libris distinctae*. Ed. Ignatius C. Brady. 4 vols. 3d rev. ed. Grottaferrata: Collegii S. Bonaventurae ad Claras Aquas, 1971–81.

Works Cited

Macrobius. *Commentarii in Somnium Scipionis.* Ed. Iacobus Willis. Leipzig: Teubner, 1963.
Marie de France. *Lais.* Ed. Karl Warnke. Trans. Laurence Harf-Lancner. Lettres Gothiques 4523. Paris: Le Livre de Poche, 1990.
Martianus Capella. *De nuptiis Philologiae et Mercurii.* Ed. A. Dick. Leipzig: Teubner, 1925.
Michault, Pierre. *Oeuvres poétiques.* Ed. Barbara Folkart. Série "Bibliothèque médiévale." Paris: Union Générale, 1980.
Ockham, William. *The Tractatus de Praedesitatione et de praescientia dei et de futuris contingentibus.* Ed. Philotheus Boehner. New York: Franciscan Institute, 1945.
Ovid, P. Naso. *Amores, Medicamenta faciei femineae, Ars amatoria, Remedia amoris.* Ed. E. J. Kenney. Oxford: Clarendon Press, 1961.
Page, Denys, ed. *Poetae melici Graeci.* Oxford: Oxford University Press, 1962.
Piché, David, with Claude Lafleur, ed. *La condamnation parisienne de 1277: Texte latin, traduction, et introduction.* Paris: Vrin, 1999.
Pindar. *Pindari carmina cum Fragmenta.* Ed. B. Snell and H. Maehler. Leipzig: Teubner, 1975–80.
Quintilian. *The Institutio Oratoria.* Trans. H. E. Butler. 4 vols. Cambridge: Harvard University Press, 1920–22.
Raimbaut d'Aurenga. *The Life and Works of the Troubadour Raimbaut d'Orange.* Ed. Walter T. Pattison. Minneapolis: University of Minnesota Press, 1952.
Rijk, E. M. de, ed. *Logica Modernorum: A Contribution to the History of Early Terminist Logic.* 2 vols. Assen: Van Gorcum and Co., 1967.
Riquer, Martín de, ed. *Los trobadores: Historia literaria y textos.* 3 vols. 1975. 3d ed. Barcelona: Planeta, 1992.
Siger of Brabant. *Écrits de logique, de morale et de physique.* Ed. Bernardo Bazán. Louvain: Publications Universitaires, 1974.
Spade, Paul Vincent. *The Mediaeval Liar: A Catalogue of the* Insolubilia-*Literature.* Toronto: Pontifical Institute of Mediaeval Studies, 1975.
Sutherland, Ronald. *The Romaunt of the Rose and Le Roman de la Rose.* Berkeley: University of California Press, 1969.
West, M. L., ed. *Iambi et Elegi Graeci Ante Alexandrum Cantati.* Vol. 1: *Archilochus, Hipponax, Theognidea.* Oxford: Oxford University Press, 1971.
William of Aquitaine. *Poesie.* Ed. Nicolò Pasero. Modena: S. T. E. M.-Mucchi, 1963.

III. Reference Works

Ernout, A., and A. Meillet. *Dictionnaire étymologique de la langue latine: Histoire des mots.* 4th ed. Paris: Klincksieck, 1959.
Godefroy, Frédéric. *Dictionnaire de l'ancienne langue française et de tous ses dialectes: Du IXe au XVe siècle.* 1884. Rpt. New York: Kraus Reprint Corp., 1961.

Greimas, A. J. *Dictionnaire de l'ancien français.* Paris: Larousse Bordas, 1997.
Lausberg, Heinrich. *Handbuch der literarischen Rhetorik: Eine Grundlegung der Literaturwissenschaften.* 2 vols. Munich: Max Huebner, 1960.
Lewis, C. T., and C. Short. *A Latin Dictionary.* Oxford: Clarendon Press, 1879.
Ménard, Philippe. *Syntaxe de l'ancien français.* 4th ed. Bordeaux: Éditions Bière, 1994.
Moignet, Gérard. *Grammaire de l'ancien français: Morphologie-Syntaxe.* 2d ed. Paris: Klincksieck, 1979.
Niemeyer, S. F. *Mediae Latinitatis Lexicon minus.* Leiden: Brill, 1976.
Pope, Mildred Katherine. *From Latin to Modern French, with Especial Consideration of Anglo-Norman: Phonology and Morphology.* 1882. Rpt. 2d rev. ed. New York: Barnes and Noble, 1973.
Rey, Alain. *Dictionnaire historique de la langue française.* Paris: Le Robert, 1992.
Tobler, Adolf, and Erhard Lommatzsch. *Altfranzösisches Wörterbuch.* Wiesbaden: Franz Steiner, 1954.
Wissowa, Georg, and Wilhelm Kroll, eds. *Paulys Real-Encyclopädie der Classischen Altertumswissenschaft.* Stuttgart: J. B. Metzlersche Buchhandlung, 1912.
Zink, Gaston. *Morphologie du français mediéval.* Paris: Presses Universitaires de France, 1989.

IV. Works on the Roman de la Rose

Antonietti, Pascal. "'*C'est li miroers perilleus*': Images et miroirs dans le *Roman de la Rose.*" *Le Moyen Âge dans la modernité: Mélanges offers à Roger Dragonetti.* Ed. Jean R. Scheidegger, Sabine Girardet, and Eric Hicks. Geneva: Champion, 1996. 33–47.
Arden, Heather. *The Romance of the Rose.* Twayne's World Author Series. Boston: Twayne Publishers, 1987.
———. *The Roman de la Rose: An Annotated Bibliography.* Garland Medieval Bibliographies 8. New York: Garland, 1993.
Badel, Pierre-Yves. *Le Roman de la Rose au XIVe siècle.* Paris: Champion, 1980.
———. "Jean de Meun, le phénix et les logiciens." *Romania* 110 (1989): 167–80.
———. "Raison 'fille de Dieu' et le rationalisme de Jean de Meun." *Mélanges de langue et de littérature du moyen âge et de la renaissance offerts à Jean Frappier.* Vol. 1. Geneva: Droz, 1970. 41–52.
Batany, Jean. *Approches du Roman de la Rose: Ensemble de l'oeuvre et vers 8227 à 12456.* Études 363. Paris: Bordas, 1973.
Baumgartner, Emmanuelle. "The Play of Temporalities; or, The Reported Dream of Guillaume de Lorris." *Rethinking the* Romance of the Rose*: Text, Image, Reception.* Ed. Kevin Brownlee and Sylvia Huot. Philadelphia: University of Pennsylvania Press, 1992. 22–38.
Blumenfeld-Kosinski, Renate. "*Overt* and *Covert:* Amorous and Interpretative Strategies in the *Roman de la Rose.*" *Romania* 111 (1990): 443–44.

Works Cited

Bouché, Thérèse. "Ovide et Jean de Meun." *Le Moyen Âge* 83 (1977): 71–87.

Brownlee, Kevin. "Jean de Meun and the Limits of Romance: Genius as Rewriter of Guillaume de Lorris." *Romance: Generic Transformations from Chrétien de Troyes to Cervantes*. Ed. Kevin Brownlee and Marina Scordilis Brownlee. Hanover: Dartmouth College–University Press of New England, 1985. 114–34.

———. "Orpheus' Song Re-Sung: Jean de Meun's Reworking of *Metamorphoses*, X." *Romance Philology* 36 (1982): 201–9.

———. "The Problem of Faux Semblant: Language, History, and Truth in the *Roman de la Rose*." *The New Medievalism*. Ed. Marina S. Brownlee, Kevin Brownlee, and Stephen G. Nichols. Baltimore: Johns Hopkins University Press, 1991. 253–71.

———. "Reflections in the *Mirroër aus Amoreus:* The Inscribed Reader in Jean de Meun's *Roman de la Rose*." *Mimesis: From Mirror to Method*. Ed. John D. Lyons and Stephen G. Nichols Jr. Hanover: Dartmouth College–University Press of New England, 1982. 60–70.

Brownlee, Kevin, and Sylvia Huot. *Rethinking the* Romance of the Rose*: Text, Image, Reception*. Ed. Kevin Brownlee and Sylvia Huot. Philadelphia: University of Pennsylvania Press, 1992.

Cherniss, Michael D. "Jean de Meun's *Reson* and Boethius." *Romance Notes* 6 (1975): 678–85.

Dahlberg, Charles. "Love and the *Roman de la Rose*." *Speculum* 4 (1969): 568–84.

———. "Macrobius and the Unity of the *Roman de la Rose*." *Studies in Philology* 58 (1961): 573–82.

Dornbush, Jean. "'Songes est senefiance': Macrobius and Guillaume de Lorris' *Roman de la Rose*." *Translatio studii: Essays by His Students in Honor of Karl D. Uitti for His Sixty-fifth Birthday*. Ed. Renate Blumenfeld-Kozinski, Kevin Brownlee, Mary B. Speer, and Lori Walters. Amsterdam: Rodopi, 2000. 105–16.

Dragonetti, Roger. *Le mirage des sources: L'art du faux dans le roman médiéval*. Paris: Seuil, 1987.

———. "Pygmalion ou les pièges de la fiction dans le *Roman de la Rose*." *Orbis Mediaevalis: Mélanges d'études de langue et de littérature médiévales offerts à R. R. Bezzola*. Ed. Georges Güntert, Marc-René Jung, and Kurt Ringger. Bern: Francke, 1978. 89–111. Rpt. *La musique et les lettres: Études de littérature médiévale*. Geneva: Droz, 1986. 345–67.

———. "Le 'Singe de Nature' dans le *Roman de la Rose*." *Mélanges d'études romanes du Moyen âge et de la Renaissance offerts à Jean Rychner*. Travaux de linguistique et de littérature romanes de l'Université de Strasbourg. 16:1. Strasbourg: University of Strasbourg, 1978. 149–60. Rpt. *La musique et les lettres: Études de littérature médiévale*. Geneva: Droz, 1986. 369–81.

Dufournet, Jean, ed. *Études sur le Roman de la Rose de Guillaume de Lorris*. Geneva: Slatkine, 1984.

Dufourny, Michel. "Observations sur la première partie du *Roman de la Rose.*" *Mélanges offerts à Rita Lejeune.* Gembloux: J. Duculot, 1969. 2:1163–69.

Eberle, Patricia J. "The Lover's Glass: Nature's Discourse on Optics and the Optical Design of the *Roman de la Rose.*" *University of Toronto Quarterly* 46 (1977): 241–62.

Faral, Edmond. "La littérature allégorique et le Roman de la Rose." *Histoire de la littérature française illustrée.* Ed. Joseph Bédier and Paul Hazard. Paris: Larousse, 1923. 1:67–75.

———. "'Le Roman de la Rose' et la pensée du XIIIe siècle." *Revue des Deux Mondes,* 7th ser., 35 (1926): 430–57.

Fleming, John V. *Reason and the Lover.* Princeton, N.J.: Princeton University Press, 1984.

———. *The Roman de la Rose: A Study in Allegory and Iconography.* Princeton, N.J.: Princeton University Press, 1969.

———. "Jean de Meun and the Ancient Poets." *Rethinking the* Romance of the Rose*: Text, Image, Reception.* Ed. Kevin Brownlee and Sylvia Huot. Philadelphia: University of Pennsylvania Press, 1992. 81–100.

———. "The Moral Reputation of the *Roman de la Rose* before 1400." *Romance Philology* 18 (1964–65): 430–35.

Freedman, Lionel J. "Jean de Meun and Ethelred of Rievaulx." *L'Esprit Créateur* 2 (1962): 135–41.

Gallent-Fasseur, Valérie. "Des deux arcs d'Amour à la maison de Fortune: Graces et disgraces selon le *Roman de la Rose.*" *Le beau et le laid au Moyen Âge: Actes du 24e colloque, Aix-en-Provence, février 1999 du Centre universitaire d'études et de recherches médiévales d'Aix.* Aix-en-Provence: CUERMA, University of Provence, 2000. 105–21.

Galpin, Stanley Leman. "Fortune's Wheel in the *Roman de la Rose.*" *PMLA* 24 (1909): 332–42.

Gaunt, Simon. "Bel Acueil and the Improper Allegory of the *Roman de la Rose.*" *New Medieval Literatures* 2 (1988): 65–93.

Gregory, Robert. "Reading as Narcissism: *Le Roman de la Rose.*" *SubStance* 12 (1983): 37–48.

Gunn, Allan M. F. *The Mirror of Love: A Reinterpretation of "The Roman de la Rose."* Lubbock: Texas Tech Press, 1952.

Hilder, Gisela. *Der scholastische Wortschatz bei Jean de Meun: Die Artes Liberales.* Beihefte zur Zeitschrift für Romanische Philologie 129. Tübingen: Max Niemeyer, 1972.

Hill, Thomas D. "Narcissus, Pygmalion, and the Castration of Saturn: Two Mythological Themes in the *Roman de la Rose.*" *Studies in Philology* 71 (1974): 404–26.

Hult, David F. *Self-Fulfilling Prophecies: Readership and Authority in the First* Roman de la Rose. Cambridge: Cambridge University Press, 1986.

Works Cited

———. "The Allegorical Fountain: Narcissus in the *Roman de la Rose*." *Romanic Review* 72 (1981): 125–48.

———. "Closed Quotations: The Speaking Voice in the *Roman de la Rose*." *Yale French Studies* 67 (1984): 248–69.

———. "Language and Dismemberment: Abelard, Origen and the *Romance of the Rose*." *Rethinking the* Romance of the Rose: *Text, Image, Reception*. Ed. Kevin Brownlee and Sylvia Huot. Philadelphia: University of Pennsylvania Press, 1992. 101–30.

———. "Words and Deeds: Jean de Meun's *Romance of the Rose* and the Hermeneutics of Censorship." *New Literary History* 28 (1997): 345–66.

Huot, Sylvia. *The* Romance of the Rose *and Its Medieval Readers: Interpretation, Reception, Manuscript Transmission*. Cambridge: Cambridge University Press, 1993.

———. "Authors, Scribes, Remanieurs: A Note on the Textual History of the *Roman de la Rose*." *Rethinking the* Romance of the Rose: *Text, Image, Reception*. Ed. Kevin Brownlee and Sylvia Huot. Philadelphia: University of Pennsylvania Press, 1992. 203–33.

———. "Bodily Peril: Sexuality and the Subversion of Order in Jean de Meun's *Roman de la Rose*." *Modern Language Review* 95 (2000): 41–61.

———. "'Ci parle l'aucteur': Rubrication of Voice and Authorship in the *Roman de la Rose* Manuscripts." *SubStance* 17 (1988): 42–48.

———. "Confronting Misogyny: Christine de Pizan and the *Roman de la Rose*." *Translatio studii: Essays by His Students in Honor of Karl D. Uitti for His Sixty-fifth Birthday*. Ed. Renate Blumenfeld-Kozinski, Kevin Brownlee, Mary B. Speer, and Lori Walters. Amsterdam: Rodopi, 2000. 169–87.

———. "Medieval Readers of the *Roman de la Rose:* The Evidence of Marginal Notations." *Romance Philology* 43 (1990): 400–420.

———. "The Medusa Interpolation in the *Romance of the Rose:* Mythographic Program and Ovidian Intertext." *Speculum* 62 (1987): 865–77.

———. "The Scribe as Editor: Rubrication as Critical Apparatus in Two Manuscripts of the *Roman de la Rose*." *L'Esprit Créateur* 27 (1987): 67–78.

———. "Seduction and Sublimation: Christine de Pizan, Jean de Meun, and Dante." *Romance Notes* 25 (1985): 361–73.

———. "Vignettes marginales comme glose marginale dans un manuscrit du *Roman de la Rose* au XIVe siècle." *La présentation du livre*. Ed. Emmanuelle Baumgartner and Nicole Boulestreau. Littérales: Cahiers du Département de Français, 2. Paris: Centre de Recherche du Département de Français, 1987. 173–86.

Huot, Sylvia, and Kevin Brownlee, ed. *Rethinking the* Romance of the Rose: *Text, Image, Reception*. Philadelphia: University of Pennsylvania Press, 1992.

Jeanroy, Alfred. "Introduction." *Le Roman de la Rose: Principaux episodes traduits*. Trans. B.-A. Jeanroy. Paris: E. de Boccard, 1928.

———. "Le Roman de la Rose." *Histoire des lettres*. Vol. 1: *Des origines à Ronsard*. Ed. Alfred Jeanroy, Joseph Bédier, and F. Picavet. Paris: Plon, 1921. (= Vol. 12 of *Histoire de la nation française*. Ed. G. Hanotaux). 404–18.

Kay, Sarah. *The Romance of the Rose*. Critical Introductions to French Literature 110. London: Grant and Cutler, 1995.

———. "The Birth of Venus in the *Roman de la Rose*." *Exemplaria* 1 (1997): 7–37.

———. "Sexual Knowledge: The Once and Future Texts of the *Romance of the Rose*." *Textuality and Sexuality: Reading Theories and Practices*. Ed. Judith Still and Michael Worton. New York: Manchester University Press, 1993. 69–83.

———. "Women's Body of Knowledge in the *Romance of the Rose*." *Framing Medieval Bodies*. Ed. Sarah Kay and Miri Rubin. New York: Manchester University Press, 1994, 210–35.

Kelly, Douglas. *Internal Difference and Meanings in the* Roman de la Rose. Madison: University of Wisconsin Press, 1995.

———. "'Li chaistieus . . . Qu'Amors prist puis par ses esforz': The Conclusion of Guillaume de Lorris' *Rose*." *A Medieval French Miscellany*. Ed. Norris J. Lacy. Lawrence: University Press of Kansas, 1972. 61–78.

Köhler, Erich. "Narcisse, la fontaine d'Amour, et Guillaume de Lorris." *L'Humanisme médiéval dans les littératures romanes du XIIe au XIVe siècle*. Ed. Anthime Fourier. Paris: Klincksieck, 1964. 147–66.

Langlois, Ernest. *Les manuscrits du Roman de la Rose: Description et classement*. Paris: Champion, 1910.

———. *Origines et sources du Roman de la Rose*. Paris: Ernest Thorin, 1890.

Lewis, C. S. *The Allegory of Love*. Oxford: Oxford University Press, 1936.

Luria, Maxwell. *A Reader's Guide to the* Roman de la Rose. Hamden, Conn.: Archon Books, 1982.

Lyons, Faith. "Some Notes on the *Roman de la Rose*—the Golden Chain and Other Topics in Jean de Meun." *Studies in Medieval Literature and Languages in Memory of Frederick Whitehead*. Ed. W. Rothwell, W. R. J. Barron, David Blamires, and Lewis Thorpe. New York: Manchester University Press, 1973. 201–8.

Mancini, Mario. "Parigi 1270: Filosofia e racconto nel 'Roman de la Rose' di Jean de Meun." *Rivista di Estetica* 34–35 (1994–95): 3–27.

McKean, Sister Faith. "The Role of Faus Semblant and Astenance Contrained in the *Roman de la Rose*." *Romance Studies in Memory of Edward Billings Ham*. California State College Publications 2. Ed. Urban T. Holmes. Hayward: California State College, 1967. 103–7.

Minnis, A. J. *Magister amoris: The* Roman de la Rose *and Vernacular Hermeneutics*. Oxford: Oxford University Press, 2001.

Müller, Franz Walter. *Der Rosenroman und der lateinische Averroismus des 13. Jahrhunderts*. Frankfurt am Main: Vittorio Klostermann, 1947.

Nichols, Stephen G. "The Rhetoric of Sincerity in the *Roman de la Rose*." *Romance Studies in Memory of Edward Billings Ham*. California State College Publications 2. Ed. Urban T. Holmes. Hayward: California State College, 1967. 115–29.

Nouvet, Claire. "A Reversing Mirror: Guillaume de Lorris' *Romance of the Rose*." *Translatio studii: Essays by His students in Honor of Karl D. Uitti for His Sixty-*

fifth Birthday. Ed. Renate Blumenfeld-Kosinski, Kevin Brownlee, Mary B. Speer, and Lori Walters. Amsterdam: Rodopi, 2000. 189–205.

Nykrog, Per. *L'amour et la rose: Le grand dessein de Jean de Meun.* Cambridge: Harvard University Press, 1986.

Ott, Karl August. *Der Rosenroman.* Darmstadt: Wissenschaftliche Buchgesellschaft, 1980.

———. "Jean de Meun und Boethius: Über Aufbau und Quellen des Rosenromans." *Philologische Studien: Gedenkschrift für Richard Kienast.* Ed. Ute Schwab and Elfriede Stutz. Germanische Bibliothek, ser. 3: Untersuchungen und Einzeldarstellungen. Heidelberg: C. Winter, 1978. 193–227.

Paré, Gérard. *Les idées et les lettres au XIIIe siècle: Le Roman de la Rose.* Montreal: University of Montreal Press, 1947.

Patterson, Lee. "Feminine Rhetoric and the Politics of Subjectivity: La Vieille and the Wife of Bath." *Rethinking the* Romance of the Rose: *Text, Image, Reception.* Ed. Kevin Brownlee and Sylvia Huot. Philadelphia: University of Pennsylvania Press, 1992. 316–58.

———. "'For the Wyves love of Bathe': Feminine Rhetoric and Poetic Resolution in the *Roman de la Rose* and the *Canterbury Tales.*" *Speculum* 58 (1983): 656–95.

Pézard, André. "Lune et Fortune chez Jean de Meung et chez Dante." *Studi in onore di Italo Siciliano.* Florence: Olschki, 1966. 2: 985–95.

Pickens, Rupert T. "*Somnium* and Interpretation in Guillaume de Lorris." *Speculum* 28 (1974): 175–86.

Poirion, Daniel. *Le Roman de la Rose.* Paris: Hatier, 1973.

———. "Alain de Lille et Jean de Meun." *Alain de Lille, Gauthier de Châtillon, Jackemart Giélée et leur temps.* Ed. H. Roussel and F. Suard. Lille: Presses Universitaires de Lille, 1980. 134–51.

———. "Narcisse et Pygmalion dans le Roman de la Rose." *Essays in Honor of Louis Francis Solano.* University of North Carolina Studies in Romance Languages and Literatures 92. Chapel Hill: University of North Carolina Press, 1970. 153–65.

Regalado, Nancy Freeman. "'Des contraires choses: La Fonction poétique de la citation et des *exempla* dans le 'Roman de la Rose.'" *Littérature* 41 (1981): 62–81.

Rowe, Donald W. "Reson in Jean's *Roman de la Rose:* Modes of Characterization and Dimensions of Meaning." *Mediaevalia* 10 (1988): 97–126.

Rychner, Jean. "Le mythe de la fontaine de Narcisse dans le *Roman de la Rose* de Guillaume de Lorris." *Le lieu et la formule: Hommage à Marc Eigeldinger.* Ed. Yves Bonnefoy. Neuchâtel: Éditions de la Baconnière, 1978. 33–46.

Ryding, William. "Faux Semblant: Hero or Hypocrite?" *Romanic Review* 60 (1969): 163–67.

Stakel, Susan. *False Roses: Structures of Duality and Deceit in Jean de Meun's* Roman de la Rose. Stanford French and Italian Studies 49. Stanford, Calif.: Anima Libri, 1991.

Strubel, Armand. *Le Roman de la Rose.* Paris: Presses Universitaires de France, 1984.

---. "La personnification allégorique, avatar du mythe: Fortune, Raison, Nature et Mort chez Jean de Meun." *Pour une mythologie du Moyen Âge*. Ed. Laurence Harf-Lancner and Dominique Boutet. Paris: École Normale Supérieure, 1988. 61-72.

---. *La Rose, Renart et le graal: La littérature allégorique en France au XIIIe siècle*. Geneva: Slatkine, 1989.

Thompson, Barbara. "The Paradoxes of Fortune in the *Roman de la Rose*." *Chimères* (1972): 13-47.

Thuasne, Louis. *Le Roman de la Rose*. Paris: Société Française d'Éditions Littéraires et Techniques, 1929.

Thut, Martin. "Narcisse *versus* Pygmalion: Une lecture du *Roman de la Rose*." *Vox Romanica* 41 (1982): 104-32.

Tilman, Mary Katherine. "Scholastic and Averroistic Influences on the *Roman de la Rose*. *Annuale Mediaevale* 11 (1970): 89-106.

Uitti, Karl D. "'Cele [qui] doit estre Rose clamee (*Rose*, vv. 40-44): Guillaume's Intentionality." *Rethinking the Romance of the Rose: Text, Image, Reception*. Ed. Kevin Brownlee and Sylvia Huot. Philadelphia: University of Pennsylvania Press, 1992. 39-64.

---. "From *Clerc* to *Poète:* The Relevance of the *Romance of the Rose* to Machaut's World." *Machaut's World: Science and Art in the Fourteenth Century*. Ed. Madeleine Pelner Cosman and Bruce Chandler. Annals of the New York Academy of Sciences 314. New York: New York Academy of Sciences, 1978. 209-16.

---. "Understanding Guillaume de Lorris: The Truth of the Couple in Guillaume's *Romance of the Rose*." *Contemporary Readings of Medieval Literature* 8 (1989): 51-70.

Vitz, Evelyn Birge. "The 'I' of the *Roman de la Rose*." *Genre* 6 (1973): 49-75.

Walters, Lori. "Author Portraits and Textual Demarcation in Manuscripts of the *Romance of the Rose*." *Rethinking the* Romance of the Rose*: Text, Image, Reception*. Ed. Kevin Brownlee and Sylvia Huot. Philadelphia: University of Pennsylvania Press, 1992. 359-73.

Wetherbee, Winthrop. "The Literal and the Allegorical: Jean de Meun and the *de Planctu Naturae*." *Mediaeval Studies* 33 (1971): 264-91.

---. "The *Romance of the Rose* and Medieval Allegory." *European Writers*. Ed. William T. H. Jackson and George Stade. New York: Scribner, 1983. 1:309-35.

Zumthor, Paul. "De Guillaume de Lorris à Jean de Meung." *Études de langue et de littérature du Moyen Âge offerts à Félix Lecoy*. Paris: Champion, 1973. 609-20.

V. Other Works

Agamben, Giorgio. *The End of the Poem: Studies in Poetics*. Trans. Daniel Heller-Roazen. Stanford: Stanford University Press, 1999.

Arendt, Hannah. *The Life of the Mind: One-Volume Edition*. New York: Harcourt Brace Jovanovich, 1978.

Works Cited

Aubenque, Pierre. *Le problème de l'être chez Aristote: Essai sur la problématique aristotélicienne.* Paris: Presses Universitaires de France, 1962.

Auerbach, Erich. *Scenes from the Drama of European Literature.* With a foreword by Paolo Valesio. Minneapolis: University of Minnesota Press, 1984.

Baransky, Zygmunt, and Patrick Boyde, eds. *The* Fiore *in Context: Dante, France, Tuscany.* William and Katherine Devers Series in Dante Studies, 2. Notre Dame: University of Notre Dame Press, 1996.

Baudry, Léon. "La prescience divine chez S. Anselme." *Archives d'Histoire Doctrinale et Littéraire au Moyen Âge* 13 (1940–42): 223–37.

Bec, Pierre. *Écrits sur les troubadours et la lyrique médiévale (1961–1991).* Paris: Paradigme, 1992.

Becker, Albrecht. *Die Aristotelische Theorie der Möglichkeitsschlüsse: Eine logisch-philologische Untersuchung der Kapitel 13–22 von Aristoteles' Analytica Priora I.* Berlin: Junker und Dünnhaupt, 1933.

———. *Die Vorgeschichte des philosophischen Terminus 'contingens': Die Bedeutungen von 'contingens' bei Boethius und ihr Verhältnis zu den Aristotelischen Möglichkeitsbegriffen.* Heidelberg: F. Bilabel, 1938.

Benjamin, Walter. *The Origin of the German Tragic Drama.* Trans. John Osborne. London: Verso, 1977.

———. *Ursprung des deutschen Trauerspiels. Gesammelte Schriften.* Ed. Rolf Tiedemann and Hermann Schweppenhäuser. Frankfurt am Main: Suhrkamp, 1974. Vol. 1, pt. 1: 203–430.

Benveniste, Émile. *Problèmes de linguistique générale.* Paris: Gallimard, 1966.

———. *Le vocabulaire des institutions indo-européennes.* 2 vols. Paris: Minuit, 1969.

Bianchi, Luca. *Il vescovo e i filosofi: La condanna parigina del 1277 e l'evoluzione dell'aristotelismo scolastico.* Quodlibet. 6. Bergamo: Pierluigi Lubrina, 1990.

Blumenfeld[-Kosinski], Renate. "Remarques sur *Songe/Mensonge.*" *Romania* 101 (1980): 385–90.

Bochenski, I. M. *Formale Logik.* Munich: Karl Alber, 1956.

Boulnois, Olivier. "Création, contingence et singularité: De Thomas d'Aquin à Duns Scot." *Création et événement: Autour de Jean Ladrière.* Ed. Jean Greisch and Ghislaine Florival. Louvain: Peeters, 1996. 3–20.

Bradley, Sister Ritamary. "Backgrounds of the Title *Speculum* in Medieval Literature." *Speculum* 29 (1954): 100–115.

Brague, Rémi. *Aristote et le problème du monde: Essai sur le contexte cosmologique et anthropologique de l'ontologie.* Paris: Presses Universitaires de France, 1988.

Bronson, B. H. "Personification Reconsidered." *English Literary History* 14 (1947): 163–77.

Bruyne, Edgar de. *Études d'esthétique médievale.* 3 vols. Brugge: De Tempel, 1946. Preface by Maurice de Gandillac. Paris: Albin Michel, 1998.

Carter, Jesse Bendict. *The Religion of Numa and Other Essays in the Religion of Ancient Rome.* London: Macmillan, 1906.

Cerquiglini, Bernard. *Éloge de la variante: Histoire critique de la philologie*. Paris: Seuil, 1989.
Cerquiglini [-Toulet], Jacqueline. *"Un Engin si soutil": Guillaume de Machaut et l'écriture poétique au XIVe siècle*. Bibliothèque du XVe Siècle 47. Paris: Champion, 1985.
Champeaux, Jacqueline. *Fortuna: Le culte de la fortune à Rome et dans le monde romain*. Vol. 1: *Fortuna dans la religion archaïque*. Rome: École Française de Rome, 1982.
Chenu, M.-D. "Involucrum: Le mythe selon les théologiens médiévaux." *Archives d'Histoire Doctrinale et Littéraire du Moyen Âge* 22 (1956): 75–79.
Chiesa, Curzio. "Symbole et signe dans le De Interpretatione." *Philosophie du langage et grammaire dans l'antiquité*. Bruxelles: Ouisa, 1986. 203–18.
Colish, Marica. *Peter Lombard*. 2 vols. Leiden: Brill, 1994.
Constable, Giles. "Forgery and Plagiarism in the Middle Ages." *Archiv für Diplomatik* 29 (1983): 1–41.
Contini, Gianfranco. *Un'idea di Dante*. Turin: Einaudi, 1970.
———. *Postremi esercizî ed elzeviri*. Turin: Einaudi, 1998.
Cormier, Philippe. *Généalogie de personne*. With a preface by Jean-Luc Marion. Paris: Criterion, 1994.
Courcelle, Pierre. *La consolation de philosophie dans la tradition littéraire: Antécédents et postérité de Boèce*. Paris: Études Augustiniennes, 1967.
———. *Les lettres grecques en Occident de Macrobe à Cassiodore*. Rev. ed. Paris: Bibliothèque des Écoles Françaises d'Athènes et de Rome, 1948.
Courtine, Jean-François. *Suarez et le système de la métaphysique*. Paris: Presses Universitaires de France, 1990.
———. "Note complémentaire pour l'historie du vocabulaire de l'être (Les Traductions latines d' ΟΥΣΙΑ et la compréhension romano-stoïcïenne de l'être)." *Concepts et catégories dans la pensée antique*. Ed. Pierre Aubenque. Paris: Vrin, 1980. 33–87.
Cropp, Glynnis M. "Le Livre de Boece de Consolacion: From Translation to the Glossed Text." *The Medieval Boethius: Studies of the Vernacular Translations of De Consolatione Philosophiae*. Ed. A. J. Minnis. Cambridge: D. S. Brewer, 1987. 63–88.
———. "The Medieval Tradition." *Boethius in the Middle Ages: Latin and Vernacular Traditions of the Consolatio Philosophiae*. Ed. Maarten J. F. M. Hoenen and Lodi Nauta. Leiden: Brill, 1997. 243–66.
Curtius, Ernst Robert. *Europäische Literatur und lateinisches Mittelalter*. Bern: Francke, 1965.
Descartes, René. *Oeuvres*. Ed. Charles Adam and Paul Tannery. 12 vols. 1897–1910. Rpt. Paris: Vrin, 1996.
Doren, Alfred. "Fortuna im Mittelalter und in der Renaissance." *Vorträge der Bibliothek Warburg*. Ed. Fritz Saxl. Vol. 2: *Vorträge 1922–1923*. Leipzig: B. G. Teubner, 1924. Pt. 1: 71–144.

Works Cited

Dragonetti, Roger. *La technique poétique dans la chanson courtoise: Contribution à l'étude de la rhétorique médiévale*. Brugge: De Tempel, 1960.

———. "Trois motifs de la lyrique courtoise confrontés avec les *Arts d'aimer* (Contribution à l'étude de la thématologie courtoise)." *Romanica Gandensia*. Vol. 7: *Études de philologie romane*. Ghent: Romanica Gandensia, 1959. 5–48.

———. *La vie de la lettre au Moyen Âge (Le Conte du Graal)*. Paris: Seuil, 1980.

Dronke, Peter. *Fabula: Explorations into the Uses of Myth in Medieval Platonism*. Leiden: Brill, 1974.

Dumézil, Georges. *La religion romaine archaïque, avec un appendice sur la religion des Étrusques*. 1966. 2d ed. Paris: Payot, 1974.

Economou, George D. *The Goddess Natura in Medieval Literature*. Cambridge: Harvard University Press, 1972.

Foucault, Michel. "Qu'est-ce qu'un auteur?" *Bulletin de la Société Française de Philosophie* 64 (1969): 77–95. Rpt. Michel Foucault. *Dits et écrits*. Vol. 1: *1954–1969*. Paris: Gallimard, 1994. 789–821.

Fowler, W. Walde. "Fortuna (Roman)." *The Encyclopaedia of Religion and Ethics*. Ed. James Hastings. 1926–76. Rpt. Edinburgh: T. and T. Clark, 1994.

Frakes, Jerold C. *The Fate of Fortune in the Early Middle Ages: The Boethian Tradition*. Studien und Texte zur Geistesgeschichte des Mittelalters 23. Leiden: Brill, 1988.

Franck, R. W. "The Art of Reading Medieval Personification Allegory." *English Literary History* 20 (1953): 237–50.

Frappier, Jean. *Étude sur la Mort le Roi Artu: Roman du XIIIe siècle*. Geneva: Droz-Minard, 1961.

———. "Variations sur le thème du mirroir: De Bernard de Ventadour à Maurice Scève." *Cahiers de l'AIEF* 11 (1959): 134–58. Rpt. Jean Frappier. *Histoire, mythes et symboles: Études de littérature française*. Geneva: Droz, 1976. 149–68.

Frege, Gottlob. *Funktion, Begriff, Bedeutung*. Ed. Günter Patzig. Göttingen: Vandenhoeck and Ruprecht, 1994.

Frontisi-Ducroux, Françoise. *Du masque au visage: Aspects de l'identité en Grèce ancienne*. Paris: Flammarion, 1995.

Gaunt, Simon. *Retelling the Tale: An Introduction to French Medieval Literature*. London: Duckworth Academic, 2001.

———. "A Martyr to Love: Sacrificial Desire in the Poetry of Bernart de Ventadorn." *Journal of Medieval and Early Modern Studies* 31 (2001): 477–506.

Gilson, Étienne. *L'esprit de la philosophie médiévale*. 2d ed. Paris: Vrin, 1948.

Glaser, R. "Abstractum agens und Allegorie im älteren Französisch." *Zeitschrift für Romanische Philologie* 59 (1953): 43–122.

Goichon, A.-M. *Introduction à Avicenne: Son épître des définitions*. Paris: Brouwer, 1933.

———. *Lexique de la langue philosophique d'Ibn Sina*. Paris: Brouwer, 1938.

Goldin, Frederick. *The Mirror of Narcissus in the Courtly Love Lyric*. Ithaca: Cornell University Press, 1967.

Gorni, Guglielmo. *Il nodo della lingua e il verbo d'amore: Studi su Dante e altro duecentisti*. Saggi di "Lettere italiane" 29. Florence: Leo Olschki, 1981.
Hamacher, Werner. "Ou, séance, touche de Nancy, ici." *Paragraph* 16:2 (1994): 216–31 and 17:2 (1994): 103–19.
Hegel, Georg Wilhelm Friedrich. *Werke in zwanzig Bänden, 13–15: Vorlesungen über die Ästhetik*. Ed. Eva Moldenhauer and Karl Markus Michel. Frankfurt: Suhrkamp, 1994.
Heidegger, Martin. *Holzwege*. 3d ed. Frankfurt am Main: Vittorio Klostermann, 1957.
———. *Poetry, Language, Thought*. Trans. Alfred Hofstadter. New York: Harper and Row, 1971.
Heinimann, Siegfried. *Das Abstraktum in der französischen Literatursprache des Mittelalters*. Romanica Helvetica 73. Bern: Francke, 1963.
Heller-Roazen, Daniel. "Language, or No Language." *Diacritics* 29:3 (1999): 22–39.
———. "The Matter of Language: Guilhem de Peitieus and the Platonic Tradition." *MLN* 113 (1998): 851–80.
Hissette, Roland. *Enquête sur les 219 articles condamnés à Paris le 7 mars 1277*. Philosophes Médiévaux 22. Louvain: Publications universitaires, 1977.
Holtz, Louis. *Donat et la tradition de l'enseignement grammatical: Étude sur l'Ars Donati et sa diffusion (IVe–IXe siècle) et édition critique*. Paris: Centre National de la Recherche Scientifique, 1981.
Huchet, Jean-Charles. *Littérature et psychoanalyse. Pour une clinique littéraire*. Paris: Presses Universitaires de France, 1990.
Hunt, Tony. "The Rhetorical Background to the Arthurian Prologue: Tradition and the Old French Vernacular Prologues." *Forum for Modern Language Studies* 6 (1970): 1–23.
Huot, Sylvia. *From Song to Book: The Poetics of Writing in Old French Lyric and Narrative Poetry*. Ithaca: Cornell University Press, 1987.
Ildefonse, Frédérique. *La naissance de la grammaire dans l'antiquité grecque*. Paris: Vrin, 1997.
Imbert, Claude. "Théorie de la représentation et doctrine logique dans le stoïcisme ancien." *Les Stoïciens et leur logique, actes du colloque de Chantilly, 18–22 Septembre 1976*. Paris: Vrin, 1978. 223–49.
Isaac, J. *Le peri hermeneias en occident de Boèce à Saint Thomas: Histoire littéraire d'un traité d'Aristote*. Bibliothèque Thomiste 39. Paris: Vrin, 1953.
Jakobson, Roman. "Shifters, Verbal Catgeories and the Russian Verb." Jakobson, Roman. *Selected Writings*. The Hague: Mouton, 1971. 2:130–47.
Jeauneau, Édouard. "L'usage de la notion d'*integumentum* à travers les gloses de Guillaume de Conches." *Archives d'Histoire Doctrinale et Littéraire du Moyen Âge* 24 (1957): 35–100.
Jolivet, Jean. *Arts du langage et théologie chez Abélard*. Études de Philosophie Médiévale 57. Paris: Vrin, 1969.

Jung, Marc-René. *Études sur le poème allégorique en France au Moyen Âge.* Romanica Helvetica 82. Bern: Francke, 1971.

Kahane, Henry, and Renée Kahane. "The Hidden Narcissus in the Byzantine Romance of *Belthandros and Chrysantza.*" *Jahrbuch der österreichischen Byzantinistik* 33 (1983): 199–219.

Kant, Immanuel. *Gesammelte Schriften* (Akademieausgabe). Vol. 20: *Kritik der Urteilskraft.* Berlin: G. Reimer, 1942.

Kantorowicz, Ernst H. "The Sovereignty of the Artist: A Note on Legal Notions and Renaissance Theories of Art." *Selected Studies.* Locust Valley, N.Y.: J. J. Augustin, 1965. 352–65.

Kay, Sarah. *Subjectivity in Troubadour Poetry.* Cambridge: Cambridge University Press, 1990.

Kennedy, Elspeth. "The Scribe as Editor." *Mélanges de langue et de littérature du Moyen Âge et de la Renaissance offerts à Jean Frappier.* Geneva: Droz, 1970. 523–31.

Kirchner, Gottfried. *Fortuna in der Dichtung und Emblematik des Barock: Tradition und Bedeutungswandel eines Motivs.* Stuttgart: Metzler, 1970.

Kittridge, George Lyman. *Chaucer and His Poetry.* Cambridge: Harvard University Press, 1915.

Kretzmann, Norman. "Nos Ipsi Principia Sumus: Boethius and the Basis of Contingency." *Divine Omniscience and Omnipotence in Medieval Philosophy: Islamic, Jewish and Christian Perspectives.* Ed. Tamar Rudavsky. Dordrecht: D. Reidel, 1985. 23–50.

Kretzmann, Norman, with Anthony Kenny, Jan Pinborg, and Eleanor Stump, eds., *The Cambridge History of Later Medieval Philosophy: From the Rediscovery of Aristotle to the Disintegration of Scholasticism, 1100–1600.* Cambridge: Cambridge University Press, 1982.

Kruger, Steven F. *Dreaming in the Middle Ages.* Cambridge: Cambridge University Press, 1992.

Lang, Helen S. *Aristotle's Physics and Its Medieval Varieties.* Albany: State University of New York Press, 1992.

Lejeune, Philippe. *Le pacte autobiographique.* Paris: Seuil, 1975.

Levêque, Pierre. *Aurea catena Homeri.* Paris: Les Belles Lettres, 1959.

Libera, Alain de. *La philosophie médiévale.* Collection Premier Cycle. Paris: Presses Universitaires de France, 1993.

Looze, Laurence de. *Pseudo-Autobiography in the Fourteenth Century: Juan Ruiz, Guillaume de Machaut, Jean Froissard, and Geoffrey Chaucer.* Tallahassee: University Press of Florida, 1997.

Lote, Georges. *Histoire du vers français.* Pt. 1: *Le Moyen Âge.* Vol. 1: *Les origines du vers français, les éléments constitutifs du vers: la césure; la rime; le numérisme et le rhythme.* Paris: Hatier, 1949.

———. *Histoire du vers français.* Pt. 1: *Le Moyen Âge.* Vol. 2: *La déclamation, art et versification, les formes lyriques.* Paris: Hatier, 1951.

———. *Histoire du vers français.* Pt. 1: *Le Moyen Âge.* Vol. 3: *La poétique, le vers et la musique.* Paris: Hatier, 1955.
Lukasiewicz, Jan. *Aristotle's Syllogistic from the Standpoint of Modern Formal Logic.* 2d ed. Oxford: Oxford University Press, 1951.
———. "On Determinism." *Polish Logic: 1920–1939.* Ed. Storrs McCall. Oxford: Clarendon Press, 1967. 19–32.
———. "On the Notion of Possibility." *Polish Logic: 1920–1939.* Ed. Storrs McCall. Oxford: Clarendon Press, 1967. 15–16.
———. "On Three-Valued Logic." *Polish Logic: 1920–1939.* Ed. Storrs McCall. Oxford: Clarendon Press, 1967. 16–18.
———. "Philosophical Remarks on Many-Valued Systems of Propositional Logic." *Polish Logic: 1920–1939.* Ed. Storrs McCall. Oxford: Clarendon Press, 1967. 40–65.
Magee, John. *Boethius on Signification and Mind.* Leiden: Brill, 1989.
Mâle, Émile. *L'art religieux du XIIIe siècle en France.* 1898. Rpt. Paris: Colin, 1958.
Malkiel, Yakov. "Ancient Hispanic *vera(s)* and *mentira(s):* A Study in Lexical Polarization." *Romance Philology* 6 (1952–53): 121–72.
Man, Paul de. *The Rhetoric of Romanticism.* New York: Columbia University Press, 1984.
Michalsky, Konstanty. "Le problème de la volonté au XIVe siècle." *Studia Philosophica, Commentarii Societatis Philosophiae Polonorum.* Leopoli: Ksazka, 1937. 2:233–365.
Milner, Jean-Claude. *L'Oeuvre claire: Lacan, la science, la philosophie.* Paris: Seuil, 1995.
Minnis, A. J. *Medieval Theory of Authorship: Scholastic Literary Attitudes in the Later Middle Ages.* London: Scolar Press, 1984.
Muralt, André de. *L'enjeu de la philosophie médiévale: Études thomistes, scotistes, occamiennes et grégoriennes.* Leiden: Brill, 1991.
Muscatine, Charles. *Chaucer and the French Tradition.* Berkeley: University of California Press, 1957.
———. "The Emergence of Psychological Allegory in the Old French *Roman.*" *PMLA* 68 (1953): 1160–82.
Nichols, Stephen G. "Why Material Philology? Some Thoughts." *Philologie als Textwissenschaft: Alte und neue Horizonte,* ed. Helmut Tervooren and Horst Wenzel, *Zeitschrift für deutsche Philologie.* Special Issue 116 (1997): 10–30.
Normore, Calvin. "Future Contingents." *The Cambridge History of Late Medieval Philosophy: From the Rediscovery of Aristotle to the Disintegration of Scholasticism, 1100–1600.* Ed. Norman Kretzmann, Anthony Kenny, and Jan Pinborg (Eleanor Stump, assoc. ed.). Cambridge: Cambridge University Press, 1982. 359–81.
Paris, Gaston. *La littérature française au Moyen Âge (Xie–XIVe siècle).* 1888. 5th ed. Paris: 1913.
Paris, Paulin. "Fin du treizième siècle. Trouvères: Le *Roman de la Rose.*" *Histoire Littéraire de la France* 23 (1856): 1–61.

Patch, Howard Rollin. *The Tradition of Boethius: A Study of His Importance in Medieval Culture*. Oxford: Oxford University Press, 1935.

———. "The Tradition of the Goddess Fortuna in Roman Literature and the Transitional Period." *Smith College Studies in Modern Languages* 3:3 (1922): 131–77.

———. "Fortuna in Old French Literature." *Smith College Studies in Modern Languages* 4:4 (1923).

Patterson, Lee. *Chaucer and the Subject of History*. Madison: University of Wisconsin Press, 1991.

Pépin, Jean. "Σύμβολα, Σημεῖα, Ὁμοιώματα: À propos de *De interpretatione* I, 16a 3–8 et *Politique* VIII 5, 1340 a 6–39." *Aristoteles Werk und Wirkung: Paul Moraux gewidmet*, vol. 1: *Aristoteles und seine Schule*, ed. Jürgen Wiesner. Berlin: De Gruyter, 1985: 22–44.

Pézard, André. *Dante sous la pluie de feu (Enfer, chant XV)*. Études de Philosophie Médiévale 40. Paris: Vrin, 1950.

Piaget, A. "Le 'Chemin de Vaillance,' de Jean de Courcy, et l'hiatus et l'*e* final des Polysyllabes au XIVe et XVe siècles." *Romania* 27 (1898): 582–607.

Pound, Ezra. *The Spirit of Romance*. 1952. Rpt. New York: New Directions Press, 1968.

———. *Translations*. Intro. Hugh Kenner. New York: New Directions Press, 1963.

Regalado, Nancy Freeman. "Villon's Legacy from *Le Testament of Jean de Meun*: Misquotation, Memory, and the Wisdom of Fools." *Villon at Oxford: The Drama of the Text, Proceedings of the Conference Held at St. Hilda's College, Oxford, March 1996*. Ed. Michael Freeman and Jane H. M. Taylor. Amsterdam: Rodopi, 1999. 282–311.

Richards, Earl Jeffrey. *Dante and the "Roman de la Rose": An Investigation into the Vernacular Context of Dante's "Commedia."* Beihefte zur Zeitschrift der romanischen Philologie, 184. Tübingen: Niemeyer, 1981.

Robertson, W. D. *A Preface to Chaucer: Studies in Medieval Perspectives*. Princeton, N.J.: Princeton University Press, 1962.

Rosenstein, Roy. "*Mouvance* and the Editor as Scribe: *Trascrittore Tradittore?*" *Romanic Review* 80 (1989): 157–71.

Siciliano, Italo. *François Villon et les thèmes poétiques du Moyen Âge*. Paris: Armand Colin, 1934.

Singleton, Charles S. *Dante Studies I: Commedia, Elements of Structure*. Harvard: Harvard University Press, 1954.

———. *Journey to Beatrice*. Baltimore: Johns Hopkins University Press, 1958.

Söder, Joachim Roland. *Kontingenz und Wissen: Die Lehre von den futura contingentia bei Johannes Duns Scotus*. Beiträge zur Geschichte der Philosophie und Theologie des Mittelaters: Neue Folge 49. Münster: Aschendorff, 1999.

Spitzer, Leo. "Note on the Poetic and Empirical 'I' in Medieval Authors." *Romanische Literaturstudien: 1936–1956*. Tübingen: Niemeyer, 1959. 100–113.

———. "The Prologue to the *Lais* of Marie de France and Medieval Poetics." *Romanische Literaturstudien: 1936–1956*. Tübingen: Niemeyer, 1959. 3–14.

Steenberghen, Fernand van. *La philosophie au XIIIe siècle.* 2d ed. Louvain: Peeters, 1991.
Stock, Brian. *Myth and Science in the Twelfth Century: A Study of Bernard Sylvester.* Princeton, N.J.: Princeton University Press, 1972.
Stock, George St. "Fortune (Greek)." *The Encyclopaedia of Religion and Ethics.* Ed. James Hastings. 1926–76. Rpt. Edinburgh: T. and T. Clark, 1994.
Stump, Eleanore, and Norman Kretzmann. "Eternity." *Journal of Philosophy* 78 (1981): 429–58.
Tobler, Adolf. *Le vers français ancien et moderne.* Trans. Karl Breul and Léopold Sudre. Paris: F. Vieweg, 1885.
Tuve, Rosemond. *Allegorical Imagery: Some Medieval Books and Their Posterity.* Princeton, N.J.: Princeton University Press, 1966.
Van der Poel, Dieuwke. *De Vlaamse "Rose" en "Die Rose" van Heinric: Onderzoekingen over Twee Middelnederlandse Bewerkingen van de "Roman de la Rose" (avec un résumé en français).* Middeleeuwse Studies en Bronnen 13. Hilversum: Verloren, 1989.
———. "A Romance of a Rose and Florentine: The Flemish Adaptation of the *Romance of the Rose.*" *Rethinking the* Romance of the Rose*: Text, Image, Reception.* Ed. Kevin Brownlee and Sylvia Huot. Philadelphia: University of Pennsylvania Press, 1992. 304–15.
Van Dyke, Carolyn. *The Fiction of Truth: Structures of Meaning in Narrative and Dramatic Allegory.* Ithaca: Cornell University Press, 1985.
Vanossi, Luigi. *Dante e il "Roman de la Rose": Saggi sul "Fiore."* Biblioteca dell' 'Archivium Romanicum,' series 1, 144. Florence: Olschki, 1979.
Vuillemin, Jules. *Nécessité ou contingence: L'aporie de Diodore et les systèmes philosophiques.* Paris: Vrin, 1984.
Wallace, David. "Chaucer and Boccaccio's Early Writings." *Chaucer and the Italian Trecento.* Ed. Piero Boitani. Cambridge: Cambridge University Press, 1983.
Weiss, Helene. *Der Zufall in der Philosophie des Aristoteles.* London: Wyndham Printers, 1935.
Wetherbee, Winthrop. *Platonism and Poetry in the Twelfth Century: The Literary Influence of the School of Chartres.* Princeton, N.J.: Princeton University Press, 1972.
Wittman, Michael. *Aristoteles und die Willensfreiheit: Eine historisch-kritische Untersuchung.* Eichstätt: Fuldaer Actiendruckerei, 1921.
———. *Die Ethik des Aristoteles: In ihrer systematischen Einheit und in ihrer geschichtlichen Stellung untersucht.* Regensburg: G. J. Manz, 1920.
Wolfson, Harry Austryn. *The Philosophy of the Church Fathers.* Cambridge: Harvard University Press, 1970.
Zaganelli, Gioia. *Aimer, sofrir, joïr: I paradigmi della soggettività nella lirica francese dei secoli XII e XIII.* (Florence: La Nuova Italia, 1982).
Zink, Michel. *La subjectivité littéraire.* Paris: Presses Universitaires de France, 1985.
Zumthor, Paul. *Essai de poétique médiévale.* Paris: Seuil, 1972.

Works Cited

———. *Langue, texte, énigme.* Paris: Seuil, 1975.
———. "From the Universal to the Particular in Medieval Poetry." *MLN* 85 (1970): 815–23.
———. "Narrative and Anti-Narrative: *Le Roman de la Rose.*" *Yale French Studies* 51 (1974): 185–204.

Index

Abelard, Peter, 16, 22–26, 31–32, 54, 75–76, 149n. 64, 152n. 12
accident. *See* contingency; fortune
action. *See* will
Alain de Lille, 58, 92, 171n. 94, 172n. 2
　Anticlaudianus, 87, 91, 171n. 91
Albert the Great, 17, 25–26, 83, 116, 124, 176n. 47
Alkman, 56
allegory, 39, 41–42, 63–66, 155n. 46, 156n. 48, 169n. 72
Ammonius, 176nn. 45, 54
Amors (love)
　as figure in *Roman de la Rose,* 49–53, 54–60, 64–66, 69, 72–73, 97–99, 160n. 68, 172n. 100
　See also desire
anaphora, 46–47
Anaxagoras, 81
annominatio. See paranomasia
Anselm of Canterbury, 16, 21–22, 109–10, 116
Anticlaudianus (Alain de Lille), 87, 91, 171n. 91
Antonietti, Pascal, 178n. 67
Apollonius Dyskolos, 32
aporia. *See* paradox
Apuleius of Madaura, 16
Archilochus, 56
Arden, Heather, 5
Arendt, Hannah, 174n. 23
Aristotle, 31, 37, 96, 145n. 11, 168n. 62
　Boethius' translation of, 11, 12, 17–21
　on contingency, 13–15, 17–21, 148n. 47
　on fortune, 79–84
　as influence on the Middle Ages, 15–17
　on language, 11–15

　on truth, 12–13
　See also De Interpretatione; Metaphysics; Physics
Aubenque, Pierre, 80
auctor. See authorship
Auerbach, Erich, 39
Augustine, Saint, 40, 43, 68, 94, 108, 123, 172n. 104, 174n. 23
authorship, 1, 4–6, 49–54, 111, 143n. 40
autobiography, 42–45, 156n. 55, 157n. 59

Badel, Pierre-Yves, 6, 42, 156n. 48
Baumgartner, Emanuelle, 45
Bec, Pierre, 158n. 64
Becker-Freysing, Albrecht, 18–19, 147n. 37, 148n. 47
Benjamin, Walter, 156n. 48
Benveniste, Émile, 31, 151n. 12, 164n. 8
Bernardus Sylvestris, 172n. 2
Bernart de Ventadorn, 57, 59, 158n. 64, 160n. 73
bivalence, law of, 13, 145n. 11
Bochenski, I. M., 22
Boehner, Philotheus, 148n. 49
Boethius, 15, 16, 22, 24–25, 26, 108, 116, 122, 123, 127, 128, 129, 153n. 25
　Aristotle's *De Interpretatione* as translated by, 11, 12, 17–21, 147n. 35, 148n. 47, 149n. 63
　Fortune as portrayed in Jean de Meun's translation of, 70–72, 75, 82, 83, 85
　and Nature's confession, as source for, 103–4
　See also De Consolatione Philosophiae
Bonaventure, 116
Bonifacio Calvo, 57

201

Index

Book of Wisdom, 128
Brague, Rémi, 80
Brownlee, Kevin, 5, 135

Capella, Martianus, 16
Cassiodorus, 18, 147n. 37
categoreme, 24
Catullus, 56
causation, 79, 80–85, 99
Cavalcanti, Guido, 58
Cerquiglini, Bernard, 143n. 40
Cerquiglini-Toulet, Jacqueline, 153n. 28
Champeaux, Jacqueline, 164n. 8
chance, 9, 25, 67, 79–80, 82. *See also* fortune
Chartres, School of, 39, 155n. 41
chiasmus, 4, 71–72
Chrétien de Troyes, 34–35, 93
Cicero, 37, 67, 68, 86, 98
citation, 26, 50–52
completion/incompletion
    of *Roman de la Rose*, 1–10
    as structures of the medieval literary work, 7
condemnations of 1277, 110–11, 175n. 37
Conrad of Hirschau, 38
contingency
    Abelard's treatment of, 22–26, 75–76
    Anselm's treatment of, 21–22
    Aristotle's definition of, 13–15, 17–21
    in Boethius' translation of Aristotle, 12, 17–21, 22
    condemnations of 1277, position in, 110–11
    and divine knowledge, 102–3, 107–11
    Fortune and personification of, 9, 28, 63–64, 97–99
    history of terminology, 17–19, 146n. 30, 147nn. 35, 39, 148n. 47
    and Nature, 102–5, 106–8, 111–17, 118–24
    and necessity, 111–17, 118–21
    and structure of *Roman de la Rose*, 7–10
    See also fortune
Contini, Gianfranco, 54–56

convertibility (*convertibilitas*), 107, 174n. 20
1 Corinthians, 125, 155n. 43
2 Corinthians, 155n. 43
Courcelle, Pierre, 87, 170n. 81, 176n. 45
Curtius, Ernst Robert, 171n. 94

Dahlberg, Charles, 154n. 33, 175n. 43
Damian, Peter, 16
Dante Alighieri, 27, 52, 54, 58, 150nn. 80, 81, 151n. 6, 160n. 69, 162n. 95
death, 10, 52, 54–60, 100–101
De Consolatione Philosophiae (Boethius), 15, 70–75, 85, 87, 103–4, 108–9, 119, 122, 125, 127, 128–29, 165n. 30, 166nn. 35, 40, 170n. 81, 171n. 98, 177n. 61
deformation. *See* formation/deformation
De Interpretatione (Aristotle), 11–15, 106
    Abelard's commentaries on, 22–24
    Boethius' translation of, 11, 12, 17–21
    translations of, 15
    transmission and influence, 15–17
de Man, Paul, 157n. 55
Democritus, 81
Descartes, René, 31, 151n. 11
desire, 54–60, 65–66, 97–98, 172n. 100. *See also* Amors (love)
digression, 3, 7, 65–66, 104–5, 130–31
disguise, 88, 92, 135, 171n. 89
divine knowledge, 176n. 47, 177n. 58
    and contingency, 102–3, 107–11
    and free will, 103–5, 106, 108–17, 118–24
    as mirror, 124–31
    Nature's discussion of, 124–31
Donatus, 32–33, 152n. 22
Dornbush, Jean, 154n. 33
doubling, 41–44, 50, 62, 87–93
Dragonetti, Roger, 4–5, 29, 30, 51, 57, 58, 158n. 64, 159n. 67
dream, 35–39, 153nn. 28, 29, 154n. 33
Dronke, Peter, 154n. 33
Dumézil, Georges, 66

Eberle, Patricia, 128
elision, 158n. 63

202

Empedocles, 100
eternity, 123–24, 177nn. 58, 61
Etymologiarum sive Originum (Isidore of Seville), 37, 41–42, 69
excluded middle, law of. *See* bivalence, law of
excursus, 3

fable, 35–40
False Seeming, as figure in *Roman de la Rose*, 132–37, 179n. 4
falsity. *See* truth and falsity
Faral, Edmond, 2, 3, 140n. 4
fate, 26, 101–2
fiction, 30, 35–40
figura (in Patristic sense), 39–40, 155n. 43
figure. See *prosopopoeia*
Fiore, Il, 54, 139n. 2
Fleming, John V., 4, 5, 142n. 30
foreknowledge. *See* divine knowledge
formation/deformation, 45, 88–94, 96–97, 171n. 90
fortune
  Aristotle's concept of, 79–84
  Boethius' treatment of, as translated by Jean de Meun, 70–72, 75, 82, 83, 85
  changing form of, 63, 87–96
  etymology of term, 66, 68–69, 164n. 8
  as figure in *Roman de la Rose*, 9, 28, 63–64, 69, 70–71, 72–78, 85–94, 96–99, 163n. 1, 172nn. 100, 103
  Lanctantius on, 94, 171n. 97
  and love, 69, 97–99, 172n. 100
  as mythological figure, 66–68, 86–87
  ontological status of, 94–95
  paradox of, 70–78
  in philosophy, thirteenth-century, 25, 26, 78–85, 86–87
  and Reason, 69, 72–73, 76–78, 85, 94–99
  Thomas Aquinas on, 81–82, 83
  wheel of, 73–76, 98–99, 166n. 39, 172n. 102
Foucault, Michel, 143n. 40
Frappier, Jean, 178n. 67
freedom. *See* will
future, 12–15, 19–24, 38–42, 102, 106–8, 123
future contingents. *See* contingency; future

Gace Brulé, 58
Gallarati, Silvia Buzzetti, 159n. 65
Genius, 100, 172n. 1
Gervais de Bus, 87
Gilson, Étienne, 174n. 23
gloss. *See* reading/writing
God. *See* divine knowledge
Godefroy, Frédéric, 163n. 101, 173n. 5, 180n. 11
Goldin, Frederick, 178n. 67
Gorni, Guglielmo, 162n. 95
Guilhem de Peitieus, 56–57
Guillaume de Lorris, 1–7, 38–39, 45, 46, 50. See also *Roman de la Rose*
Gunn, Alan M. F., 4, 141n. 22

Hegel, Georg Wilhelm Friedrich, 33, 151n. 5
Heidegger, Martin, 156n. 48
Henry of Settimello, 170n. 81
Hilder, Gisela, 78, 103, 167n. 47
Hult, David F., 5, 6, 143nn. 40, 42, 153n. 28, 157n. 60
Huot, Sylvia, 5, 60, 135, 143n. 40, 157n. 60

incompletion. *See* completion/incompletion
indeterminacy/indistinction, 21–24, 62, 63, 80, 81, 94, 98, 99, 102, 108, 111, 121, 133
integumentum, 39, 155n. 41
involucrum, 39, 155n. 41
Isaac, J., 15, 16, 145n. 16
Isidore of Seville, 37, 41–42, 69, 170n. 76

Jacob of Venice, 167n. 48
Jakobson, Roman, 31, 151n. 12
Jean de Meun, 175n. 41
  as author of *Roman de la Rose*, 1–7, 45, 46, 47, 49–50, 103–5, 157n. 60, 179n. 70
  Boethius as translated by, 71–72, 165n. 30, 166n. 35, 176n. 45, 177n. 61

Index

Jean de Meun (*cont.*)
   Fortune in text by, 70–71, 73–75
   Reason in text by, 64–66
   See also *Roman de la Rose*
Jeanroy, Alfred, 2, 3, 8, 141n. 13

Kantorowicz, Ernst H., 143n. 40
Kay, Sarah, 5, 30, 33, 156n. 55
Kelly, Douglas, 5
Kennedy, Elspeth, 143n. 40
Kittridge, George Lyman, 141n. 13
knowledge. *See* divine knowledge

Lactantius, 94, 171n. 97
Langlois, Ernest, 2, 3, 4, 8, 65, 73, 103–4, 153n. 28
Lecoy, Félix, 73, 104, 120, 172n. 2
Lejeune, Philippe, 45, 157n. 59
Lewis, C. S., 2, 3, 8, 135, 141n. 13
lies. *See* truth and falsity
Lombard, Peter, 109–11, 118, 176n. 47, 177n. 58
Lommatzsch, Erhard, 163n. 101
Lorris, Guillaume de. *See* Guillaume de Lorris
Lote, Georges, 158n. 63
love. *See* Amors (love)
Lukasiewicz, Jan, 145n. 11, 148n. 49
Lyons, Faith, 103
lyric poetry, 26–28, 56–60

Machaut, Guillaume de, 87
Macrobius, 39, 154n. 33
manuscripts, 143n. 40
   of *Roman de la Rose*, 1, 6, 46, 142n. 37, 157n. 60, 159n. 67, 172n. 103
Marie de France, 41
martyrdom, 48, 158n. 64
Matthew of Vendôme, 35
McKean, Sister Faith, 179n. 4
metanomasia, 53
Metaphysics (Aristotle), 17, 18, 80, 82–83, 84, 146n. 30, 147n. 33, 169n. 70
Meun, Jean de. *See* Jean de Meun
Michalski, Konstanty, 148n. 49
Michault, Pierre, 87

Minnis, A. J., 5
mirrors, 124–31, 177n. 67, 179n. 70
mise en abîme. See self-reference
Montaigne, Michel de, 2–3
Muscatine, Charles, 135, 179n. 4

naming, 49–54, 160n. 69
Narcissus, 98, 130, 172n. 101, 178n. 68
Nature
   discussion of contingency, 102–5, 106–8, 111–17, 118–24
   discussion of phoenix, 61–62, 162n. 99
   and divine knowledge, 106, 124–31
   and fate, 101–2
   as figure in *Roman de la Rose*, 100–105, 106–8, 111–31
   and Genius, 100, 172n. 1
necessity, 12–14, 20–24, 101, 103, 111–24, 146n. 25, 176n. 45. *See also* contingency
Nichols, Stephen G., 143n. 40, 157n. 55
nothing, 12–14, 94–96, 99
Nouvet, Claire, 45

Origen, 100
Ovid, 52, 67, 160n. 68, 172n. 101

paradox
   of contingency, 22, 75–76, 84
   of fortune, 70–71, 75–76
   of Liar, 133, 179n. 1
paranomasia, 35–36, 47–48, 62
Paré, Gérard, 78, 92, 103, 105, 127
Paris, Gaston, 2, 3, 140n. 4
Paris, Paulin, 2–3
Patterson, Lee, 5, 135
Paul, Saint, 125, 155n. 43
Peirce, C. S., 31
perjury, 133
persona, 32–34, 53, 54, 60, 62, 86–87, 91, 97, 152n. 24
personal pronouns
   in ancient and medieval grammar and theology, 31–33, 152nn. 17, 21, 22, 24, 153n. 25
   in Dante, 151n. 6

204

in *Roman de la Rose*, 34–35, 53–54, 60–61, 62
personification. See *prosopopoeia*
Philo Judaeus, 155n. 43
Physics (Aristotle), 79–85, 167n. 48
Piaget, A., 158n. 63
Pindar, 56
Plato, 172n. 104
Plautus, 67
Pliny the Elder, 67
Poirion, Daniel, 78, 104
Porphyry, 31
possibility. See contingency
predication, 11–15, 21–24, 27–28, 106–7
Priscian, 152nn. 22, 24
prologue, 34–45
pronouns. See personal pronouns
prosopopoeia, 86–87, 91, 96–97, 169n. 72, 171n. 90
providence. See divine knowledge
Prudentius, 63
Pygmalion, 59, 162n. 97

Quintilian, 86

reading/writing, 41–42, 51, 155n. 47
reason, 172n. 104
　concept of, 68, 81–82, 86
　as figure in *Roman de la Rose*, 64–66, 69, 72–73, 76–78, 163n. 1
　Fortune as viewed by, 69, 72–73, 76–78, 85, 94–95, 97–99
Regalado, Nancy Freeman, 5, 159n. 65
Roman de la Rose
　allegorical structure of, 41–42, 63–66
　Amors as figure in, 49–53, 54–60, 63–66
　bipartite structure of, 1–2, 54–60, 64–66
　completion and incompletion of, 1–10
　death in, 10, 54–56
　dream in, 35–45, 52, 153nn. 28, 29
　False Seeming as figure in, 132–37
　Fortune as figure in, 9, 28, 63–99, 163n. 1
　interruptions in, 10, 46–49
　manuscripts of, 1, 6, 46, 142n. 37, 157n. 60, 159n. 67, 172n. 103
　medieval reception of, 6, 139nn. 1, 2
　mirrors in, 124–31, 177n. 67
　modern reception of, 2–8, 65, 103–5, 135, 140n. 4, 141nn. 13, 19, 22, 28, 142n. 30
　naming in, 49–54
　narrator of, 34, 40, 42–45, 47–54, 59–61
　Nature as figure in, 100–105, 106, 111–31
　phoenix in, 61–62, 136, 162n. 99
　prologue of, 34–45
　Reason as figure in, 64–69, 72–73, 76–78, 97–98, 163n. 1
　subjectivity in, 9, 28, 34–62, 98–99
　textual division of, 46–49
　translations of, 1, 115–16, 135–36
Ryding, William, 135, 179n. 4

Sappho, 56
self-reference, 35–36, 61–62, 93–94, 130–31, 133, 179n. 2
senefiance (signification), 40–43
Sententiae (Lombard), 109–11, 118, 177n. 58
shifters, 31, 151n. 12
Siger of Brabant, 79
Singleton, Charles S., 29
songe/mensonge. See dream
speculum. See mirrors
Spitzer, Leo, 29, 151n. 6
Stakel, Susan, 5, 135, 179n. 4
statement, 11–15, 20–24, 27–28, 106–7, 144nn. 3, 4, 145n. 11, 148n. 49
Stoics, 81, 168n. 62
Strubel, Armand, 47, 65, 104, 136, 158n. 61, 164n. 5, 175n. 43
subjectivity
　concept of in literary criticism, 29–34, 151n. 5
　in *Roman de la Rose*, 34–69, 98–99
　terminology, 31–34, 151n. 11
　in troubadours, 56–57
　in *trouvères*, 57–58, 161n. 87

Index

supplement, 3–4, 120–21. *See also* surplus
surplus, 41, 155n. 47. *See also* supplement
syncategoreme, 24

Tempier, Étienne, 110
Terence, 67
Tertullian, 39
testament, 49, 159n. 65
Thomas Aquinas, Saint, 17, 25, 81–82, 83, 128–29
Thuasne, Louis, 3
Tobler, Adolf, 158n. 63, 163n. 101
translation, 85, 102, 104, 115–16, 129–30, 131, 146n. 29, 148n. 63
  of *De Consolatione Philosophiae,* 71–72, 129–30, 165n. 30, 176n. 45, 177n. 61
  of *De Interpretatione,* 17–19, 147nn. 35, 37, 39, 148nn. 47, 63
  of *Metaphysics,* 84, 169n. 70
  of *Physics,* 79, 167n. 48
  of *Roman de la Rose,* 1, 115–16, 135–36, 173n. 5, 180n. 11

truth and falsity, 12–13, 14, 20–28, 35–39, 71, 106–7, 114–15, 144n. 3, 145n. 11, 148n. 49, 154n. 30

Van Dyke, Carolyn, 135, 179n. 4
Varro, Marcus Terentius, 37
vernacular, 9, 26–28, 115–16, 150nn. 80, 81
verse, 136–37, 158n. 63, 180n. 11
Victorinus, Marius, 15, 18, 19, 147n. 38
Vitz, E. B., 42, 156n. 55

Walters, Lori, 157n. 60, 158n. 63
will, 13, 21, 26, 100–102, 174n. 23
  and divine knowledge, 9, 28, 103–5, 106, 108–17, 118–31
William of Moerbeke, 15, 82–83, 147n. 39
Wisdom, Book of, 128
Wittman, Michael, 174n. 23
writing. *See* reading/writing

Zink, Michel, 29, 30, 33, 43, 44, 151n. 5, 156n. 55
Zumthor, Paul, 6, 29, 30, 60, 156n. 55